Nguyen Cong Khanh
Nguyen Thi My Linh

n Solving Test for Adolescents

Nguyen Cong Khanh
Nguyen Thi My Linh

Social Problem Solving Test for Adolescents

LAP LAMBERT Academic Publishing

Publisher:
LAP LAMBERT Academic Publishing
is a trademark of
International Book Market Service Ltd., member of OmniScriptum Publishing Group
17 Meldrum Street, Beau Bassin 71504, Mauritius

Printed at: see last page
ISBN: 978-3-659-53390-7

Table of Contents

Chapter 1

SOCIAL PROBLEM SOLVING:
AN OVERVIEW OF APPROACHES AND CONCEPTS

Researchers, practitioners, educators and psychologists have recognized that life is full of problems to be solved and that humans are problem-solvers. When personal and interpersonal problems arise in all aspects of life and one is inevitably faced with social dilemmas, the study of problem-solving ability is especially necessary because it has been generally assumed that problem-solving ability contributes to social competence (or social intelligence) which helps one to deal with everyday real-life problems so as to maintain an adequate level of personal-social functioning (D'Zurilla, 1986; D'Zurilla, & Maydeu-Olivares, 1995; D'Zurilla, Nezu, & Maydeu-Olivares, 1996; Frauenknecht, & Black, 1995; Guilford, 1977; Nguyen, 2019; Nguyen, & Nguyen, 2017, 2019; Parnes, Noller, & Biondi, 1977). Research on problem solving shows that deficits of problem-solving skills can contribute to psychological and behavioural disorders that may lead to learning difficulties (D'Zurilla & Sheedy, 1992; Semrud-Clikeman 2007; Wentzel, 1991), depression (Craighead, 1991; Desjardins and Leadbeater 2011; Joffe, Dobson, Fine, Marriage, Haley, 1990), suicidal behaviour (Orbach, Bar-Joseph, & Dror, 1990; Sadowski, & Kelly, 1993), peer bullying (Offrey and Rinaldi 2017; Fitzpatrick and Bussey 2011), early school leaving or even violent behaviour in schools (D'Zurilla, 1986; Kathryn 2011). Consequently, in the educational, clinical and counselling areas, social problem solving has been enthusiastically adopted as an important factor in adjustment, and social problem-solving training is a promising method for improving a person's adaptive functioning so as to reduce and prevent psychological and behavioural disorders (D'Zurilla, & Maydeu-Olivares, 1995; McMurran and McGuire 2011; Kasik 2014; Nguyen, & Nguyen 2017; Zsolnai & Kasik, 2016; Zsolnai, Kasik, & Braunitzer, 2014). In a forum about school violence at University of Western Australia, 20th June, 1996, it was hypothesized that modern behavioural training programs can help considerably cut violence in schools. One strategy of these programs is to provide strong conflict resolution skills so that when youngsters are faced with hatred or aggression they have a more positive way of coping with it than to be violent. The other effective practice is to work through underlying values (or beliefs) and attitudes, challenge them and help the development of more positive attitudes and values (Ludowyke, 1996)[1].

---

[1] Student Values the Keys, In: *The West Australian*, June, 20th, 1996.

However, researchers, practitioners and teachers still lack reliable and valid measures that identify deficits of conflict resolution skills (social problem-solving skills) and assess the effects of behavioural training programs. As indicated by D'Zurilla et al (1996), "for many years, one of the major deficiencies in research on social problem solving was the lack of a specific, comprehensive, theory-based measure of social problem-solving processes that would allow an investigator to isolate, study, and compare specific strengths and deficits in problem-solving attitudes and skills among different individuals" (p. 5). In an attempt to meet the need for such a measure in Vietnam, this project involved the development and validation of a multidimensional measure of Vietnamese adolescents' competences in dealing with interpersonal problems.

The structure of this study includes six chapters. Chapter 1 addresses approaches underlying social problem-solving approach, main concepts and factors influencing an individual's performance of social problem solving. Chapter 2 presents methodological issues in social problem-solving assessment. Chapter 3 identifies interpersonal difficulties in adolescents to develop a taxonomy of adolescent interpersonal problems, while chapter 4 points to modifying an empirically supported, multidimensional model of social problem solving to design test subscales/scales and standardizing testing procedures which base on a cognitive-behaviour-analytic approach to develop test items. Chapters 5 and 6 present evidence concerning test reliability and validity and discussions of psychological testing properties, as well as implications for practice and future research.

Conceptual Antecedents and Approaches

Research on human problem solving has a history in experimental psychology starting from the 1960s, (Kleinmuntz, 1966; Newell & Simon, 1972; Parnes, Noller, & Biondi, 1977). The research began with impersonal intellectual problems such as jigsaw puzzles, anagrams, mechanical problems, water-jar problems, mathematical problems, and concept-formation tasks (Spivack, Platt, & Shure, 1976; Sarason, 1981; Spivack & Shure, 1974) that do not include many social abilities (such as social problem solving). Then, research in experimental psychology focused on descriptive models of problem solving or decision making which attempted to identify how individuals typically go about solving problems. However, these models were not suitable for personal and interpersonal problem solving that involves handling daily difficulties, seeking help, planning a course of action to obtain a social goal and so on. These types of problem solving require prescriptive or normative models which attempt to specify and predict how individuals can solve problems so as to maximize their problem-solving effectiveness (D'Zurilla, 1986).

Current problem-solving approaches to clinical intervention and prevention in social behavioural problems, according to D'Zurilla (1986), have been considerably influenced by four different areas of research: (a) discovering the nature and nurturance of creativity, (b) the social-competence approach to psychopathology as a challenge to the medical model, (c) the development of the cognitive-behavioural approach within behaviour modification, and (d) the transactional theory of stress. These four areas are now discussed briefly.

The constitution of creativity. Various researchers in the area of creativity maintained that the traditional concept of general intelligence (IQ) fails to include many of the abilities which are important for creative performance and "social intelligence". Several studies attempted to investigate the relationships between social problem-solving ability and general intelligence and found low correlations (Heppner & Petersen, 1982; Spivack, Platt, & Shure, 1976). It is possible that IQ might put an upper limit on social problem-solving ability, but high IQs may not ensure high problem-solving ability. However, low IQs may involve low problem-solving ability (D'Zurilla, 1986). Researchers investigating the intellectual abilities that constitute creative thinking and creative performance, found that problem solving and creative thinking, abilities work together, contributing to creative performance and social competence, and that there is much overlap between creativity and problem solving of any kind (Guilford, 1977; Spivack, Platt, & Shure, 1976). The majority of the basic cognitive abilities (such as social information-processing abilities and generation of alternative solutions) which are found in the Structure-of-Intellect model (Guilford, 1977) and in the programs of Parnes and his colleagues (Parnes, Noller, & Biondi, 1977) are also the most important abilities for social problem solving. For example, the Structure-of-Intellect Problem-Solving model includes five kinds of informational content (visual, auditory, symbolic, semantic, and behavioural), six kinds of products (units, classes, relations, systems, transformations and implication), and five kinds of operation (memory, cognition, convergent production, divergent production, and evaluation). Each factor in the model represents a specific ability. Within the informational content dimension, the abilities associated with the categories labelled semantic (ie. verbal and meaningful information) and behavioural (personal-social information) are most relevant for social problem solving (D'Zurilla, 1986).

3

The social competence approach to psychopathology. Investigators in this area (D'Zurilla & Goldfried, 1971; Spivack, Platt, & Shure, 1976) hypothesised that social competence and psychopathology might be related, and that increases in social competence might be associated with decreases in psychopathology. Also, some researchers assumed that problem solving is positively related to social competence (positive adjustment) and inversely related to psychopathology or maladaptive behaviour (Nguyen, 2016, 2017; Semrud-Clikeman, 2007;). Several studies strongly supported the inverse relationship between social competence and psychopathology (Levine & Zigler, 1973; Nguyen, 2016, 2017). However, the relationship between social competence and psychopathology has been differently recognized since then. For example, D'Zurilla (1986) has argued that "social competence has been viewed as both a "buffer" against psychopathology and as a preventative factor" (p. 6). Some researchers (e.g., D'Zurilla & Goldfried, 1971; Phillips, 1978; Spivack, Platt, & Shure, 1976) have argued that the concept of psychopathology should be broadened to recognize that maladaptive responses may result from generalized deficiencies in social competence which in turn involve deficits in social problem-solving skills. Thus, they suggested that social-skills training programs should also include problem-solving skills training to facilitate generalized improvements in social competence. Experimental and correlational studies have supported this assumption (Kasik 2014; McMurran & McGuire 2011; Zsolnai & Kasik, 2016; Zsolnai et al, 2014). In addition, significant relationships have been found between various measures of social problem solving and a variety of measures of positive adjustment and maladjustment (Heppner et al, 1982; Sherry et al, 1984; Nezu, 1985; Heppner et al, 1984, 1985; Heppner & Anderson, 1985). It would appear then that an overlap exists between social competence and social problem solving. Social problem solving can be viewed as one component of social competence, albeit a very important one (Tisdelle & St. Lawrence, 1986).

The cognitive-behavioural approach to behaviour modification. Within the field of clinical psychology, an approach to modifying behaviour was developed whereby intervention programs focused on the direct facilitation of performance skills in specific problematic situations by manipulating the consequences of specific target behaviours through using a set of procedures, such as prompting, modelling, behaviour rehearsal, performance feedback, positive reinforcement, and shaping. For example, Asher (1978) identified three social skill training procedures: (1) contingency management strategies that teach the learner new ways of behaving by reinforcing desirable behaviours while ignoring undesirable ones, (2) modelling strategies that teach through demonstrating competent performance in specific social situations, and (3)

4

coaching strategies that provide general principles, along with behavioural examples, which the learner is expected to employ to generate appropriate social behaviour in a variety of future situations.

Although these procedures have been demonstrated to be effective and useful in improving performance, behaviour changes are often limited to the specific training situations (Kazdin, 1975; Sarason, 1981). For example, D'Zurilla and his colleagues (1986, 1995, 2001) indicated that while the approach is useful for specific behavioural deficits, it is less effective with clinical problems which are assumed to concern generalized deficiencies in social competence because generalized improvements in social competence do not tend to occur. An empirical study reported by Bramston and Spence (1985) indicated that, for adult intellectually handicapped clients, training in the performance of specific, overt social skills did not lead to improvements in covert-cognitive social skills.

The limitations of this approach appeared to instigate a new trend in behaviour modification that now tends to focus on cognitive activities ranging from specific thoughts or self-statements, through a broader level of underlying beliefs, motivations, and assumptions, to more complex processes such as information processing and covert thinking processes (i.e., problem solving) (D'Zurilla & Goldfried, 1971, Murphy, 1985; Spivack & Shure, 1974; Spivack, Platt, & Shure, 1976; Turk & Salovey, 1985). D'Zurilla and Goldfried (1971) noted the introduction of "the operation of cognitive strategies or learning sets…which enable an individual to create or discover symbolically solutions to a variety of unfamiliar problems" (p. 108). Thus, the cognitive-behavioural perspective, as Kendall and Hollon (1979) have argued, represented "an attempt to preserve the demonstrated efficiencies of behaviour modification… and to incorporate the cognitive activities of the client in the efforts to produce therapeutic change" (p.1).

Using a cognitive-behavioural perspective and based on research on children and adolescents in the field of interpersonal problem solving, Spivack and Shure and their associates (Shure & Spivack, 1978; Spivack, Platt, & Shure; 1976; Spivack & Shure, 1974) were among the first to propose a model of social problem-solving although they employed the term *interpersonal cognitive problem solving*. According to these authors, the following cognitive abilities were required for effective problem solving: (a*) recognition of or sensitivity to problems* (recognizes that problems exist), (b) *alternative thinking* (ability to generate alternative solutions to solve these problems), (c) *means-ends thinking* (ability to conceptualize the step-by-step means to a goal), (d) *consequential thinking* (ability to identify or anticipate consequences), and (e) *perspective thinking* (ability to perceive another person's perspective, empathic ability). Hence, their assessment and training of interpersonal cognitive problem-solving (ICPS) skills in children concentrate on developing and integrating these critical cognitive skills.

D'Zurilla and Goldfried (1971) were instrumental in defining social problem solving as a cognitive-affective-behavioural process through which an individual identifies or discovers solutions to a problem. Based on a theoretical and empirical review of the literature, they proposed a *prescriptive* or normative model of social problem solving for adults. Their social problem-solving model attempts to specify how individuals *should solve* problems so as to maximize their effectiveness, in contrast to a *descriptive* model that focuses on how individuals typically *go about* solving problems. The D'Zurilla and Goldfried model originally included two main components (or processes): *problem orientation* and *problem-solving proper*. The model, as later revised by D'Zurilla and Nezu (1982), consists of five components or stages as follows: (1) *problem orientation*; (2) *problem definition and formulation*; (3) *generation of alternative solutions*; (4) *decision making (i.e., evaluation of alternatives and selection of solution)*; and (5) *solution verification (i.e., analysis of actual outcome of implementing a solution)*.

These components (or stages) include skills and abilities that imply the mentioned cognitive abilities described in Spivack et al's model as well as in Guilford's model, but each has a definite purpose/function in the problem-solving process (D'Zurilla, 1986; D'Zurilla & Nezu, 1982). These functions are described below.

Problem orientation as defined by D'Zurilla and his colleagues (D'Zurilla and Goldfried, 1971; D'Zurilla & Nezu, 1982) is a set of facilitative, problem-solving cognitive variables that relate to: (a) increased sensitivity to problems; (b) a focus of attention on *positive* problem-solving expectations; (c) maximized effort and persistence when faced with obstacles and emotional distress; and (d) minimized disruptive emotional distress while attempting to maximize the likelihood of positive, facilitative emotional states. Problem definition and formulation involves (a) gathering as much relevant, factual information about the problem as possible; (b) clarifying the nature of the problem; (c) setting a realistic problem-solving goal; and (d) reappraising the significance of the problem for personal-social well-being. The purpose of the generation of alternative solutions is to generate as many solutions as possible, because in such a way the problem solver can maximize the likelihood of discovering the "best" solution among them. Decision making involves evaluating the available solution alternatives in order to select the "best" one(s) for implementation in the problematic situation. The judgement may be based on four cost/benefit criteria (expected utility theory): problem resolution (likelihood of obtaining the problem-solving goal), emotional well-being (quality of expected emotional outcome), time/effort (expected time and effort), and overall personal-social well-being (total expected cost/benefit ratio). Solution implementation and verification relates to the assessment of the solution outcome and to examination (verification) of the "effectiveness" of the chosen solution strategy in solving the real-life problem.

As indicated by these authors, the order of these five components represents a logical and useful sequence for training and systematic, efficient application. The sequence means that a problem solving process should begin with a positive problem orientation, since such an orientation is likely to facilitate a general problem-solving performance. Also, a well-defined problem is likely to facilitate the generation of alternative solutions. However, it is not an orderly, one-directional sequence that begins with the first step and ends with the final step. Instead, these steps usually overlap and interact with each other. An effective problem-solving process is likely to involve movement back and forth from one task to another before it is finally terminated with an effective solution (D'Zurilla, 1986).

There is much empirical support for the component skills outlined in D'Zurilla and Gold-fried's problem-solving model from studies assessing the efficacy of training in individual problem-solving component skills as well as in different combinations of components. For example, a study conducted by Nezu and D'Zurilla (1981a) indicated that college students who had been trained in problem definition and formulation skills, performed significantly better on a decision-making test than a control group.

Cormier, Otani, and Cormier (1986) conducted a study to evaluate the problem-orientation component. In this study, the subjects (including experimental and control groups) were presented with a problem-solving task requiring that they select the best alternatives from a list of solution alternatives to several social oriented problematic situations. They found that the subjects in the experimental group (who received instructions in the content of problem orientation) performed significantly better than the control-group subjects.

Another study that has investigated the efficacy of the generation of alternative solutions indicated that college subjects who had been instructed in the content of this step produced significantly more effective solutions to two problematic situations than control-group subjects (D'Zurilla & Nezu, 1980). The efficacy of the decision-making component has been found when comparing experimental-group subjects who were trained in decision making with control-group subjects. Both these groups were asked to complete tasks requiring selection of the "best" solution to various social problems (Nezu & D'Zurilla, 1979, 1981b). There have been no experimental studies specifically investigating the solution implementation and verification component. However, as D'Zurilla (1986) argued, "an objective assessment of outcome is necessary to establish clearly the success of any behaviour-modification procedure. Thus, the evidence supporting the use of self-monitoring and self-evaluation in behavioural assessment in general can be used to support the efficacy of solution implementation and verification" (p. 45).

In sum, although there are some variations in wording, categorization, or specific skills mentioned among these theorists, there has been a remarkable degree of agreement among them as to the general kinds of operations that are involved in *effective problem solving* (e.g., Brim et al, 1962; Crutchfield, 1969; D'Zurilla & Goldfried, 1971; Parnes, 1967; Spivack et al, 1976).

Effective problem solving interventions place greater emphasis on training covert thinking processes (identifying problems, generating alternative solutions, decision making, etc.), whereas behavioural intervention methods (contingency management, modeling, coaching, shaping, etc.) are designed to specifically train discrete behavioural responses to various situations (Ubrain & Kendall, 1980). Problem solving interventions do, nonetheless, share with behavioural interventions an emphasis on the social learning processes involved in response acquisition (Bandura, 1977).

The transactional/problem solving approach to stress. This is the last of the four areas of inquiry which have influenced current problem-solving approaches to social behavioural problems. The transactional theory of stress and coping (Lazarus, 1966, 1981; Lazarus & Folkman, 1984; McGrath, 1970, 1976; Sch"-npflug 1983; Schulz & Sch"npflug, 1982) defines stress as a particular type of person-environment encounter or "transaction" in which environment factors (e.g. task demands) and person factors (e.g., coping responses or cognitive capabilities) interact and influence each other. This particular type of person-environment transaction is very similar to the concept of a problem in social problem-solving approaches. According to D'Zurilla (1986), the transactional approach of stress has influenced the present problem-solving approach as follows: (a) it has suggested that problems in everyday living and the social problem-solving process can best be understood by viewing them within a transactional perspective; (b) it has indicated that life problems are often stressful, and that emotional variables may significantly affect the problem-solving process; and (c) it has suggested that problem-solving training might be useful as a stress-management approach. Within the transactional model of stress, as Lazarus (1981) suggested, there are two critical processes: *cognitive appraisal* and *coping*. Cognitive appraisal is a process in which an individual evaluates the significance of an encounter for his or her well-being, such as (a) harm/loss, (b) threat (anticipated harm and loss), and (c) challenge (opportunity for personal growth or mastery). This procedure is labelled the "decision-making process" (McGrath, 1970).

Coping relates to the responses or activities by which a person attempts to reduce, minimize, control or prevent stress. This process can be emotion-focused, involving regulation of distressing emotions, and problem-focused, oriented to alter the troubled person-environment relationship that is causing the distress.

Stress usually occurs when there is concern about a problem (Sch"npflug, 1983). The "problem" in a stressful situation is viewed as an imbalance between perceived task demands and perceived coping capacity, which taxes or exceeds capacity. Thus, coping is considered a problem-solving activity which attempts to increase coping capacity (coping response availability) or reduce demands (D'Zurilla, 1986).

Based on the assumption that problem solving may be useful as a stress management strategy, D'Zurilla (1986) has proposed a transactional/problem-solving model of stress that includes four critical factors: (a) *problem*, (b) *emotion*, (c) *coping*, and (d) *problem solving*. The problem (problematic situation) is defined here as a person-environment transaction in which imbalance or discrepancy occurs between "what is" (the transaction as it exists) and "what should be" (the transaction that is demanded or desired), under conditions in which the means or resources for reducing the imbalance are not immediately available. Emotion (emotional arousal) involves autonomic activity as well as subjective affective experience. Coping refers to the general strategy that the subject uses to deal with life stressful situations. The most effective and adaptive general coping strategy is labelled by D'Zurilla (1986) as problem-solving style (or problem-solving oriented coping).

From the transactional perspective, the links between these factors (i.e., problem, emotion, and coping) are mediated by different components of a problem-solving process (see Figure 1). D'Zurilla (1986) indicated that: the relationships between a problem, emotional arousal, and coping are conceived as reciprocal. Problem solving is the process that mediates these reciprocal relationships (P. 88).

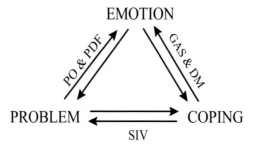

Figure 1: Reciprocal relationships between problem, emotion, and coping. PO = problem orientation; PDF = problem definition and formulation; GAS = generation of alternative solutions; DM = decision making; SIV = solution implementation and verification (D'Zurilla, 1986, p. 89)

The link between problem and emotion is mediated by problem orientation (PO) and problem definition and formulation (PDF). Some variables associated with the objective problematic situation (such as task demands) or variables involving problem orientation (such as problem appraisal, personal-control expectations) may influence emotional arousal, which in turn is able to influence the perception of the problem (depending on how the individual interprets and appraises it). The relationship between emotion and coping is mediated by the generation of alternative solutions (GAS) and decision making (DM). The link between problem and coping is mediated by the solution implementation and verification (SIV). These relationships are illustrated in Figure 1.

Social Problem Solving: Operative Concepts

The term social problem solving has been differently conceptualized across studies. However, one of the most useful definitions of social problem solving has been provided by D'Zurilla and Maydeu-Olivares (1995): "Social problem solving is defined as the self-directed cognitive behavioral process by which a person attempts to identify or discover effective or adaptive ways of coping with problematic situations encountered in everyday living" (D'Zurilla & Maydeu-Olivares, 1995, p. 410). Social problem solving is perceived by these authors as a social-learning process, a self-management technique, and a general coping strategy. When the problem solving involves the use of cognitive strategies to produce a change in performance, it is a learning process (Bandura, 1977). When a person applies problem solving skills in encountering a wide variety of life's problems, it is a self-management technique (D'Zurilla, 1986). When problem solving is applied as a general strategy by an individual as an approach to life's stressful problems which attempts to find effective coping responses, it is an active, versatile coping strategy (D'Zurilla, 1986; D'Zurilla & Goldfried, 1971; D'Zurilla & Maydeu-Olivares, 1995; D'Zurilla, Nezu, & Maydeu-Olivares, 2004; Lazarus & Folkman, 1984).

Problem solving is conceived as a cognitive-affective-behavioural process that refers to the discovery of a solution to a problem. The process is described at three different levels: problem-orientation cognitions, specific-problem skills, and basic problem-solving abilities. At the most general level, the problem-orientation cognitions consist of a set of cognitive variables which help an individual define a general orientation to problems such as problem perception (the recognition and labelling of the problem), causal attributions, problem appraisal, beliefs about personal control, values, and commitments concerning real-life problems.

The intermediate level is a set of relatively specific problem-solving skills which must be performed in order to solve a particular problem successfully. They include the tasks of defining and formulating the problem, generating alternative solutions, making a decision, implementing the solution, and evaluating the solution outcome (D'Zurilla & Goldfried, 1971). Basic problem-solving abilities, that appear at the most specific level, are a set of abilities to learn and implement the problem-solving operations. They are likely to include cognitive abilities, such as sensitivity to problems (ability to recognize that a problem exists); alternative thinking (ability to generate alternative solutions); means-ends thinking (ability to conceptualize relevant means to a goal); consequential thinking (ability to anticipate consequences); and perspective taking (ability to view a problem from another person's perspective or empathic ability) (D'Zurilla,1986; D'Zurilla & Goldfried, 1971; Spivack, Platt, & Shure, 1976).

A *problem* is defined as a life situation (i.e., problematic situation) in which no effective or adaptive coping response is immediately apparent or available to the individual. The individual in such a situation is required to engage in problem-solving behaviour (D'Zurilla, 1986; D'Zurilla & Goldfried, 1971; D'Zurilla & Maydeu-Olivares 1995; D'Zurilla & Nezu, 1982). In their Manual for the Social Problem Solving Inventory-Revised, D'Zurilla, Nezu, & Olivares, (1996) defined a problem as: "something important in your life that bothers you a lot but you don't know immediately how to make it better or stop it from bothering you so much. The problem could be something about yourself (such as your thoughts, feelings, behavior, health, or appearance), your relationship with other people (such as your family, friends, teacher, or boss), or your environment and the things that you own (such as your house, car, property, money)" (D'Zurilla, Nezu, & Olivares, 1996, p. 11).

The problem is conceived here as not only a personal or interpersonal problem, but also a problem of person-event/environment encounter, or transaction. The demands in the problematic situation may originate in the environment (e.g., objective task demands) or within the individual (e.g., personal goal, need, commitment). Hence, a problem should not be considered as a characteristic of the environment alone, nor as a characteristic of the individual alone. Instead, it is best perceived as a person-environment transaction in which there is a perceived imbalance or discrepancy between demands and response availability.

Problems are likely to be stressful if they are at all difficult, because difficult problems appear to involve more conflict, uncertainty, and/or perceived uncontrollability (D'Zurilla, 1986; Epstein, 1982; Janis, 1982; Phillips, 1978).

A solution is perceived here as the product or outcome of the problem-solving process when the individual is faced with a specific problematic situation. This means that a solution is a situation-specific coping response or response pattern that is effective (i.e., a positive response) in altering a problematic situation and/or one's own personal reactions to the situation, so that it is no longer problematic to the individual. At the same time, the solution maximizes other positive consequences (benefits) and minimizes other negative consequences (costs) (D'Zurilla, 1986; D'Zurilla & Goldfried, 1971). The relevant benefits and costs may include personal and/or interpersonal effects as well as short-term and/or long-term effects.

Various studies of problem solving have shown that there are wide differences among individuals in the manner in which they go about social problem solving (Schroder, Driver, & Streufirt, 1967; Semrud-Clikeman, 2007; Zsolnai & Kasik, 2016). In addition, the effectiveness of any particular solution may vary across different individuals or different environments depending on various factors such as norms, values, emotional arousal, beliefs, etc.

In theory, research, and practice, it is necessary to distinguish between the concepts of problem solving, solution implementation, and social competence. As the above definition showed, problem solving refers to the process by which an individual attempts to find, or discover a solution to a specific problem, whereas solution implementation relates to the performance of the solution response (i.e., the process of carrying out the solution in the actual problematic situation). Hence, the solution implementation process is a function not only of problem solving, but also of other factors involving the individual's learning history, such as performance skill deficits, anxiety, emotional inhibitions, motivational deficits and so forth. Depending on the particular problem domain, solution implementation skills may require the full range of possible coping performance skills (adaptive functioning) (D'Zurilla, 1986; D'Zurilla & Goldfried, 1971; D'Zurilla & Maydeu-Olivares, 1995).

Coping performance, according to Lazarus and Folkman (1984), refers to the cognitive and behavioural activities by which a person attempts to manage specific stressful situations (reduce, minimize, prevent stress) and at the same time tries to control the emotions that they generate. A general coping strategy can be identified by two forms: (a) goal-oriented coping and (b) facilitative coping (Lazarus, 1981). Goal-oriented coping involves a person's attempts to reduce stress by achieving a problem-solving goal. Facilitative coping refers to a person's attempts to remove or eliminate cognitive and emotional obstacles to effective problem-solving. In such a definition, problem solving is the equivalent of a coping process, but not all coping is problem solving.

Based on process analyses of coping, some investigators (e.g., Logan, 1988, 1989; Epstein, 1990, 1994; Epstein & Meier, 1989; Epstein et al, 1992) have identified two qualitatively different information-processing systems which play a significant role in coping performance: (a) an automatic or experiential system and (b) a nonautomatic/rational system (which includes rational problem solving). The first system operates primarily at the preconscious level. It is rapid (oriented toward immediate action), effortless, unintentional, emotional, and intuitively validated for example, "It feels right". The second system works at the conscious level. It is slower (oriented toward delayed action), deliberate (or thoughtful), purposeful, effortful, analytic, logical, and objectively validated (requiring validation through logic and evidence). These authors have assumed that these two systems are based on different underlying mechanisms. The automatic/experiential system is based on obligatory (i.e., unintended) memory retrieval in contrast to the nonautomatic/rational system that is based on the deliberate, intentional use of algorithms (e.g., using problem-solving techniques).

Within this framework, rational problem solving, as D'Zurilla and Goldfried (1971) have suggested, is most likely to occur in problematic situations where automatic memory retrieval has failed to generate an effective coping response. With regard to this view-point, D'Zurilla and Maydeu-Olivares (1995) stated: "rational problem solving does not replace the experiential system at this point but, rather, the problem-solver attempts to control automatic processing (e.g., inhibiting automatic action, screening out poor quality responses) while conducting a rational search for a more effective or adaptive coping response" (p. 412).

Social competence is not an easy psychological construct to define for it has a multidimensional nature. In general, however, social competence refers to a wide range of social skills, behavioural competencies, and coping behaviours which enable an individual to deal effectively with the demands of day-to-day living (Goldfried & D'Zurilla, 1969; Kasik, 2014; McFall, 1982; Semrud-Clikeman, 2007; Wrubel, Benner, & Lazarus, 1981). According to Conger and Conger (1982), social competence is defined as the degree to which a person is successful in interactions or transactions taking place in the social sphere. Under this view, effective problem-solving performance is only one component of social competence and social problem solving can be viewed as one identified sub-set of social competence (D'Zurilla, 1986; Tisdelle & St.Lawrence, 1986), albeit a very significant one (Sarason, 1981).

As noticed previously, social-skills training and problem-solving training are both interventions. Early social-skills training programs focused on specific social performance skills (Bellack, 1979), then the concept of social skills was broadened to include cognitive skills (Kagan, 1984; McFall, 1982; Shujja & Malik, 2011). Problem solving has been demonstrated to be an important cognitive skill. Thus, it should be incorporated into social skills training programs (D'Zurilla & Goldfried, 1971; D'Zurilla & Maydeu-Olivares, 1995; Kagan, 1984; Kasik, 2014; McFall, 1982; Sarason, 1981; Trower, Bryant, & Argyle, 1978).

In the clinical and counselling psychology literature, along with real-life problem solving that has been recognized as social problem solving (D'Zurilla, 1986; D'Zurilla & Nezu, 1982; Krasnor & Rubin, 1981), the terms *interpersonal problem solving* (Shure, 1981), *interpersonal cognitive problem solving* (Spivack et al, 1976), *personal problem solving* (Heppner & Petersen, 1982), and *applied problem solving* (Heppner, Neal, & Larson, 1984) have also been used. These terms are very similar to, or very compatible with, the term *social problem solving* used by D'Zurilla and his colleagues, but the term *problem* as defined by D'Zurilla and Maydeu-Olivares (1995) is equivalent or broader than the term *problem* defined by these authors. For example, Heppner et al (1982) used the term *applied problem solving* or *personal problem solving* to refer to how people solve real-life personal problems. The real-life personal problems were divided into *interpersonal problems* and *intrapersonal problems*. These authors defined interpersonal problems as difficulties between individuals (e.g., with boy/girl friends, parents, authority figures, peers), whereas intrapersonal problems are difficulties within an individual (e.g., study problems, being overweight, low self-concept). In their Problem Solving Inventory (PSI), Heppner & Petersen (1982) suggested that, "we are not talking about math or science problems, but rather about personal problems that come up from time to time, such as feeling depressed, getting along with friends, choosing a vocation, or deciding whether to get a divorce" (cited in D'Zurilla, 1986, p. 233).

Factors Influencing Social Problem Solving

There are a variety of factors which may influence an individual's social problem solving process either in a positive or a negative way. For example, emotional factors can play an important role in problem-solving performance when dealing with real-life problems. Awareness and control of these factors is thus essential for effective social problem solving, however, the subject has received very little empirical attention to date (D'Zurilla, 1986; Nguyen, 2016, 2017). Spence (1988, 1991) has suggested that an individual may have an adequate skill repertoire (i.e., possess social-cognitive and performance skills) and yet behave inappropriately with others (interpersonal difficulties). In clinical assessment, it is important to distinguish between the two major groups. The first group consists of people whose interpersonal difficulties are a result of social problem solving skills deficits (or other social skills deficits). The second group involves those who possess appropriate requisite social skills, but who fail to use such skills and thus experience skill inhibition (due to such factors as emotional arousal or depression).

According to McFall (1982) and Spence (1988, 1991), interpersonal difficulties may result from three deficient cognitive aspects or stages of information processing which can be seen as social-cognitive skills involving the receipt of social responding. The first aspect or stage refers to an inappropriate social perception process in which social information has been received or interpreted incorrectly. Social information involving the situational context and the social cues (verbal or nonverbal) elicited by other subjects in the interaction is perceived, which in turn permits determination of the demands, requirements, and expectations of the social task at hand. The second aspect involves all stages of the social problem-solving sequence. At these stages, the subject's knowledge involving social rules and meaning of social information may play an important role in determining appropriate social perception. Hence, subjects who have difficulty in the determination of social information, such as individuals with sensory handicaps or attention deficit disorders (Morrision & Bellack, 1981), or whose social information is limited, may have difficulty in the social perception process which leads them to experience interpersonal problems. The stage involving the characteristics of the social task identified, thus requires the subject to produce a range of alternative responses (solutions). Difficulties may arise if the subject is limited in their range of solution options and/or if the person is unable to evaluate the consequences of various response choices. Even after selecting an appropriate response strategy, the subject may still perform the action unsuccessfully because of deficient microskills, such as eye contact, tone of voice, body posture, facial expression, etc. As Spence (1991) noted: "it is not just the overall strategy used to deal with the situation, nor the content of what is said and done, but how the response is performed that determines judgements of social competence" (p. 150). The third and last stage of social information processing concerns the monitoring of the subject's personal performance and the reaction of other persons to the response strategy selected. In this stage, a social perception would be influenced by the skills of attention, correct interpretation, and social knowledge.

A child or adolescent may possesses a good skill repertoire (both problem-solving skills and other specific overt social skills), yet selects an inappropriate social response strategy because of the presence of a variety of maladaptive cognitions which restrict selection of an appropriate social response. These maladaptive cognitions may involve beliefs, self-concept, self appraisal (such as "no-one likes me"; "they will laugh at me") and so forth. Spence (1988) noted: "Possession of the overt and covert skills necessary for appropriate social response is therefore not the sole determinant of how successful a child will be in social interaction. The degree of social competence will be determined partly by skill ability and partly by the response the child elects to make, response selection being influenced by cognitive appraisal of events" (p. 12). The author provided a case study as a good example supporting this idea: "Mary is 10 years old. She has no friends at school after four years with the same peer group. During assessment it emerges that she has a competent knowledge about how to approach peers and yet rarely does so. Her microskill usage is adequate in the few situations that she does interact with peers suggesting that her difficulties are not due to social skill inadequacy. Assessment within the cognitive domain however reveals a series of negative evaluations concerning her own ability to talk to peers, her prediction of their likely response and her own physical attractiveness. Her thoughts while hovering on the side of the playground are frequently "no-one likes me; I am hopeless; they will laugh at me if I go up to them; why am I so useless?". Given such mala-daptive cognitions it is perhaps not surprising to find her avoiding peer interactions whenever possible" (p. 12).

Thus, interpersonal problems may result from a failure to use skills that are already within the subject's repertoire. Some researchers (e.g., D'Zurilla 1986; Kennedy, Spence, & Hensley, 1989; Nguyen & Nguyen, 2017) have indicated a pool of various factors that may result in skill inhibition. These factors involve lack of motivation, low or very high emotional arousal, external reinforcement of inappropriate behaviour, and interference from anxiety or negative emotional states, especially cognitive and affective processes concerning stress, anger, and depression (Desjardins, & Leadbeater, 2011; Spence, 1988). For example, a child or adolescent may avoid entering a stressful situation, or he/she experiences an aversive feeling of discom-fort that inhibits skill usage when having to deal with the situation.

D'Zurilla (1986) has suggested that there are three possible sources of emotional arousal in-volving social problem solving: (a) *the objective problematic situation* (e.g., the importance or complexity of a problem to an individual; loss or deprivation of reinforcers, etc.), (b) *the problem-orientation cognitions* (e.g., problem perception, problem appraisal, etc.), and (c) *the specific problem-solving tasks* (e.g., problem definition and formulation, generation of alter-native solutions, decision making, etc.). Emotional variables from these sources may facilitate or inhibit problem-solving performance, depending on such bio-psychological factors as the subjective quality of the emotional response (pleasure vs. pain) and the intensity of emotional arousal (autonomic nervous system activity), and the duration of emotional stress. The effects may be situationally specific (e.g., effects on some preferable solution in a specific situation) or generalized (e.g., effects on performance efficiency in various situations).

The *objective problematic situation* is likely to generate "conditioned" and/or "unconditioned" emotional responses. The conditioned emotional responses may refer to prior emotional con-ditioning or associative learning experiences concerning the particular problem. For example, a mother feels depressed and disappointment about her 13 year old son because he does not care about her expectations involving keeping his room clean, doing the chores, and complet-ing his homework, and in the fact she feels that the son acts just like her husband. These emo-tional responses vary in nature and intensity with various situations and different individuals, depending on the individual's past associative learning experiences. In contrast, unconditioned emotional responses are generated by stimulus conditions that are independent of any prior associative learning experiences involving those particular conditions. Some investigators have indicated that some of these stimulus conditions are problematic because they are usually perceived as "aversive" or stressful. This can lead to frustration (i.e., an obstacle preventing a goal response), loss or deprivation of customary reinforcers and unpredictability or uncontrollability of aversive events (Hamberger & Lohr, 1984). Additionally, there is empirically significant evidence that personal characteristics (such as physical attractiveness, grooming, cleanliness, style of dress, physique, school attainment, presence of physical handicaps, etc.) may influence whether an individual is judged to be socially competent or not (Cartledge & Milburn, 1986; McFall, 1982; Rathjen, 1980; Spence, 1988). For example, a child or adolescent who dresses inappropriately, or who has inadequate personal hygiene (to which other people react in a negative way), may be judged as socially incompetent by others or rejected by their peers. A judgement based on such characteristics may "identify" subjects with interpersonal difficulties, but in fact they do not have deficits of social problem-solving skills or other social skills.

The *problem-orientation cognitions* may generate emotional responses. For example, when a boy is spat at by one of his peers in a canteen, his cognition may appraise (label) this as unintentional or intentional behaviour that leads to different emotional responses (a little bit of distaste but tolerable, or upset and anger). These emotional responses may be categorized into (a) conditioned emotional responses to the verbal labels used to identify a problem, and (b) emotions involved in the perceptual characteristics (i.e., meaning and significance) of the problem-orientation cognitions (Lazarus, 1982). For example, a person may feel unwell; his cognition may label this as a "health problem" that leads to a conditioned anxiety response if the person has had a serious illness in the past. Problem-orientation cognitions that contain positive expectations are believed to produce positive affects, such as hope, relief, feeling of confidence, whereas those that contain negative expectations are believed to generate negative affects, such as fear, disappointment and depression (D'Zurilla, 1986; Nezu, 1985; D'Zurilla & Sheedy, 1991). For example, D'Zurilla and Sheedy (1991) suggested that "a positive problem orientation may be sufficient to reduce psychological stress - even though solutions for current problems have not yet been discovered or implemented - because it allows a person to anticipate a less problematic and threatening future"(p. 845). The following example may clarify this idea: An adolescent girl has been cut off from an intimate friendship without any word to explain the reason. Although she is not immediately aware of how she can solve the problem, she approaches the problem with an optimistic and confident attitude. The attitude is the result of the way she thinks about the problem. First, she could think that the problem may be a misunderstanding and that the problem could happen to anyone. Second, she believes that the problem is solvable. Third, she thinks of a solution to the problem (e.g., look for an opportunity to meet her friend so as to identify the problem). Fourth, although she realizes that solving the problem might take time, effort and persistence, she values independent problem solving and is willing to commit time, persistence and effort to the problem.

Cognition-produced emotional responses and problem-produced emotional responses may interact and influence each other. A strong anxiety response generated by a problematic situation might affect problem-orientation cognitions such as: (a) attribution of the cause of the problem to an internal defect or abnormality (emotional hypersensitivity; psychological "weakness"); (b) appraisal of the problem as a significant threat to well-being; (c) doubt of ability to cope with the problem successfully; and (d) feelings that the problem is too demanding or the person cannot afford a sufficient amount of time and effort to problem solving (D'Zurilla, 1986). Empirical research reported by Bandura and Wood (Bandura & Wood, 1989) indicated that subjects with optimistic self-appraisals of problem solving tended to perform more effectively in complex problem-solving situations. In contrast, those who had pessimistic expectancies tended to be more erratic and inefficient in their problem-solving process.

The *specific problem solving tasks,* as D'Zurilla (1986) suggested, might generate emotional responses that are categorized as: (a) conditioned emotional responses to the verbal labels used to define and formulate the problem and to identify solutions and outcomes; (b) emotional arousal involving the perceptual characteristics of particular problem formulations, solution frames and outcome frames (Tversky & Kahneman, 1981); (c) emotions concerned with the expected outcomes or consequences of problem-solving task performance such as reinforcement and punishment (Smith & Lazarus, 1990; Semrud-Clikeman, 2007); and (d) unconditioned emotional responses generated by conflict involved in information processing and decision making (e.g., ambiguity, uncertainty, or decisional conflict) (Janis, 1982; Janis & Mann, 1977). These emotional variables are assumed to be more important during the final problem solving task (i.e., solution implementation and verification) because they may facilitate or inhibit solution performance, depending on the quality and intensity of emotional arousal (D'Zurilla, 1986; D'Zurilla & Maydeu-Olivares, 1995).

Emotional arousal from all mentioned sources can combine to produce a significant generalized effect on performance efficiency across the problem-solving process. The effects of emotional factors may depend to a considerable extent on the intensity of emotional arousal. D'Zurilla (1986) suggested that low emotions may involve poor performance efficiency, but as emotional arousal increases, performance should increase to an optimal level, after which a

further rise in arousal may result in a deterioration in performance, and that as emotions increase (over an optimal level) a narrowing or restriction in attention occurs, decreasing the
number of cues attended to.

Some studies of problem solving deficiencies have suggested the negative influence of emotional arousal. For example, a study conducted by Mandler (1982) indicated that the narrowing
of thought processes generated by high stress influences the generation of solution alternatives
and decision making. Under high stress, individuals frequently focus their attention on task-
irrelevant cues (such as their own threatening interpretations) and reduce attentional capacity
on a target problem-solving task, in such a way that only obvious solution alternatives and
outcomes are considered, thus considerably limiting the range of available solutions and the
range of outcomes affecting solution selection. Another study (Janis, 1982) found a similar
result whereby high stress may produce cognitive deficiencies, which include narrowing the
range of perceived solution alternatives and thus failing to take into account the full range of
values relevant to the choice. Gotlib and Asarnow (1979) found mildly and clinically depressed university students, in comparison to normal students in the control group, to be significantly less effective in their ability to engage in the "means-end thinking" component of
the problem-solving process (which is defined as the ability to orient oneself to and plan a
series of specific actions of moving toward a solution).

Other investigators (e.g., Doerfler, Mullins, Griffin, Siegel, & Richards, 1984) examined the
relationship between social problem-solving skills and depression in children, adolescents and
adults. Their results indicated that subjects classified as moderately to severely depressed in
all groups did not differ significantly compared with control-group subjects on the total number of relevant means generated on the measure of social and emotional means-ends problem
solving. One possible explanation, as Doerfler et al (1984) suggested, is that depressed individuals' social problem solving may be characterized by poor performance, as opposed to skill
deficits. That is, depressed and non-depressed subjects may possess comparable problem-solving ability, however the depressed subjects' inherent motivational deficits (i.e low emotional
arousal) might affect problem-solving performance.

Marx and Schulze (1991) examined whether depressed subjects suffer from interpersonal
problem-solving deficits and attempted to specify such deficits. Subjects consisted of 20 depressed university students who had a mean score of 24.95 (SD = 4.95) on the Beck Depression
Inventory (BDI), and 20 non-depressed university students who had a mean BDI score of 3.30
(SD = 1.81). Measures included the Situation Specific Problem-Solving Inventory (Falken-
stein, Kolb, & Stubellvoll, 1983, cited in Marx and Schulze, 1991) and a problem-orientation

measure. Results showed that depressed subjects developed significantly less effective problem-solving strategies than non-depressed subjects (these findings are consistent with Gotlib and Asarnow's (1979) findings, yet contradictory to Doerfler et al.'s (1984) non-significant results). In particular, most of the strategies used by the depressed subjects were passive, not action-oriented. In addition, depressed subjects showed significantly lower subjective competency than non-depressed counterparts, providing some evidence for the existence of a negative problem orientation in the depressed subjects. However, depressives did not evince higher stressfulness ratings or a stronger external control orientation. Depressed subjects appeared to have an adequate recognition of problems and a clear idea about targets, but they failed to indicate strategies to solve the problem. These authors concluded that the problem-solving deficit in the depressives may not have been due to a lack of knowledge of appropriate strategies but an inability or lack of motivation to retrieve potentially available strategies due to a depressed mood.

Summary

It is generally recognized that life is full of problems to be solved, and that social problem solving is a construct which refers to problem solving as it occurs in the real world. This construct has been defined by D'Zurilla and his colleages as the self-generated cognitive-behavioural process by which a person attempts to identify or discover effective or adaptive ways of coping with problematic situations encountered in life.

Social problem solving is at the same time a social-learning process, a self-management technique, and a general coping strategy, which makes an important contribution to social competence that helps a person successfully deal with real-life problems and maintain an adequate level of personal-social functioning.

Social problem-solving ability has a multidimensional nature which includes a number of different kinds of abilities and skills. These abilities and skills may have different adaptational outcomes in both different subject populations and different social contexts, and their demonstration may be influenced by emotional factors in terms of facilitation and inhibition. The definition of social problem solving and its determining variables are important in attempting to develop a valid measure of social problemsolving.

Chapter 2

APPROACHES AND ISSUES IN THE ASSESSMENT OF
SOCIAL PROBLEM SOLVING

Assessment of an individual's social problem-solving abilities or skills is important for identifying specific skill deficits, planning an appropriate training program and assessing training progress and outcomes. This chapter will focus on a discussion of various approaches and issues for assessing social problem-solving processes.

Approaches to Assessment

Research on the assessment of social competence including social problem solving has proliferated recently. For adults, assessment approaches have typically relied upon self-report procedures, or on the observation of behaviour in naturalistic or analogue situations (Bellack & Hersen, 1977). With regard to children, assessment approaches that have become available and familiar to professionals and researchers include peer sociometric assessment techniques, teacher rating judgements and observational procedures (O'Connor, 1969, 1972).

Sociometric assessment techniques typically used in identifying students with peer-relationship problems, involve peer nominations (both positive and negative) and peer ratings. Positive nominations are obtained by asking the subject to name "three best friends" or "whom the subject is most likely to work (or play) with", whereas negative nominations are obtained by asking the subject to specify those children "whom he/she dislikes" or "with whom he/she does not like to interact" (French & Tyne, 1982).

With regard to peer ratings, the subjects are typically presented with a list of their peers and are asked to rate each peer along some social or interpersonal dimension based on a Likert-type scale. For example, Tyne & Flynn (1979) used this procedure by asking each student in a class to rate every classmate on a 6-point Likert-type social distance scale ranging from "don't like them" to "one of my best friends".

Teacher judgements that are frequently used to identify children experiencing peer-relationship difficulties, are obtained through the use of nomination, checklist, or rating procedures (French & Tyne, 1982). Nomination procedures require the teacher to specify the students who fit a particular criterion (e.g., shy or aggressive). With the checklist approach the teacher is required to determine which descriptors reflect each student's behaviour, while with ratings, the teacher quantitatively estimates the extent to which a given descriptor is characteristic of each student.

The above mentioned assessment approaches have proven useful in identifying students with peer relationship difficulties. However, these assessment approaches have not contributed a great deal to treatment programs because they identify neither the social context which presents a problem for a particular subject nor the component process skills in which the subject may be deficient (Dodge, McClaskey, & Feldman, 1985). Furthermore, they may be biased by subjective factors such as the personal characteristics as indicated in chapter 1. Shuller and MacNamara (1976) indicated that ratings by teachers are rather susceptible to experimenter biases. Hence, some researchers have attempted to find a new approach - called a situational approach - which is assumed to provide more detailed assessment that is more diagnostic in nature and thus is useful for social skills training of the individually maladjusted child in educational or clinical settings (Freedman, Rosenthal, Donahoe, Schlundt, & McFall, 1978; Gaffney & McFall, 1981; Dodge, McClaskey, & Feldman, 1985).

Within the situational approach, some authors (e.g., Dodge & Murphy, 1984; McFall & Dodge, 1982) have suggested that a three-step assessment model should precede any effective treatment plan for a maladjusted child. The first step, as they indicated, is to identify the maladjusted child (which previous assessment procedures are likely to do). The second step is to identify the particular social contexts, tasks, or situations where the child displays disruptive behaviour. The last step is to identify the sources of deficiency by assessing the child's particular component skills in each of the problematic situations.

The importance and power of assessing social problem solving or social competence in specific situations have been emphasized early by the "cognitive-behavior-analytic" model of Goldfried and D'Zurilla (1969). These authors proposed a set of guidelines for the construction of verbal problem-solving performance tests. Their guidelines consist of the following steps: (1) situational analysis (identifying significant problematic situations); (2) response enumeration (determining a range of possible responses or solutions for each situation); (3) response evaluation (judging the responses or solutions); (4) development of a measuring instrument format (e.g., pencil-and-paper questionnaires, free-response, multiple-choice, etc); and (5) evaluation of the measure (reliability and validity studies). They conducted an empirically based situational analysis and found it powerful in assessing social incompetence in college freshmen and in planning treatments for the population (Goldfried & D'Zurilla, 1969).

McFall and his colleagues (1978, 1981) have employed a similar approach. Based on Goldfried and D'Zurilla's model, these authors developed the Adolescent Problem Inventory (API) including 44 items (i.e., various problematic situations) (Freedman, Rosenthal, Donahoe, Schlundt, & McFall, 1978) and the Problem Inventory for Adolescent Girl (PIAG) including

23

52 problematic situation items (Gaffney & McFall, 1981). These measures have been found to be useful in identifying situation-specific social skills deficits in delinquent adolescents. For example, in a study referring to 60 adolescent boys (who were delinquents, non-delinquents, and student leaders), Freedman et al (1978) found that the API could differentiate between delinquents and non-delinquents. Another study that involved 30 institutionalized delinquent boys who were known to differ in their disruptiveness within an institution also indicated that the subjects were significantly different in their API performance (Freedman et al, 1978).

Spence (1980) also identified the specific interpersonal situations which children and adolescents mostly experienced as difficult, uncomfortable, or hard to handle. The List of Social Situation Problems (LSSP) includes 60 interpersonal problematic situations to which subjects answer "yes" or "no" depending on whether they view the situation as a problem for them. Factor analysis of the LSSP reported by Spence and Liddle (1990) revealed 8 factors, each of which focused on a specific type of social problem, such as social anxiety/assertiveness, dealing with strangers, temper control, social discomfort, conflict situations, problems with parents, making friends, and dealing with persons of the opposite gender. These factors were found to be useful in the identification of specific situations which an individual found problematic. Thus, they may serve as target areas in social skills training programs. For example, when they compared the responses of matched groups of depressed and non-depressed children on the LSSP, Spence and Liddle (1990) found a higher level of social problems amongst the depressed group than non-depressed group, particularly on factors relating to social discomfort and conflict situations.

Dodge et al (1985) have used a cross-situational approach to identify the situational contexts that are most likely to lead deviant elementary school children to experience social difficulties. These authors were successful in constructing the Taxonomy of Problematic Situations for Children (TOPS) that contained 44 situational items in six categories. The TOPS has provided a rich description of the contexts in which children experience peer difficulties and the instrument appears to be useful in the second step of Dodge and Murphy's (1984) model of clinical assessment, i.e., the identification of social situations that are particularly problematic for a particular child. Moreover, these authors identify specific component skill deficits (e.g., accurate encoding and interpretation of social cues, generation and evaluation of response alternatives and so on) in a particular child within these situations (the third step of Dodge and Murphy's model) by asking socially rejected, aggressive and adaptive children to role-play their probable responses for each situation. Dodge et al (1985) conducted a study that involved two groups of socially rejected and adaptive children. They found that the TOPS successfully distinguished a socially rejected group of children from an adaptive group, and that socially rejected children responded less competently overall than adaptive children. In this study, aggressive children were found to be significantly deficient in response to the categories: 'being provoked by peers' (such as being teased, hit, or insulted) and 'social expectations'. They have proposed that children's social behaviours are best understood as responses to specific situations or tasks, and that the clinical assessment of socially maladjusted children could benefit from taking a profile approach (i.e., a profile of assessments in each situation) to identify skills and deficits.

Evidence from empirical studies (Dodge, McClaskey, & Feldman; Freedman, Rosenthal, Donahoe, Schlundt, & McFall, 1978; Spence & Liddle, 1990) supports the cross-situational approach which is useful in both the clinical assessment and the design of intervention or prevention training programs. However, the approach may have a problem of external validity if the problematic situations do not represent a full range of the domain being measured. This issue will be discussed in the second part of this chapter.

Process versus outcome assessment

In considering the research on social problem solving, it is important to distinguish between two major types of problem-solving measures: (a) *process measures* and (b) *outcome measures*. According to D'Zurilla and Maydeu-Olivares (1995), process measures refer to the assessment of the general cognitive and behavioural activities which facilitate or inhibit a person's attempts to discover effective or adaptive problem-solving solutions, whereas outcome measures assess the quality of specific solutions to specific problems. Process measures are most useful for evaluating problem-solving attitudes and skills, whereas outcome measures are most useful for assessing problem-solving performance or a person's ability to employ his/her problem-solving skills effectively to specific problems.

Process measures may be divided into *inventories* (questionnaires) and *performance* tests. An inventory is a broad survey of problem-solving attitudes, strategies, and techniques. Most problem-solving inventories are pencil and paper questionnaires that use Likert-type items. However, some other formats can be used for this purpose, such as a structured personality/structured interview, audiotape procedures, and computer-assisted implementation. As indicated by D'Zurilla and his colleagues (1986, 1995), the disadvantage of inventories is that they do not actually test a person's problem-solving skills and abilities. Instead, they estimate the quality of the person's problem-solving skills or abilities. Whereas a performance test, that is classified as a process measure, directly assesses the ability to apply problem-solving skills to solve a particular problem-solving task. The performance format presents the subject with a problem-solving task which requires use of a specific ability or skills (e.g., problem orientation, problem definition and formulation, generation of alternative solutions, decision making). Such a performance test is perceived as a tool to indicate the level of ability in that particular area (D'Zurilla, 1986; D'Zurilla & Nezu, 1980; Nezu & D'Zurilla, 1979, 1981a, 1981b; Spivack, Platt, & Shure, 1976).

All outcome measures are classified as performance tests. These measures test overall problem-solving performance by presenting the person with a problematic situation and requiring that person to solve it (D'Zurilla & Maydeu-Olivares, 1995). Therefore, the assessment of problem-solving performance focuses on the product or outcome of the problem-solving process (the chosen solution). Most outcome measures use hypothetical test problems or real-life problematic situations presented orally or in written format. The subject may be asked to report his/her solution verbally or his/her actual solution performance may be observed (D'Zurilla & Maydeu-Olivares, 1995; Marx, William, & Claridge, 1992; Schotte & Clum, 1987). In general, performance measures are assumed to have greater external validity because they assess the subject's knowledge of the content of the problem-solving process and the ability to apply this knowledge to specific problematic tasks. Furthermore, they more closely approximate real-life problem-solving behaviour than inventories. However, the external validity of these measures is still an issue (such as problematic situations do not represent a full range of the domain being measured) that requires more empirical research.

Instead of estimating process and outcome separately, some investigators have proposed a conjoint approach (Goddard & McFall, 1992; Plienis et al, 1987). Within this approach, skills and abilities of a problem-solving process are directly assessed by presenting the subject with a particular problem-solving task, then these process measures are related to solution quality. For example, the 'think aloud' method described by Meichenbaum et al (1982) is a useful method for assessing covert processes during or following a problem-solving task. Likewise, the Articulated Thoughts during Simulated Situations (ATSS) procedure developed by Davison, Robins and Johnson (1983) is an example of this approach.

Verbal versus observational assessment

There are two approaches that can be used to assess problem-solving processes as well as outcome: (a) self-report or verbal problem-solving measures, and (b) observational measures. The former focuses on the individual's oral or written problem-solving responses. These measures

employ such methods as questionnaires, pencil-and-paper scales, inventories, structured interviews and verbal or written problem-solving tests, using real-life or hypothetical test problems.
The latter involves the direct observation of the subject's actual problem-solving behaviour in
the natural environment or in simulated problematic situations, e.g. role-play situations (quasi-
naturalistic, problem-solving situations) in an experimental or clinical setting (D'Zurilla &
Maydeu-Olivares, 1995). Verbal problem-solving assessment has two major advantages as follows: (1) it is the most practical, efficient, and cost-effective method to assess the problem-
solving skills and abilities of a large number of subjects across a wide range of problems; (2)
it is the only way to obtain a direct, comprehensive measure of covert problem-solving processes (D'Zurilla, 1986; D'Zurilla & Maydeu-Olivares, 1995).

The major disadvantages of verbal problem-solving assessment are threats to validity that are
related to any other self-report measure. Several investigators have indicated that verbal
measures of social problem solving lack clear-cut evidence of the relationship between these
measures and actual problem-solving behaviour in the real-life setting (Butler & Meichenbaum, 1981; D'Zurilla & Nezu, 1982; Kendall & Fischler, 1984). Some factors or variables
that limit the validity of verbal measures were discussed in the previous chapter. They may
include deliberate distortions, expectancy effects, response sets, comprehension problems,
emotionality, and motivations which are less likely to influence the individual's problem-solving performance in a test situation than in a real-life problem-solving situation (D'Zurilla,
1986; D'Zurilla & Maydeu-Olivares, 1995).

Another set of methodological factors that may reduce ecological validity involves test construction and administration. For example, some researchers found that the specific content or
types of solutions that children use may be influenced by the interpersonal context of the problem situation and by the level of apparent hostile intent that others display (Elias, Larcen,
Zlotlow, & Chinky, 1978; Dodge, Murphy, & Buchsbaum, 1984). Also, other studies have
indicated that children's behavioural problem-solving strategies in a natural setting differ from
their verbal responses to test social problem-solving situations (Asher, 1983; Gesten, Weissberg, Amish, Smith, 1987). In addition, there are possible differences in reinforcement contin-
gencies between a verbal test situation and a real-life problem-solving situation. For example,
when problems arise in the natural environment they tend to be more ambiguous than experimental situations (Tisdelle & St.Lawrence, 1986). Hence, it is better to view a verbal problem-
solving measure in most cases as an indication of a person's problem-solving potential, that
may not necessarily correlate highly with the person's current problem-solving behaviour in
the real-life setting (D'Zurilla, 1986).

In order to avoid the limitations of verbal assessment, some investigators have recommended that social problem-solving assessment should employ observational methods (Butler & Meichenbaum, 1981; Krasnor & Rubin, 1981; Tisdelle & St.Lawrence, 1986). Observational measures avoid most of the disadvantages of verbal assessment. However, as argued by D'Zurilla and Maydeu-Olivares (1995), these measures do have their own problems. This approach is considered as being costly, inefficient, time-consuming, and not practical for a large number of subjects. For example, it is clear that the frequency of relevant target behaviours is often low, especially in social settings such as the classroom, and that natural social problems (e.g., peer provocations) may appear similar yet are essentially different in terms of causation, duration, and outcome (Shantz, 1987; Vitaro & Pelletier, 1991). Moreover, the observational approach also has some serious threats to validity. For example, it is not possible to distinguish problem-solving solutions from experiential coping responses. Hence, an observer who records overt coping responses in real life or role-play stress situations, could not conclude that problem-solving ability is being measured (D'Zurilla & Maydeu-Olivares, 1995). In addition, a person's problem-solving performance in real-life problematic situations may be influenced significantly by other factors, such as emotional inhibitions or motivational deficits as noted earlier. Another potential problem of this approach is that solution outcomes might be confounded by the quality of the person's solution-implementation skills, namely, a potentially good problem-solving solution might have a poor outcome because the subject has a deficit in solution-implementation skills (which would reduce the validity of the outcome measure) (D'Zurilla & Maydeu-Olivares, 1995).

It would be useful to integrate these two approaches. Some researchers (e.g., D'Zurilla and his colleagues, 1986, 1995) have proposed a possible integrative strategy. For example, verbal measures might be used first to identify critical problematic situations for a particular target population, then observational measures could be employed to examine the individuals' overt problem-solving performance in these situations. Another form of this integrative approach is that of self-observation or problem-solving self-monitoring (Barlow, Hayes, & Nelson, 1984; D'Zurilla, 1986). Within this view, the subject identifies, observes, and records significant problematic situations, followed by mediation of cognitive-behavioural problem-solving activities and solution-implementation activities as they happen in the real-life world.

It is generally realized that assessment of problem-solving skills and abilities is important for identifying specific problem-solving deficits and subsequent planning of interventions as well as for assessing progress during training and intervention outcome. Hence, in order to maximize a test's reliability and validity, test issues will be identified in the following section.

Procedures and Issues in Test Design and Development

There is a practical need for a reliable and valid measure of general problem-solving abilities for children. Such a measure should consist of subtests that assess the full range of problem-solving abilities, including problem-orientation abilities, specific problem-solving skills, and basic problem-solving abilities. However, up to date, it has not yet been possible to develop such a measure.

The measures that are currently being used to assess problem-solving skills and abilities focus on only a limited number of component skills or abilities. The validity of these measures may be reduced because they fail to measure all of the component abilities required for effective problem solving. For example, the Means-Ends Problem-Solving Procedure (MEPS) (Platt & Spivack, 1975) designed to measure *means-ends thinking*. The hypothetical social situations used in the MEPS have fixed endings, and subjects are asked to tell what steps the protagonist would take to obtain the fixed problem solutions. Such a measure taps only one course of action per story. It does not identify indices of the subject's knowledge of possible alternative social problem-solving behaviour (e.g., the selection of irrelevant stimuli for the problem definition or an insufficient production of alternatives would result in ineffective problem-solving) and the subject's outcome expectations in the problematic situations (e.g., a negative problem orientation that inhibits effective problem solving would not be detected) (Joffe, Dobson, Fine, Marrigage, & Haley, 1990). Hence, it should not be surprising that these measures often fail to indicate a significant relationship with real-life problem-solving performance (Butler & Meichenbaum, 1981; D'Zurilla & Nezu, 1982; Kendall & Fischler, 1984). Some investigators have proposed suggestions for test construction and administration to maximize the reliability and validity of social problem-solving measures (Bellack & Hersen, 1977; D'Zurilla & Maydeu-Olivares, 1995; Goldfried & D'Zurilla, 1969). Their suggestions are discussed below.

Firstly, there is the *construction of content sampling and validity*. As these authors indicated, the first condition required is that the items of a problem-solving measure must be a representative sample of the domain being measured. In the development of process measures, the target domain would be some theoretical model of the social problem-solving process, or some specific component of that process (such as generation of alternative solutions). Regarding outcome measures, the relevant domain would be the range of everyday problems which the particular target population usually encounters. D'Zurilla and Maydeu-Olivares (1995) have suggested that a test developer firstly *identifies a target population*, secondly *defines the domain* to be measured, thirdly *specifies the goal* of the measuring instrument, and then *constructs items* in order to adequately represent the content of the target domain.

The procedures of sampling representativeness of items, as these authors suggested, include: (1) collection of items generated by people who are very familiar with the particular theoretical construct or problem domain (e.g., members of the target population; people who interact regularly with the members of the target population); (2) development of procedures to screen the items and retain the most representative ones; and (3) validation of the content sampling procedures (examining and checking the items against the relevant domain).

For outcome measures, it is important to sample all types of problems within the targeted domain. So far research has not yet determined if social problem-solving abilities are the same or different across different kinds of problems (Tisdelle & St.Lawrence, 1986).

Secondly, there are *procedures to distinguish between rational problem solving and experiential coping*. Process measures may satisfy these procedures if they are based on some theoretical model of rational problem solving. However, it is difficult for outcome tests to determine from the form or quality of situation-specific-coping responses alone whether they are actually problem-solving solutions, mediated by a rational problem-solving process, or automatic coping responses directly retrieved from memory (D'Zurilla & Maydeu-Olivares, 1995).

In order to overcome this difficult task, the test developer must identify possible difficult situations and retain only the most difficult situations during the test construction so as to ensure that the test items will be problematic, and thus, likely to generate rational problem-solving behaviour. D'Zurilla and his colleagues (1969, 1971, 1995) have provided productive guidelines for accomplishing the task. They recommend that the test problems should be administered to a sample of subjects from the target population using the think aloud method, interview, self-monitoring procedures, or questionnaires designed to obtain a report of their problem-solving processes during or following the problem-solving task. Then, investigators should analyse these reports to determine the extent to which rational problem-solving activities occurred. Test items would be retained only if they involved significant problem-solving thinking in all, or, the majority of subjects.

In another approach, based on the assumption that perceived problem-solving difficulty may be involved in generating problem-solving activities, D'Zurilla and Maydeu-Olivares (1995) suggested that subjects should be asked to solve each test problem and then rate how difficult the problem-solving task was immediately after reporting each solution. Test items would be considered problematic and retained if they are difficult for all or the majority of the subjects.

Item difficulty is assessed on the basis of independent solution effectiveness ratings. D'Zurilla and Maydeu-Olivares (1995) indicated that "test items are considered too easy if the effectiveness rating for all, or some high percentage of subjects is above some arbitrarily chosen high number, and too difficult if the rating for all or some high percentage of subjects is below some arbitrarily chosen low number"(p. 415). The elimination of extremely easy items discards many ordinary and routine stressors which may generate only experiential coping responses. However, this procedure alone is not sufficient to ensure that all of the remaining items will generate rational problem solving. Thus, other procedures are required. For example, asking individuals from the target population to report familiar and routine tasks or (pressures) which are likely to produce only experiential coping responses or to determine whether these individuals feel puzzled, perplexed, stumped, etc. which are important cues in order to determine whether or not problem solving will occur.

Thirdly, there are *procedures for instructions and format*. The instructions of social problem-solving measures can affect the validity of test responses. For example, subjects may understand the term "problem" (in inventories) in different ways and may respond inappropriately. Some studies have found that the quality of test responses varies with different test instructions (Freedman et al, 1978; Marx et al, 1992; Penn, Spaulding, & Hope, 1993). Freedman et al (1978) found that different instructions affected the API performance of both delinquents and non-delinquents, such as when told to respond with "the best" solution, all subjects did better than when they were told to say what they would actually "do". Although it is not clear from these studies what responses are most valid (with what kinds of instructions, under what conditions) some investigators have argued that the responses produced by self and actual solution instructions (such as, what would you *actually* do?) might have greater ecological validity (Camp, Doherty, Moody-Thomas, & Denney, 1989) because they increase the likelihood that the test problem will be received as personally relevant.

The validity of a test can also be influenced by the test format. For example, a study conducted by Freedman et al (1978) indicated that all subjects (delinquents and non-delinquents) did better when given the API items in a multiple-choice format than when given the items in a free-response format. Most social problem-solving measures use a pencil-and-paper format (D'Zurilla & Nezu, 1990; Heppner & Petersen, 1982; Platt & Spivack, 1975). Some tests use an audiotape procedure (Freedman et al, 1978; Goddard & McFall, 1992) or a structured interview (Heppner, Hibel, Neal Weinstein, Rabinowitz, 1982; Plienis, Hansen, Ford, Smith, Stark, & Kelly, 1987). All three of these formats involve verbal communication, and thus their validity may be influenced by poor comprehension of test items (in particular, for individuals with lower educational and intellectual levels). Hence, the best way to resolve the issue, as D'Zurilla and Maydeu-Olivares (1995) recommended, is for test developers to check the readability level of these tests.

Several investigators have reported that a free-response format and a forced choice format may produce different responses. For example, Freedman et al (1978) found that a multiple-choice version of their problem-solving test produced more effective responses than a free-response version. In contrast, the free-response version had the ability to distinguish between delinquents and non-delinquents, whereas the multiple-choice format did not have that ability. One possible explanation for these results is that in a free-response format the subject can use a broader range of problem-solving skills and abilities than in a multiple-choice format, where the subject is forced to choose between two or more given alternatives (D'Zurilla & Maydeu-Olivares, 1995).

Lastly, there are *scoring procedures*. There are two general types of scoring procedures that have been used in problem-solving measures: *quantitative scoring* and *qualitative scoring* (D'Zurilla & Maydeu-Olivares, 1995). In the former, some relevant solution variables are identified and a frequency count is viewed. For example, in the scoring system for the MEPS, quantitative scores are computed for relevant means (the sequenced steps that enable the protagonist to approach a particular problem-solving goal), obstacles (interferences with goal attainment), and time (references to the fact that effective problem solving takes time or appropriate timing is an important component of effective solution implementation) (Platt & Spivack, 1975; Spivack, Shure & Platt, 1985). In the latter, qualitative scoring usually involves a rating of a person's overall solution on some dimension of solution quality such as effectiveness, appropriateness, passivity, or avoidance (Fischler & Kendall, 1988; Freedman, Rosenthal, Donahoe, Schdlundt, & McFall, 1978; Getter & Nowinski, 1981; Marx, Williams, & Claridge, 1992).

Some investigators have argued that quantitative scoring may not provide adequate relevant information about the subject's solutions so as to distinguish between different levels of problem-solving competence and adjustment. For example, Fischler and Kendall (1988) indicated that only qualitative scores (i.e., appropriateness ratings) were related to adjustments in school children. Also, Marx et al (1992) suggested that only qualitative scores (i.e., effectiveness ratings) distinguished between depressed psychiatric patients and non-depressed patients. However, research has not yet determined whether qualitative scoring usually has more validity for certain purposes than quantitative scoring. Hence, as D'Zurilla and Maydeu-Olivares (1995) indicated, the best recommendation at the present time is that researchers should analyse their data using both types of scoring procedures.

D'Zurilla and Maydeu-Olivares (1995) have warned that a potential threat to the validity of social problem-solving measures, using solution effectiveness ratings, may occur when these ratings are performed by unqualified raters, who are not sufficiently familiar with the criteria that are generally used to estimate coping performance in the particular target environment. Qualified raters would consist of authority figures and experts such as supervisors, instructors, and counsellors who routinely evaluate coping behaviour in a particular setting. Qualified raters also include members of the target population who have previously been judged as competent on the basis of some criteria (such as grades, peer ratings, nominations, or scores on a valid measure of social problem-solving ability).

Recently, Yoman and Edelstein (1993) examined the external validity of solution effectiveness ratings by relating them to actual solution outcomes in a role-play situation (the raters were undergraduates who were judged to be socially competent on the basis of a score < 25 on the Social Introversion Scale of the MMPI). These authors failed to find any significant relation-ship between solution effectiveness ratings and actual-problem-solving goal accomplishment. Although the negative results increase questions about the validity of solution effectiveness ratings in general, it is possible that the Social Introversion Scale might not be a sufficient criterion for selecting socially competent solution raters (D'Zurilla & Maydeu-Olivares, 1995).

Summary

Assessment of problem-solving ability is important for identifying specific problem-solving deficits and subsequent planning of interventions and preventions, as well as assessing progress during training and intervention outcome. Major goals during the assessment phase are not only to identify problem-solving skill deficits (pin-pointing specific areas of the deficits), but also to determine whether a person's problems directly concern problem-solving skill deficits or whether they result from skill inhibitive variables which suggest intervention programs should focus on training skills or elimination of skill inhibition. Empirical evidence has endorsed that a combined cross-situational and behaviour-analytic approach is useful for identifying indices of the subject's knowledge of possible alternative social problem-solving behaviour, behaviour the subject would select in his/her own personal social problem solving, or the subject's out-come expectations in the problematic situations. Hence, the combined approach may satisfy the major goals of assessment.

In the assessment of social problem solving skills, it is important to distinguish between process measures and outcome measures, and between problem-solving ability and problem-solving performance. Process measures refer to the assessment of the general cognitive and behavioural activities which facilitate or inhibit one's problem-solving skills and abilities. Inventories are popular process measures that do not actually test one's problem-solving skills or ability, but test the quality of the person's problem-solving skills or abilities. In contrast, performance measures refer to the ability to apply these skills and abilities to particular problems.

Two general approaches to the assessment of problem solving are verbal assessment and observational assessment. Each approach has its own advantages and disadvantages which involve test validity and reliability. A promising strategy is to combine the advantages of these assessments. Then, there must be adequate attention to the procedures and issues of test construction and administration to maximize the reliability and validity of problem-solving measures.

Research Goals

The primary purpose of the present research was to utilise the combined cross-situational and behaviour-analytic approach to construct a social problem-solving measure specifically for Vietnamese adolescents. The measure would be able to pin-point specific deficient areas of interpersonal problem-solving. In order to achieve this purpose, five component goals were identified:

(1) to identify a taxonomy of interpersonal problems in adolescents;

(2) to identify a multi-dimensional model of social problem solving that functions as a valid theoretical basis for the development of this social problem-solving measure;

(3) to design an adolescent interpersonal problem-solving scale that is matched to the selected multi-dimensional problem-solving model;

(4) to design an additional behavioural measure for use by teachers to identify interpersonal problems in adolescents and assess their problem-solving behaviours;

(5) to evaluate the reliability and the validity of the problem-solving measure.

Chapter 3 presents material used to accomplish goal 1. Work pertaining to the remaining 4 goals is presented in chapters 4, 5 and 6.

Chapter 3

INTERPERSONAL PROBLEMS
IN ADOLESCENCE

In order to construct items for a social problem solving scale, a first task was to identify the interpersonal difficulties of adolescents from different aspects in order to find a relatively full range of possible interpersonal problems that confront them. This was considered very important for test construction which requires that the items of an interpersonal problem solving measure must be a representative sample of the domain being measured and that the relevant domain is the full range of interpersonal problems that confront the target population. This chapter firstly presents a general view of problems in adolescence and then discusses how a taxonomy of adolescent interpersonal problem situations was constructed.

Adolescence as Developmental Transition

Adolescence is defined as the developmental transition from childhood to adulthood (Nguyen, 1994; Nguyen, 2016; Petersen, Silbereisen, & S"rensen, 1996). The developmental transition, as some researchers have indicated, is a period of life in which there is a great deal of change, both within the individual and within the individual's social environment (Eichorn, Mussen, Clausen, Haan, & Honzik, 1981. Nguyen & Nguyen, 2017). A cross-national perspective reveals that there is not one universal age range which can be defined as the adolescent period, but that pubertal change is the best way to index adolescent development (Nguyen, 1991, 2016; Nguyen & Nguyen, 2019; Offrey & Rinaldi, 2017; Petersen & Hamburg, 1986; Petersen et al, 1996). However, adolescence is often divided into two main phases: early adolescence that is between 12 and 15 years, and late adolescence is from 16 to 20 years (Kagan & Coles, 1972; Nguyen, 2016). Early adolescence is often recognized as the most difficult and challenging period because, for the first time, the child is faced with new social environments which involve new developmental tasks and require more complex social skills (Kelly, 1982).

The adolescent period involves a great deal of change including physical-social-cognitive changes and relationship changes that may make it more difficult than the years which precede or follow it (Conger, 1973). For many adults, adolescence is seen as a tumultuous phase of development (Petersen & Ebata, 1987; Petersen & Hamburg, 1986; Petersen et al, 1996; Rabichow & Sklansky, 1980). Some mental health professionals have used the term *adolescent turmoil* to describe both disturbed adolescents and processes of normal development (Offer,

1987). There are many studies that have reported the proportion of young people who experience difficulties, such as psychological disorders or involvement in various kinds of substance abuse (e.g., Green & Horton, 1982; Petersen & Hamburg, 1986), that increase during the adolescent years (Kaplan, Hong, & Weinhold, 1984; Rutter et al, 1976; Weiner, 1980).

However, during the last two decades, Offer and his colleagues have examined normal adolescent development across diverse populations of adolescents (Offer, 1969; Offer & Offer, 1975; Offer, Ostrov, & Howard, 1981; Offer, Ostrov, Howard, & Atkinson, 1988) and they indicate that the majority (approximately 80 %) of adolescents do *not* experience turmoil or psychological disturbance. Another study of young adolescence conducted by Petersen and her colleagues (Petersen & Ebata, 1987; Petersen at al, 1987) revealed that 11% of young adolescents had serious, chronic difficulties, 32% had more situational and intermittent difficulties, and 57% had positive healthy development. In contrast, studies of the problems of elementary school students reported that between 5% and 15% of the population experienced significant interpersonal relationship problems (Asher & Renshaw, 1981).

A consensus view would be that adolescent behavioural problems are related to coping with developmental tasks, decreasing controls by adults, and increasing peer-related activities, which are probably characteristic of the transition to adulthood (D'Hondt & Vandeweile, 1983, 1984; Kandel & Adler, 1981; Morales & Atilano, 1977; Teichmann, Rahav, & Barnea, 1987).

Identification and A Taxonomy of Adolescent
Interpersonal Problems

It has been accepted that the importance and power of interpersonal relationships in adolescence are far greater than in childhood or in any other age group (Furman & Gavin, 1989; Mitchell, 1974). Interpersonal relations take an increasingly important role in the socialization process during adolescence. For example, peer relationships are believed to serve a variety of functions which contribute to adolescents' social development and learning, and cognitive-emotional development (Berndt, 1982; Dusek, 1991; Hendry et al, 1993, Nguyen & Nguyen, 2017, 2018). Hartup & Sancilio (1986) indicated that friendships function as the "context" in which specific basic competencies emerge. These specific basic competencies consist of cooperation skills, group entry behaviour, impulse controls, self-evaluation, self-knowledge, general knowledge, and social communication skills. Some researchers found that adolescents report spending more time talking to peers than on any other activity and describe themselves as most happy when so engaged (Hamilton & Darling, 1989; Hendry, 1989; Hendry et al, 1993;

Montemayor, 1982). For example, a study by Hendry et al (1993) suggested that about 80 % of teens aged 13-14 viewed peer group acceptance as important. With increasing importance of peer relationships, adolescents may suffer more difficulties than younger children when there is a break in a relationship (e.g., a close friend moves away). Poor interpersonal relationships and deficits of interpersonal problem solving have been associated with suicide (Rotherham-Borus, Trautman, Dopkins, & Shrout, 1990; Sadowski & Kelly, 1993; Semrud-Clikeman, 2007, Nguyen, 2017, 2019), psychiatric problems (Cowen et al, 1973; Joffe, Dobson, Fine, Marriage, & Haley, 1990), school drop out (Barclay, 1966; Wentzel, 1991), academic failure (Dishion, 1990; Kathryn, 2011; Wentzel, 1991) and delinquency (Roff & Wirt, 1984). It is clear that those adolescents who experience problems in their interpersonal relationships may be missing a large part of their social and personal developmental progress (Fine, 1981, Nguyen & Nguyen, 2017, 2019) and that the high levels of aggressive and inappropriate behaviour in adolescents in a rejected group usually place them at risk of delinquency and school dropout (Gottlieb, 1991). This is why a majority of social problem-solving training programs in high schools focus on interpersonal problems in adolescents.

Interpersonal problems are defined as *difficulties between individuals* such as difficulties between an individual and boy/girl friends, parents, authority figures, and peers (Heppner, Hibel, Neal, Weinstein, & Rabinowitz, 1982; Nguyen, 2016, 2017, 2019; Nguyen & Nguyen, 2017, 2019). In this view, interpersonal problems in adolescents are perceived as interpersonal difficulties that occur in interpersonal relationships between an adolescent with his/her peers (same sex and opposite sex), parents, teachers, other adults, and younger children. Within the interpersonal relationship domain, family relationships in adolescence are also of high emotional and social importance because one of the developmental tasks during adolescence is to become emotionally, socially, and economically detached from the important reference group that the family represents (Hurrelmann, 1996; Nguyen & Nguyen, 2017, 2019). Some studies suggest that adolescents tend to move away from their parents and toward closer relationships with their peers (Hamilton & Darling, 1989; Hendry, 1989; Montemayor, 1982). Klagholz (1987) reported a study in which 223 adolescents (aged 15-18) indicated that peers were the most frequent choice as "significant people in their lives" and mothers the second most frequent choice.

A study of urban and suburban high school students (Offer et al, 1990, cited in Offer & Boxer, 1991) revealed that when normal adolescents have an emotional problem, they often discuss it with a friend (> 70%) and with their parents (> 60%), but rarely discuss it with their teachers (< 10%). For disturbed adolescents, the rates were the same for peers and for teachers, but less than 35% of the youths would discuss an emotional problem with parents. Another study of nomination (who is your confidential communication partner?) conducted by Bois-Reymond and Ravesloot (1996) involving 119 adolescents indicated that 57% of the respondents maintained confidential relationships with peers, whereas 17.65% of the respondents shared their personal thoughts and problems with mothers and less than 4% mentioned their fathers or both their parents. The data from a report of the Youth Psychological Counselling Centre in Hanoi (Vietnam) (Nguyen, 1994) suggested that a majority of adolescents' difficulties involve peers and parents. Approximately 80% of 965 letters that the centre received (from 1990 to 1993) from Vietnamese youths throughout Viet Nam aged 12-22 years complained about difficulties relating to peers and their parents, whereas only a small percentage (less than 8%) of these letters involved problems with other adults.

Although there are various findings in the literature, peer and family relationships in adolescence are generally believed to be the most important interpersonal relationships that serve various functions in the socialization process. Thus, adolescent difficulties in these relationships are considered to be the most significant influence on future negative adjustments. For example, an adolescent girl who is constantly rejected by her peers may become anxious and withdraw into lonely isolation. A boy who has been subjected to harsh or inconsistent discipline and to rejection or ridicule by his parents in the course of growing up may emerge as an angry and destructive adolescent (Conger, 1979).

Some studies of parent-adolescent conflict have suggested that high levels of conflict are related to adolescents' moving away (Gottlieb & Chafetz, 1977), running away (Blood & D'Angelo, 1974; Singh, 1984), marrying or becoming pregnant early (McKenry, Walters, & Johnston, 1979), dropping out of school (Bachman, Green, & Wirtanen, 1971), developing psychiatric disorders (Rutter et al, 1976; Hurrelmann, Engel, Holler, & Nordlohne, 1988; Desjardins & Leadbeater, 2011), and attempting suicide (Sadowski & Kelly, 1993).

Difficulties with teachers and other adults, as indicated above, seem to occupy a relatively low rank in adolescent interpersonal difficulties. However, there are very few studies in this field, thus it is not clear whether the impact of these difficulties is less important. In fact, some studies have indicated that, when disengagement from the family occurs, contact with an interested, supportive adult plays a particularly important role in "buffering" the adolescent against his/her behavioural problems (Hetherington, 1989). Among significant adults, teachers and coaches were most likely to be nominated by adolescents (Bois-Reymond & Ravesloot, 1996).

The typical environments for adolescent activities are class, school, family, streets or neighbourhood, and social groups where the most important interpersonal relationships of adolescent life are present. For the purpose of the present study, in order to identify a range of possible problematic areas for adolescents, a search was made of potentially problematic situations from a variety of sources: (1) problem inventories developed especially for adolescents which used problematic situations as items, eg. the Adolescent Problem Inventory (API) developed by Freedman[2] (1978) and the Problem Inventory for Adolescent Girls (PIAG) developed by Gaffney and McFall[3] (1981); (2) studies involving adolescents such as "Stress management for teenagers" (Bunnell, 1988) and studies conducted by the author and his colleagues (Nguyen; 1991; Nguyen, 1993; Pham, Nguyen & Nguyen, 1991)[4]; (3) a large pool of 967 letters sent to the Youth Psychological Counselling Center (YPCC) complaining about problematic difficulties[5]; (4) problem situations collected in the author's interviews or talks on adolescent psychology with adolescents, teachers, parents, and psychologists; (5) the literature on adolescent interpersonal difficulties in general developmental text books.

After analysing the difficulties identified from these sources, especially from those identified by the adolescents in our studies, it was found that difficulties in adolescent years had a broader range and more variety than those in the years which precede adolescence. For example, these adolescents worried about subjects such as behaviours threatened their well-being (e.g., being teased or rejected by peers) or threats to their life, such as pollution of the environment, famine or plague. One explanation is that adolescents expand the domain of "what matters". As Larson and Asmussen (1991) have suggested, "adolescents' experiences of anger, worry, and hurt can be understood as responses to breaches of what really matters, as the difference between life as they expect and want it and life as it actually is" (p. 23).

---

[2] API includes 44 situational items designed to measure social competence (personal and interpersonal skills) among adolescent boys.
[3] PIAG consists of 52 situational items designed to assess girls' strengths and weaknesses in interpersonal situations and measure social competence among adolescent girls.

[4] These studies include: (1) a study of values and oriented values (Nguyen, 1993) that involved 369 high school students at 3 regular high schools (urban and suburban) aged from 15 to 19; (2) a survey of the psychology of puberty that concerned 2000 high school students aged 14 to 20 from 18 high schools in north Viet Nam and 21 high schools in the south of Viet Nam (Nguyen, 1991); and (3) a study of an anticipated model for Vietnamese youths in the year 2000 and later that concerned over 10.000 adolescents and youths throughout Viet nam (Pham et al, 1991) in which we asked subjects the following questions: "What are the greatest difficulties that you were confronted with during the last three months?; (b) What are the most things that you worry about?; (c) List the greatest difficulties you have or have experienced with your friends, parents or teachers (no more than three)?".

[5] The YPCC which is situated in Hanoi (Viet Nam) received 967 letters from Vietnamese youths throughout this country from 1990-1993 (Nguyen, 1994).

Further analysis of adolescent difficulties also revealed that there are differences in quantity and quality between adolescent boys and girls concerning difficulties. That is, adolescent girls seem to have more problems than boys, and the problems identified by girls appear to be more concerned with being hurt and are more emotional than those identified by boys or, girls are more willing to report/discuss their difficulties. For example, about two thirds of the YPCC's letters came from adolescent girls. Moreover, the most serious and complex difficulties found in these letters belonged to teen-age girls (see the example p 61-62). According to Offer and Boxer (1991), adolescent girls are more attached to their relatives and friends and are more sensitive to social problems than adolescent boys and thus they have more problems or are more likely to feel hurt than adolescent boys. This is consistent with some researchers' conclusions that adolescent girls are more likely to report significant depressed affect or that they are easier to hurt than boys (Earls, 1986; Offer & Boxer, 1991).

With regard to interpersonal difficulties, a majority of difficulties are familiar to primary and secondary school students. The majority of these difficulties usually involve problematic situations such as being teased or bullied and rejected by peers, being nagged by parents, being treated unfairly by teachers and so on. However, a significant number of adolescents' problematic situations were strange or unfamiliar to primary school students, such as the difficulties involving a "love-emotional affair", a "peaceful family being threatened" or "occupational selection". Analysis of these difficulties revealed that many of these situations seem to be of low consequence for adults in terms of stress, importance, and resolution, yet are "big" problems for the adolescent (see the examples p. 60-61). In most all problematic situations occurring in adolescence, the presence of emotional beliefs, emotional arousal and personal-interpersonal expectations are important components of the perceived underlying causes of the problems or social contexts in which they occur. One possible explanation is that adolescents experience difficulties that may be a result, not of an objectively harder or harsher world, but of subjective changes which make it seem harder (Larson & Asmussen, 1991).

In conducting assessments, based on a combined cross-situational and behaviour-analytic approach, several researchers (Freedman et al, 1978; Gaffney & McFall, 1981, Dodge et al, 1985) first generated a taxonomy of problematic social situations for their targeted populations and then evaluated competence within each situation. The Taxonomy of Problematic Situations for Children (TOPS) developed by Dodge et al (1985) contained 44 items (problematic situations) in eight categories: (a) responding to peer group norms (when this child is working on a class project that requires sharing or cooperation); (b) being identified as different from one's peers (when peers notice that this child is somehow different, such as walking funnily or dressing peculiarly); (c) attempting to initiate entry into the peer play group (when this child wants to play with a group of peers, but the peers tell the child to wait); (d) responding to ambiguous provocation by a peer (when another child takes this child's turn in a game); (e) being excluded or rejected by peers (when peers have started a game and not included this child); (f) being identified as superior to the peer group (when this child has won a game against peers); (g) responding to failure (when this child loses a game against peers); and (h) responding to negative statements about oneself made by peers (when peers call this child a bad name). The eight categories were then revised and reduced to six factors (based on analysing the items with loadings greater than .30): (1) Peer Group Entry where the child's task is to initiate inclusion into the peer group (items from the original "group entry" factor and "being excluded from peer group" factor); (2) Response to Peer Provocations, in which the task is to preserve self-integrity while maintaining peer status (items from the original "provocation" factor, the "being identified by peers as being different" factor, and the "negative peer statements" factor); (3) Response to Failure (items from the original factor of the same name); (4) Response to Success (items from the original factor of responses to "being identified as superior"); (5) Social Expectations where clear social norms for the child's behaviour are stated (some of the items from the original "peer group norms" factor); and (6) Teacher Expectations where the classroom teacher has stablished clear norms for child behaviour (also some of the items from the "peer group norms" factor).

Based on the work described about, in the present study, adolescent interpersonal difficulties were ordered into five domains based on the following major relationships: *adolescent - peers, adolescent - parents, adolescent - teachers, adolescent - other adults, and adolescent - younger children.*

The interpersonal difficulties of adolescents were characterized and categorised as representative groups within these five domains. These were:

1. Difficulties faced by adolescents in peer relationships:
   - Having difficulty in peer group entry (being boycotted by the class, being excluded from the peer group or being rejected by the peer group).
   - Being teased/bullied/insulted by other peers.
   - Having personal wishes frustrated or prevented by other peers.
   - Being cut off from intimate friendships.
   - Being involved in love-emotional affairs.

- Being involved in illegal or dangerous behaviour (in an anti-social friendship group or a criminal gang) where the subject didn't want to engage in group behaviour, but found it difficult to object or refuse.
- Being accused unjustly or being misunderstood.

2. Difficulties in relationships with parents:
   - Being nagged by parents (e.g., not doing chores, eccentricity of dress or hair, having "strange" behaviour).
   - Being neglected by parents.
   - Being treated/blamed unfairly or being punished/threatened unjustly.
   - Being insulted or being condemned in front of one's friends.
   - Feeling depressed about conflict in the family or worried about a peaceful family being disrupted by something or somebody.
   - Complaining of parents' "strict" authority, despair of parent's behaviour, and personal wishes or occupational intentions being prevented by parents.

3. Difficulties in relationships with teachers:
   - Being treated unfairly or being punished/threatened/accused unjustly.
   - Being insulted or condemned in front of the class.
   - Being prevented from doing favourite work or participating in favourite activities.
   - Having trouble/conflict or aversion to teacher(s).

4. Difficulties with other adults:
   - Having one's work (or wishes) frustrated or disturbed by adults.
   - Being insulted by adults.
   - Being involved in anti-social behaviour by adults, but finding it difficult to escape or refuse.
   - Being depressed about a significant adult where admiration has been lost or challenged.
   - Witnessing threats or dangers to adults.

5. Difficulties with younger children:
   - Being disturbed by children's behaviour.
   - Having one's work or activity disrupted by children.

Although we attempted to characterize and classify the adolescent interpersonal difficulties into representative categories, some problematic situations that are relatively complicated may represent more than one category, or even more than one domain. The following problematic situation quoted from one of the letters noted above is a typical example:

"I am writing a letter to you in a hopeless state... and the only one way I can escape is to end my life, although more than once I have tried to suicide unsuccessfully... My name is Thanh Hang (i.e., moon light), year 11, 17 years old. I had been a top student at secondary school. However, my study has gone down hill in the last few years, and I am currently, as my teacher has said, a "idle-worthless" student with "intermittent-aggressive problems". The reason for my decreasing study is that I have been suffering a long serious torment... my Mum always "sings old blaming songs" day by day. In addition, my Dad only cares about money and alcohol (or beer), characterized by intermittent anger...

They inhibit me of many things (such as dress and hairstyle), whereas they are free to do these things (e.g., my Mum is over forty years old, yet often dresses in a fashionable way that is suitable for youths). Like other adolescent girls, I have friends (both male and female). Although many opposite sex friends like me (which may be due to my pretty form, as my friends said), I haven't accepted one as a boy-friend because I realize that the love-affair is too early at high school time. However, my Mum doesn't like me to have a lot friends, especially boy-friends. She usually refuses socially entertaining offers or healthy activities from my friends and several times has asked my friends to get out in provocative ways (after my parents' unhospitality, I have several times got into trouble from their boycotts that made me more depressed... and I did not want to live, because I can not live without friends).

Recently, I have been blamed by my teacher who seems to care only about "disciplinary norms" and would like to get me out of her class (she has more than once asked the school to punish me by suspending my study and refusing to allow me to come back to her class after that, because I cut class three days without permission). For this fault, my mum took her spite out on me with all the worst damned words which are suitable for a non-human being delinquent only... My name is "moon light", yet I haven't had a moment of my youth with joy and sadness being shared (I have often hidden my sadness so as to communicate with my friends). In fact, I have been living in a family that is like prison and its members like jailers" (N. T. H, Hanoi city).

This situation represents the characterized categories: "being treated/blamed unfairly by parents", "being insulted or being condemned in front of one's friends by parents" and "being depressed by parent's behaviour, or personal wishes being prevented by parents".

Here are some more typical examples of the variety of interpersonal difficulties that face adolescents:

"I have a big problem which has kept me from concentrating on my studies. It is about my classmate who is one of my close friends. I knew him from the first high school opening day, but we were close friends only after our class picnic a few months ago. Then, as time passed, I found my infatuation for him growing. Whenever we are in the classroom, I often look at him, and I am usually surprised to find him looking me... Now, he has suddenly stopped talking to me. He seems to be avoiding me if possible... I don't know what to do. Please give me your advice" (P. T. N, Haiphong city). This situation represents the characterized category: "being involved in love-emotional affairs".

"I am suffering torment...my parents are so busy with their work. They rarely talk to me except during meals, but they often have angry attitudes toward me when they have trouble with work. Although they support me, what I need is their love, I really thirst for fondness...One day I wheedled my mum by leaning on her shoulder, nevertheless she pushed me aside and shouted at me: "Are you a baby?". I felt upset and self-pitying. I am not a baby, but not adult. I have some pleasant things from my school, my friends but no one to share...", (N. T. L, Namdinh city). This situation is a representative of the category: "being neglected by parents".

"I am 15 years old, successful in my study, and a pretty girl (as my friends said). I have many opposite-sex friends, but none that is considered a boyfriend since I really regard my study. However, my parents are very strict, they don't like me to have boyfriends. Once my opposite-sex friends come to see me, my parents get them out of my house. I feel ashamed and insulted, and tormented with what my parents have done. In addition, my friends have set up a boycott against me. Now I feel lonely, and down in my study...I have every thing (from my parental support) except friendships. Instead of being with my parents, I feel I am under my parents' surveillance..." (N. T. V, Hue city). This represents the groups: "Being insulted or condemned in front of one's friends by parents" and "Being boycotted by peers".

44

Other typical examples of interpersonal difficulties identified by adolescents in the author's interviews or talks were:

"A group of boys are resting under the shade of a tree on the school-ground. They have just sweated out one game of soccer. A, one of players playing in the first line, teases B as instead of kicking the ball he seems to care about chopping C (another first-line player) down. B blushes and returns the teasing, this time directing it at D, who, caught unawares, stands up and angrily throws the ball at B…" (V. T. N, Cantho city). This situation is a representative of the category: "being teased by peers".

"I was finally admitted to a gang which I have wanted to join for a long time. However, as days pass, I begin to disagree with some of the practices of the gang like cutting classes when the lesson is not interesting or smoking marijuana. As a member, I am supposed to do as the rest do but I have been trained in self-discipline by my parents…" (P. V. T, Hochiminh city). This situation belongs to the category: "Being involved anti-social or illegal behaviour".

"Once I washed my Dad's clothes, I suddenly found a letter from a strange woman in his pocket. Out of curiosity, I read it…I found that the woman had fallen in love with my dad and they have had dates… I felt upset and worried, because I realise that it appears to threaten our peaceful family" (N. T. L, Vinh city). This situation may represent the category: "Peaceful family being threatened".

"A teacher accuses me of writing swear words on the toilet wall, and is threatening to put me down to a lower class. I know I didn't do it, but my close friend did" (T. V. H, Laocai city). This is a representative of the group: "Being accused unjustly by a teacher".

The problematic situations identified by adolescents seem not to be similar to those identified by parents. When we asked 47 parents of regular high school students (from year 10 to year 12) and 106 parents of maladjusted or disruptive high school students (from years 8 to year 12) to identify frequently occurring problematic difficulties between them and their children, we found that several categories were distinct from the categories of difficulties that were identified by adolescents. The categories of difficulties that were identified by parents were:

- Feeling loss of parental authority

- Feel depressed/upset about the teenager's disruptive behaviour at school
- Having conflicts/aversion in the relationship between an adolescent and his/her parent
- Parents' work or activities disrupted by children
- Assigned household-work or chores were not completed
- Having bad habits or non-acceptable behaviour similar to a parent

Typical kinds of difficulties complained about by parents are exemplified in these accounts:

"Since my husband and I split up, my children have gotten worse and worse grades at high school. I am really worried about my oldest daughter, 14 years old. She used to be a top student…but now she is failing math and science. On top of that, she has had a real sullen, angry attitude toward me… In her mind I seemed to be solely responsible for the divorce that led to her Dad leaving. I tried to talk to her but I failed since she stick to her opinion. I need advice from you" (N. T. L, Hanoi city). This represents the category: "having conflits/aversion in the adolescent-parent relationship".

"I have two children, a 13 year-old daughter and a 6 year-old son. I've told my daughter over and over that I expect her to keep her room clean and do the chores, but she doesn't do a thing without being reminded again and again. In fact, the daughter acts just like my husband". This is a representative of the group: "having bad habits or non-acceptable behaviour similar to a parent".

"I am worried about my 16 year-old son. He is all I have, thus I want him only to concentrate on his study at high school so as to enter university in the future. I supervise him carefully and often refuse or do not allow him to attend any social group…However, recently his teacher advised me that my son cut his afternoon class and that he seemed to involve in smoking marijuana" (P. T. H, Hanoi city). This situation may represent the category: "feel depressed/upset about the teenager's behaviour at school".

The categories of difficulties that were identified by teachers also seem to differ from those identified by adolescents. Two samples including 25 teachers at a regular high school and 41 teachers at a special high school were asked to identify their difficulties in relationships with their students by describing the three most problematic difficulties that they or their colleagues were confronted with during a school year. These difficulties were categorized as follows:

- Difficulty in eliminating bad or foul language in class or school

- Disrupting/violating classroom discipline (in which the teacher has established clear norms or rules for student's behaviour, but some students violate, such as cutting classes or not doing homework or talking without permission)
- Having conflicts/aversion in the student-teacher relationship
- Difficulty in getting parents to cooperate to prevent anti-social or illegal behaviour of students.

Below are some typical problematic situations that were identified by high school teachers:

"I have one student in my eighth-grade class who worried me a lot. He has no problem with his learning, but he talks too much in the classroom and often disrupts the class by clowning around or teasing other classmates. He is sometimes involved in fighting. When I talked to his parents, they said he had no disruptive behaviour at home...I don't know why and what I should do with him" (T. T. V, Haiphong city). This situation may represent the category: "disrupting classroom discipline".

"Some students in my tenth-grade class always use bad language in class. I've warned them several times and set punishments if they violate the rule...Recently, some teachers found that swear words were written on the toilet wall and they thought these students did it (because they have been involved more than once in this action). I thought so, and expected to punish those who did it. When I asked all my students who did it, no one admitted to it...These students also said that they didn't do it. They even laughed to annoy me" (L. T. H, Hanoi city). This is a representative of the group: "using foul language at school".

Some problematic situations were found to overlap categories and could represent more than one of the categories outlined above.

Summary

The adolescent period is defined as the developmental transition from childhood to adulthood which involves a great deal of change that may make it more difficult than the preceding years. About one in five adolescents experience problems which are related to coping with development tasks, decreasing controls by adults, and the increasing peer-related activities. Interpersonal problems are the most significant part of social problems, influencing the adolescent's socialization. They are perceived as difficulties with others, including peers, parents, teachers, younger children, and other adults. Interpersonal difficulties in adolescence occur over a broader range than those in childhood and they are judged and identified discrepantly through different populations and social contexts. Hence, in conducting adolescent social problem-solving assessments, it is necessary first to generate a taxonomy of social problematic situations for the targeted populations and then evaluate social problem-solving abilities within each situation. The identification and categorization of adolescent interpersonal problematic situations presented in this chapter are useful for the construction of representative problematic situations in the next chapter.

Chapter 4

RATIONALE FOR THE DESIGN AND DEVELOPMENT OF THE SOCIAL PROBLEM SOLVING SCALE

The need for the development of a reliable and valid measure of problem-solving ability for adolescents has been noted since the 1970s (D'Zurilla & Goldfried, 1971; Spivack & Shure, 1974; Spivack et al., 1976). Such a measure should be based on an empirically supported theoretical model and then should be administered to different samples to evaluate its psychometric properties. However, as indicated by researchers (e.g., D'Zurilla et al., 1996; Frauenknecht & Black, 1995), one of the difficulties in research on social problem solving was the lack of a comprehensive, theory-based, and multi-dimensional measure of social problem solving. The absence of such a measure is particularly acute in the research on social problem solving in adolescence. In order to meet the need, the Social Problem Solving Scale (SPST) was designed to pinpoint interpersonal problem-solving deficits in adolescents.

The development of the SPST is based on the theories of social problem solving developed by D'Zurilla and colleagues (D'Zurilla, 1986, D'Zurilla & Goldfried, 1971; D'Zurilla & Maydeu-Olivares, 1995; D'Zurilla & Nezu, 1982, 1990; Goldfried and D'Zurilla, 1969). The SPST is a multi-dimensional problem-solving measure that is designed specifically for adolescents. The measure is classified as an outcome performance test designed to assess facilitative (adaptive) and inhibitive (dysfunctional) dimensions of interpersonal problem solving competence in adolescents.

The SPST employs a cross-situational approach and incorporates guidelines for test construction based on the "cognitive-behaviour-analytic" approach proposed by D'Zurilla and his colleagues (D'Zurilla & Goldfried, 1971; Goldfried and D'Zurilla, 1969). It starts from choosing and modifying an empirically supported theoretical model of social problem solving and then based on the modified model to develop particular procedures to test construction including: (a) situational analysis (identifying significant interpersonal problematic situations); (b) response enumeration (generation of possible responses and solutions); (c) response evaluation (judging the solutions); (d) development of a test format (e.g., pencil-and-paper and free response); and (e) evaluation of the measure (reliability and validity studies). These phases are presented in this chapter, with the exception of the psychometric evaluation of the SPST which will be discussed in the next chapter.

A Modified Model of Social Problem Solving

The development of the SPST is based on the empirically derived, five-dimensional model of social problem solving (D'Zurilla et al., 1996) that is linked to the original theory-driven social problem-solving model introduced by D'Zurilla and Goldfried (1971). The model of social problem solving originally developed by D'Zurilla and Goldfried (1971) stated that problem-solving outcomes in the natural environment are generally determined by two main, but partially independent processes: (1) *problem orientation* and (2) *problem-solving proper*.

Problem orientation is primarily a motivational process that involves the operation of a set of cognitive-emotional schemas (both constructive and dysfunctional) that include the generalized thoughts and feelings of a person involving real-life problems, as well as the person's own problem-solving ability. Problem orientation, however, does not consist of specific problem-solving skills.

Problem-solving proper refers to the rational search for a solution through the application of specific problem-solving strategies or skills and techniques (e. g., problem definition and formulation, generation of alternative solutions, etc.) that help the person to discover the best or most effective solution or coping response for any problematic situation in life.

The two-factor model was expanded into a hierarchical model with seven first-order factors and two second-order factors to develop the Social Problem-Solving Inventory (SPSI) (D'Zurilla & Nezu, 1990). However, empirical studies have indicated moderate support for the two-factor model but not for the hierarchical model (Maydeu-Olivares & D'Zurilla, 1996; Sadowski, Moore & Kelly, 1994).

Further analyses, using exploratory and confirmatory methods, have found that a five-dimensional model is most appropriate for the SPSI in terms of goodness-of-fit, parsimony, and cross-validation criteria (Maydeu-Olivares, & D'Zurilla, 1996). This five-dimensional model has been chosen as the theoretical basis for the Social Problem Solving Scale. The five dimensions of the revised social problem-solving model are: (1) *positive problem orientation*, (2) *negative problem orientation*, (3) *rational problem solving*, (4) *impulsivity/carelessness style*, and (5) *avoidance style*. The first two dimensions involve problem orientation, whereas the remaining three dimensions relate to problem-solving proper.

As defined by D'Zurilla & Maydeu-Olivares (1995), positive problem orientation is described as a constructive, problem-solving cognitive "set", which concerns the general tendency to: (a) view a problem as a challenge; (b) believe that problems are solvable (optimism); (c) have confidence in one's own personal ability to solve problems successfully (self-efficacy); (d) have a belief that successful problem solving takes time, effort, and persistence; (e) have commitment to solving problems with dispatch rather than avoiding them. In contrast, negative problem orientation is perceived as a dysfunctional cognitive-emotional set that generally tends to: (a) appraise a problem as a significant threat to well-being, (b) believe that problems are unsolvable (pessimism), (c) have doubts about one's personal ability to solve problems successfully (low self-efficacy), and (d) became frustrated and upset when faced with problems in life (low frustration tolerance).

In relation to problem-solving skills, rational problem solving is defined as the rational, deliberate, systematic, and efficient application of effective or adaptive problem-solving skills and techniques (i.e., problem definition and formulation, generation of alternative solutions, decision making, and solution implementation verification).

In contrast, the impulsivity/carelessness style is a dysfunctional dimension that involves active attempts to apply problem-solving skills and techniques, but these attempts tend to be impulsive, careless, hurried and incomplete. Avoidance style is defined as another dysfunctional dimension characterized by procrastination (putting off solving problems), passivity (waiting for problems to resolve themselves), and dependency (passing the responsibility for problem solving to others) (D'Zurilla et al., 1996).

Based on the assumption that how people think or feel can affect what they do, it can be argued that each problem-solving dimension may be defined as a separate construct including two layers (or levels): (a) *affect-cognition* and (b) *action.* The affect-cognition level involves what the problem-solver thinks or feels (problem orientation). The action level involves what the problem-solver does (problem-solving skills). Hence, the five-component model of social problem solving developed by D'Zurilla and his colleagues can be modified as presented in Figure 2.

Figure 2. (Figure 2 about here)

Figure 2:

MULTIDIMENSIONAL MODEL OF SOCIAL PROBLEM SOLVING

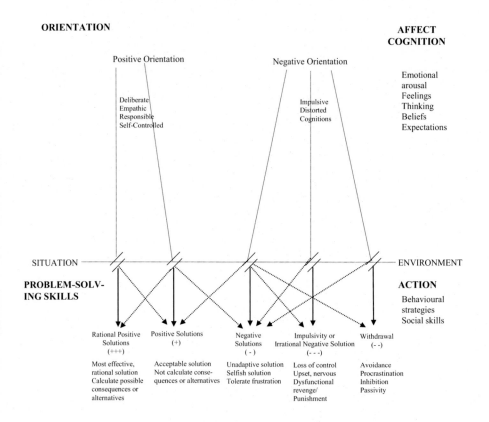

The modified model consists of five dimensions as follows: (1) *positive problem solving*, (2) *negative problem solving*, (3) *rational problem solving*, (4) the *impulsivity style*, and (5) the *withdrawal style*. Each dimension is defined as a relatively separate process (within problem solving) that includes two levels: *problem affect-cognitions* (problem orientation) and *problem-solving actions* (problem- solving skills)

The *problem affect-cognitive level* has orientational functions which automatically or rationally occur in the problem solver's mind when he/she is confronted with a problem in daily living. It is assumed to work as "leading clues" in the form of cognitive-emotional schemas (both facilitative or inhibitive) for action, and has been conceptualized as being challenged by problematic situations and driven or motivated by feelings, expectancies, situational emotions, thoughts, and beliefs.

The *problem-solving action* level involves the application (both efficient/rational and unadaptive/dysfunctional) of specific problem-solving skills and techniques (i.e., problem definition and formulation, generation of alternative solutions, etc) so as to obtain the goal of problem solving. Both positive problem solving and rational problem solving dimensions are constructive or facilitative but are different problem-solving processes. So too, all negative problem solving, including impulsivity style and avoidance/carelessness style dimensions, are dysfunctional or inhibitive but different problem-solving processes.

Positive problem solving involves (a) admitting and viewing a problem as a challenge; (b) believing that problems are solvable ("optimism"); (c) believing that problem solving takes time and persistence; (d) perceiving a problem from another person's perspective ("empathy"); and (e) applying specific problem-solving skills (acceptable solution) in terms of coping strategies (both problem-focused coping and emotion-focused coping) or controlled primary reactions (automatic/experiential processing). As presented here, positive problem solving differs from the positive problem orientation of D'Zurilla et al. (1996)'s model in that positive problem solving is conceptualized as relating to the application of specific problem-solving-skills and abilities when the problem solver views a problem as a challenge, appraises a problem from another person's perspective and attempts to control problems in a logical way (e.g inhibiting automatic action, screening out negative quality responses).

It is proposed that *rational problem solving* has characteristics of both positive problem orientation and the rational problem solving as defined in D'Zurilla et al. (1996)'s model. This dimension involves constructive or facilitative approaches to a problem as in the positive problem solving, but points to (a) understanding why problems occur like they are, (b) recognizing self-responsibility to resolve problems as soon as possible, and (c) knowing how to keep it under self-control. On the other hand, the process involves the rational, deliberate, and efficient application of adaptive problem-solving strategies and techniques (such as, generation of possible solutions, calculating consequences, selection of the best solution). There are differences in the *quality* of problem-solving solutions (responses) between positive problem solving and rational problem solving. Rational problem solving has higher qualitative responses than positive problem solving although both of these processes are positive (facilitative).

In contrast, *negative problem solving* is conceived here as a dysfunctional dimension that includes negative orientation variables such as (a) viewing a problem as a significant threat or danger to one's well-being; and (b) believing that a problem generates as the fault of another person. In addition, it involves the inefficient or unadaptive application of specific problem-solving skills or negatively coping strategies. For example, instead of identifying the problem, discovering alternative solutions, screening out negative/poor quality responses, and evaluating consequences of a selected solution, the person focuses on identifying who causes the problem or who takes responsibility for the problem, on generating self-advantageous solutions and selecting a solution that gains personal advantage over another (selfish solution), or tends to tolerate frustration. This dimension differs from the negative orientation dimension in D'Zurilla et al's model although there are overlaps.

The *impulsivity style* is another dysfunctional dimension characterized by distorted cognitions or revenge motivated by emotional arousal such as: (a) a problem is appraised as a serious threat or an unforgivable insult, (b) the person becomes upset and nervous when confronted with problems, and though may attempt to apply problem-solving strategies, these attempts tend to be impulsive, provocative (irrational negative solution), and involve dysfunctional revenge or punishment. Although this dimension has several overlapping parts with the negative orientation and impulsivity/carelessness style dimensions in D'Zurilla et al's model, it differs from these dimensions by only focusing on distorted cognitions such as feeling upset/nervous, loss of emotional control, and thoughts of revenge or punishment. This construct also differs from the negative problem-solving dimension since the problem-solver is influenced by high provocation (nervous, upset) and motivated by revenge or punishment.

The *withdrawal style* (avoidance) is an other dysfunctional dimension characterized by negative orientations such as: (a) believing that problems are unsolvable (pessimism); (b) doubting one's own ability to solve problems successfully (low self-efficacy); and (c) the unadaptive application of specific problem-solving strategies that tend to be careless, delaying solving problems (procrastination or inhibition), waiting for problems to resolve themselves (passivity), and attempting to shift problem-solving responsibility to others (dependency or avoidance). This construct differs from the avoidance style dimension in D'Zurilla et al's model, although they do overlap.

Given this modified model, it follows that problem-solving outcomes in real life problematic situations may be largely influenced by two general factors (levels): (1) a problem orientation that involves what people think and feel (problem affect-cognitions); and (2) problem-solving proper that involves what people do (problem-solving actions). This is consistent with the original model of problem solving (D'Zurilla and Goldfried, 1971). The first factor functions as a problem orientation process that reflects the generalized thoughts and feelings of a person concerning problems in living, as well as the person's own problem-solving ability (e.g., generalized appraisals, beliefs, expectancies, emotional responses). The second factor, on the other hand, functions as problem-solving proper in that it involves the application of specific problem-solving skills or strategies. When a person is confronted with a problematic situation in everyday living, the problem-solving outcomes are assumed to be determined via these two processes that involve the five relatively separate dimensions.

Thus, the SPST was based on the modified five-dimensional model of social problem solving. Its subscales are designed to assess problem-solving outcomes of both the constructive and dysfunctional dimensions including the two levels of each dimension (problem affect-cognitions and problem-solving actions).

The SPST: A measure of Social Problem-Solving Competence in Adolescents

The SPST consists of 24 interpersonal problematic situations, set in two parts, 12 stories in Part A (Stories-a) and 12 stories in Part B (Stories-b) that cover five main relationships of adolescent life: *adolescent - peers, adolescent - parent, adolescent - teacher, adolescent - other adults, and adolescent - children*. These stories are representative and characteristic of interpersonal problem situations that can occur in typical environments (i.e classroom, school, family, street or neighbourhood, and in public) surrounding an adolescent in Vietnam.

The SPST stories in Part A (SPST-A) were organized into five subscales that were designed to assess the five components of the modified multi-dimensional problem-solving model as outlined above. These five subscales include: (1) *Positive Problem Solving* (PPS), (2) *Negative Problem Solving* (NPS), (3) *Rational Problem Solving* (RPS), (4) *Impulsivity Style* (IS), and (5) *Withdrawal Style* (WS). Each subscale can be broken down into two further sub-subscales to assess problem orientation (problem affect-cognitions) and problem-solving proper (problem-solving actions) within each dimension. Thus, PPS includes Positive Orientation (PO) and Positive Problem-Solving Skills (PPSS); NPS includes Negative Orientation (NO) and Negative Problem-Solving Skills (NPSS); RPS divides in Rational Orientation (RO) and Rational Problem-Solving Skills (RPSS); IS consists of Impulsivity Orientation (IO) and Impulsivity Problem-Solving Style (IPSS); and WS includes Withdrawal Orientation (WO) and Withdrawal Problem-Solving Style (WPSS). The SPST-a can be condensed into two main scales which allow assessment of two problem-solving processes (i.e., the problem affect-cognitive level and problem-solving action level): Problem Affect-Cognitions (PAC-A) and Problem-Solving Actions (PSA-A).

Each subscale consists of 24 performance items. Twelve items assess problem affect-cognition (problem orientation) and 12 items assess problem-solving action (problem-solving proper). The items in the SPST-A are 3-point Likert-type items (0 = not true at all; 1 = sometimes true; 2 = usually true). They were designed either as (a) *potential affect-cognitive cues* (both constructive and dysfunctional) that reflect a person's general awareness and perceptions of everyday problems (i.e., the generalized thoughts and feelings of a person concerning interpersonal problematic situations) as well as his or her own problem-solving ability (i.e., the generalized threat or challenge appraisals, beliefs, expectancies, emotional arousals) to approach a particular problem orientation task, or as (b) *potential solution responses* (both constructive and dysfunctional) that imply the application of specific problem-solving strategies and abilities so as to obtain a particular problem-solving goal.

The SPST stories in Part B (SPST-B), on the other hand, were designed as alternatives of Stories-a. Instead of being organized into five subscales, the Stories-b were divided into two scales: *Problem Affect-Cognitions* (PAC-B) (assessing problem orientation) and *Problem-Solving Actions* (PSA-B) (assessing problem-solving proper) using a free-response format. In Stories-b, no affect-cognitive cues or solution responses are suggested. They require the subject to propose his/her own affect-cognitive cues or solutions (free responses). The Stories-b were hypothesised to work as a "double check" version (alternative version) so as to re-confirm the social problem solving ability performed in Stories-a.

Situational analysis

The original pool of the SPST contained close to 500 problematic situations that exemplified personal and interpersonal difficulties encountered by youths in everyday living. These situations were collected or gleaned from the following sources: (1) A large pool of letters sent to the Youth Psychological Counselling Center in Hanoi (see chapter 3); (2) The author's interviews or talks on adolescent psychology with adolescents, teachers, and parents[6]; (3) the author's studies that include values and oriented values (Nguyen, 1993) and psychological characteristics of puberty (Nguyen, 1991), and a theoretical model of personality for Vietnamese youths in the year 2000 and later that concerned over 10.000 adolescents and youths throughout Viet Nam (Pham et al, 1991); (4) problem ratings involving adolescence which included situations in training programs or situations in adolescent problem inventories (for example, the Adolescent Problem Inventory (API) developed by Freedman (1978)[7] or the Problem Inventory for Adolescent Girls (PIAG) developed by Gaffney and McFall (1981))[8]; and (5) the literature on adolescent interpersonal difficulties in general developmental text books.

An initial procedure was to eliminate redundancies, condensing similar situations into a single version, and excluding situations that seemed less related to typical adolescents (e.g., these that were mentioned only once in the pool of items). Consequently, situations that satisfied three of the following conditions were retained: difficulties (a) occurred in relationships with peers, parents, teachers, children, and other adults; (b) involved youths aged 12 to 20; and (c) appeared at least twice in the above sources.

The initial screening to eliminate redundancy reduced the pool to 101 situations. These situations were then split into five major relationship types (i.e., peers, parents, teachers, other adults, and children) and only the situations that best represented the categories of interpersonal difficulties in adolescence were retained (see chapter 3, p. 41-47). The second procedure eliminated 43 situations and retained 58 situations which comprised the following: 20 peer relations, 15 relationships with parents, 11 relationships with teachers, 6 relationships with other adults, and 6 relationships with children.

The 58 situations were transcribed into a uniform format so that each was worded in a 'standardized' way. They were divided into two groups and administered to two pilot samples of high school students (20 students in year 10 and 20 students in year 11) who were asked to rate their difficulty and familiarity from an adolescent perspective. The two samples included 21 boys

---

[6] Over 700 talks and interviews were conducted by the author from 1986 to 1994. In order to generate problematic situations as the topics for talks, the following questions were usually asked:
(a) What are the most difficult situations that you (or your friends) encounter in your lives?
(b) What are the things that you mostly worry about?
(c) Please list the 3 most difficult situations that you or your friends face in relationships with friends, parents, teachers, children or other adults.
(d) What are the greatest difficulties encountered between you and your students (or your children)? Can you give an example to illustrate those difficulties?
[7] See chapter 3, p. 39.
[8] See chapter 3, p. 39.

and 19 girls, aged 15-18 (6 of them were classified by their teachers as "disruptive" students). The two groups were asked to rate:

(1) The level of difficulty of every situation using a 4-point scale ranging from 0 *"this situation is easy to solve"* to 3 *"this situation is very difficult to solve"*;

(2) The level of familiarity of every situation using a 4-point scale that ranged from 0 *"this situation is strange to adolescents"* to 3 *"this situation is very familiar to adolescents"*.

Situations that had a mean rating of ≥ 2 for both the difficulty and the familiarity were retained. A list of 26 situations met this criterion. However, none of them represented problematic situations in relationships with other adults. Hence, two new situations covering this category were added and tested as with other items.

In sum, 28 problematic situations were validated so as to represent interpersonal problematic situations in five main areas of adolescent relationships.

Here are two examples:

"You like dressing well and you like a fashionable way of dressing. However, your parents don't like the way you dress and always nag you about it"; *"Your teacher accuses you of writing swear words on the toilet wall, and is threatening to put you down to a lower class. You know you didn't do it but your close friend did"*.

Construction of items

In order to develop items that represented potential affect-cognitive cues (problem orientation) or potential solution responses (problem-solving strategies) the following steps were taken. The first step was to generate as many potential affect-cognitive cues and potential solution responses to each of the 28 situations as possible. Toward this end, 28 of these situations were administered to five groups of students in years 10 and 11 aged 16 to 18. Each group consisted of 20 students (10 male and 10 female) randomly chosen from class lists. In each group, 2 to 4 "disruptive" students (as rated by their teachers) were included. Each group was asked to solve 5 or 6 problematic situations. For each situation the subjects were required to answer two questions, as in this example:

"On the occasion of your birthday, your friend of the opposite sex gives you a bunch of roses and a valuable present, implying "I like you…I love you". However, you want to maintain a friendship only at this moment".

(1)   What would you think or feel?   (2) What would you do?

The second step was to categorize and condense the freely generated responses (both potential affect-cognitive cues and potential solution responses) by scoring them in the five domains (i.e., positive problem solving, negative problem solving, rational problem solving, impulsivity style, and withdrawal style) with two levels (i.e., problem affect-cognition and problem-solving action) according to the modified model outlined above. They were then transcribed into a standard format, so that each situation was structured as a "mini-test" including 5 items that involved problem orientation (i.e., potential affect-cognitive cues) and 5 items that referred to problem-solving actions (i.e., potential solution responses). A sixth item was added as a free-response item that would be only used for subjects who stated a response not included in the given five responses (see the example of Story # 4 (a) below).

Twelve situations that had the most sufficiently generated responses (both affect-cognition cues and solution responses) and could best represent the specifically charaterized categories of in-terpersonal difficulties, were chosen for inclusion in 'Stories-a'. Consequently, Stories-a in-cluded: five situations that represented difficulties in peer relationships: (*being cut off from intimate friendships, personal wishes being disrupted or prevented, being teased or insulted by other peers*, and *being involved in a love-emotional affair*); three situations that reflected diffi-culties with parents: (*being nagged about something, personal wishes being prevented or dis-rupted by parents*, and *peaceful family being threatened*); two situations that referred to diffi-culties with teachers: (*being accused unjustly* and *having trouble or aversion with a teacher*); one situation that was representative of problems with children (*being disturbed by children's behaviour*); and one situation that involved difficulties with other adults (*witnessing a threat or risk to others*). These twelve situations occur in a variety of social contexts from prosocial, accidental, to hostile or provocative ways, and across different circumstances (i.e., classroom, school, family, street or neighbourhood, and in public).

Twelve of the remaining situations that could pair with each situation in 'Stories-a', made up 'Stories-b'. Each situation in Stories-b was required to satisfy the following criteria: (1) the situation was an alternative to the situation in Stories-a (i.e., a similar version in the same dif-ficulty and familiarity category); and (2) the situation had been varied slightly in terms of social context, that is, it was similar to a situation in 'Stories-a' but occurred in a different social context. This procedure aimed at preventing a simple transfer of recommended solution re-sponses from one setting to the other.

Following is a pair of problematic situations (an example of Story-a and Story-b) that represents the category: "*being cut off from an intimate peer relationship*".

Story # 4 (a)

Your friend suddenly stops an intimate relationship with you without any explanation. He/she has also made fun of you or made unfriendly comments about you and avoided you if possible.

What would you think or feel?	What would you do?
I would (think or feel):	I would (do):

1. My friend may have personal reasons or has made a mistake that is "reasonable"	0 1 2	
2. My friend is not good or is shallow	0 1 2	
3. About why my friend acts like that or about the underlying causes of the misunderstanding	0 1 2	
4. Insulted and / or upset	0 1 2	
5. The friendship is over	0 1 2	
6. Others	0 1 2	

1. Tolerate or ignore my friend 's attitude	0 1 2
2. Demand the friend explains the reason	0 1 2
3. Find a chance to meet to identify the problem and discuss it with my friend	0 1 2
4. Violently criticise or blame my friend	0 1 2
5. Cut off any relationship with my friend without asking him/her what the problem was	0 1 2
6. Others	0 1 2

(Notes: 0 = *not at all;* 1 = *sometimes;* 2 = *usually*)

Story # 4 (b)

You have a close friend (A) of the opposite sex. Since you want to expand your friendship, you help A make friends with B, a close, same -sexed friend. As time passes, you feel A and B become more intimate and leave you out. They usually avoid you, and are even unpleasant when you are present. You also heard their unfriendly comments about you.

What would you think or feel?	What would you do?
------------------------------------	----------------------------------
------------------------------------	----------------------------------
------------------------------------	----------------------------------
------------------------------------	----------------------------------

Test format and instruction

The SPST uses a structured rating (Stories-a) and a free-response format (Stories-b). The combination of these formats is expected to make the SPST more useful in assessment both the subject's ability to distinguish or recognize an effective, rational solution among dysfunctional solutions, and to identify a broader range of problem-solving skills and abilities that the subject may possess.

In order to ensure that test instructions are similar for all subjects, and are as realistic and natural as possible, the SPST has used *self*-focussed instructions accompanied by an example (i.e., the pronoun "you" is used to instruct the subjects to place themselves in the situation). Here are the instructions for the SPST:

Instructions

Below are short stories about social problem situations. Please read each story carefully and for each statement, choose (circle) ONE of the numbers (0 = not at all; 1 = sometimes; 2 = usually) that best shows to what extent the response is true of you when responding to the questions: What would you think (or feel) and do?

For example: During break time some students come up to you in the playground, teasing you and calling you stupid and dumb.

What would you think or feel and what would you actually do?

I would				I would		
1. Think they are bad people	0 1 2			1. Avoid playing with them	0 1 2	
2. Feel frightened	⓪ 1 2			2. Tolerate their behaviour	0 1 2	
3. Think about why they are behaving like they are	0 1 2			3. Ask them to stop behaving like they are	0 1 2	
4. Feel insulted or upset	0 1 2			4. Hit them or throw a tantrum	⓪ 1 2	
5. Other (describe)** <u>Eg. Feel u happy</u>	0 1 2			5. Other reaction (describe) ** <u>Eg. Stay in classroom during break-time</u>	0 1 2	

Story (b):

You are playing in the playground when two students who are chasing each other run into you and fall down. When they stand up, they yell bad words at you.

** These free-response items are other feelings or solutions that are beyond the given. The subject can describe them

What would you think or feel?	What would you do?

Eg. I would think these students have lost their temper due to being hurt	*Eg. I would leave without saying any-thing*
Eg. I would think their behaviour is not intentional	*Eg. I would ignore their bad language*
Eg.They are rude and I don't like them	*Eg. I would pick a quarrel with them*

Some investigators have warned that a potential threat to validity is poor comprehension of test items by the individuals and thus test developers should check the readability level of the measure (D'Zurilla & Maydeu-Olivares, 1995). With this in mind, 10 randomly chosen high school students from years 7 and 8 (6 males and 4 females) were asked to read the stories and point out what words or statements they did not understand. The pilot administration indicated that some words and statements were unclear or made it difficult to understand the situation. These words and statements were then rewritten until these pilot testees had no more difficulty in reading and understanding the SPST.

The pilot administration showed that the test completion time could be from 52 minutes to 65 minutes. This testing time was considered relatively long for a clinical assessment, thus the SPST has been divided into Form A and Form B. Form A includes all Stories-a and 7 Stories-b (i.e., Stories-b # 1, # 3, # 5, # 7, # 9 # 10.1 and # 11) (see Appendix B), Form B also includes all Stories-a and the remaining Stories-b (i.e., Stories-b # 2, # 4, # 6, # 8, # 9, # 10.1, # 10.2, and # 12) (see Appendix C).

Test scoring

The SPST employs both quantitative and qualitative scoring methods that involve either a rating of the subject's response quality (both affect-cognitive cues and specific solutions) in each situation on each dimension, such as effectiveness (positive and rational), passivity (negative), impulsivity, and withdrawal (avoidance), or a rating of the subject's response quality in each situation on two main components (problem orientation and problem-solving skills). The SPST-A and SPST-B are scored separately.

The SPST-A is designed to measure five partially independent dimensions and thus the score of each of 5 subscales is individually calculated within the same dimension across 12 situations (Stories-a). Similarly, two sub-subscales of each dimension are individually scored and summed up across 12 item scores (situation scores) within each domain. The SPST-A total score can be calculated in each situation. The scoring of the free responses (the sixth items) is included only when the subject describes a new response which is *absolutely different* from the five given responses. The free-response score is added (if positive) to the SPST-A total score of the subject.

Each sub-subscale assessing problem affect-cognitions and problem-solving actions in each dimension (i.e., positive problem solving, rational problem solving, negative problem solving, impulsivity, and avoidance) can give a profile of assessment in each situation: this information is specialy beneficial in clinical settings (Dodge, McClaskey, & Feldman, 1985). Such an assessment includes indices of the subject's knowledge at an affect-cognitive level (problem orientation) and the ability to find a rational, effective solution response (problem-solving skills). Hence, it may pin-point specific deficient problem-solving areas and indicate particular social problematic contexts that can provide a useful basis for intervention training programs.

Also, a global social problem solving score (where a higher score indicates greater social problem-solving abilities) can be calculated in the following way as an overall unweighted Social Problem Solving (SPS) Index 1[9]:

$$SPS\text{-}1 = PPS + (48 - NPS) + RPS + (48 - IS) + (48 - WS)[10]$$

To obtain this index, the NPS, IS, and WS subscales are reversed-scored by subtracting the actual scores of these subscales from the maximum scores. Similarly, the scoring of the two main scales of SPST-A can be calculated by using the following formulas:

$$PAC = PO + (24 - NO) + RO + (24 - IO) + (24 - WO)$$
$$PSA = PPSS + (24 - NPSS) + RPSS + (24 - IPSS) + (24 - WPSS)$$

---

[9] The formula was adapted from the Social Problem-Solving Index suggested by D'Zurilla, Nezu, & Maydeu-Olivares (1996).

[10] Notes: PPS = Positive Problem Solving; NPS = Negative Problem Solving; RPS = Rational Problem Solving; IS = Impulsivity Style; WS = Withdrawal Style.

Here is an example of scoring an actual case:

Sub scales	Sub-subscales	Problem Affect-Cognitions (PAC-A) Items # (Stories-a) Scores	Sub-sub-scales	Problem-Solving Actions (PSA-A) Items # (Stories-a) Scores
		1 2 3 4 5 6 7 8 9 10 11 12		1 2 3 4 5 6 7 8 9 10 11 12
		--		--
PPS	PO 1.	2 2 1 1 2 1 1 1 2 1 0 1 = 15	PPSS 1.	1 2 1 1 2 1 1 2 2 1 0 2 = 16
NPS	NO 2.	1 0 0 1 1 0 2 2 0 1 1 2 = 11	NPSS 2.	0 0 1 1 0 1 1 1 0 2 0 1 = 8
RPS	RO 3.	2 2 1 1 1 2 0 1 2 1 2 1 = 16	RPSS 3.	2 2 2 1 0 2 1 1 2 1 2 2 = 18
IS	IO 4.	0 1 1 0 0 0 1 1 0 1 0 1 = 6	IPSS 4.	0 1 1 0 2 0 0 0 1 1 0 1 = 7
WS	WO 5.	1 1 1 1 0 1 0 1 0 0 2 1 = 9	WPSS 5.	1 1 1 2 0 0 2 0 0 1 1 0 = 9
	Other 6.	1 (positive) = 1	Other 6.	2 (positive) = 2

The subject's scores on *the sub-subscales/subscales/scales* of the SPST-A are:

PO = 15   PPSS = 16   PPS = PO + PPSS = 31
NO = 11   NPSS = 8   NPS = NO + NPSS = 19
RO = 16   RPSS = 18   RPS = RO + RPSS = 34
IO   = 6   IPSS   = 7   IS   = IO + IPSS   = 13
WO = 9   WPSS = 9   WS = WO + WPSS = 18

PAC-A = PO + (24 - NO) + RO + (24 - IO) + (24 - WO) = 77
PSA-A = PPSS + (24 - NPSS) + RPSS + (24 - IPSS) + (24 - WPSS) = 82
SPST-A = PPS + (48 - NPS) + RPS + (48 - IS) + (48 - WS) = 159

(the subject scored 3 points on two free-response items and thus the SPST-A score = 162)

Another scoring version can be obtained by applying the following overall weighted Social Problem Solving Index 2:

SPS-2 = PPS + (48 - NPS) + (2 * RPS) + (48 - IS) + (48 - WS)

The overall weighted scoring doubles the score of the RPS which is the most

important component of social problem solving. Thus, it is hypothesized that such a scoring will be useful for assessing the discrimination between a group of good problem solvers and a group of poor problem-solvers.

The SPST-B is designed to measure two problem-solving processes and thus the score of each scale can be individually computed and the score of the PAC-B (Problem Affect-Cognitions) and the PSA-B (Problem-Solving Actions) scales are calculated separately. This is achieved by adding the particular score of each situation within the domain. Such a score may indicate specific deficient areas that involve either problem affect-cognitions (problem orientation) or problem-solving actions (problem-solving skills), but it does not provide the information of social contexts (i.e., specific situations) that affect the deficiencies. Hence, a profile of the scoring in each situation may be beneficial for clinical assessment. However, the overall score of the SPST-B is necessary to discriminate between different individuals. The SPST-B score can be found by summing the PAC-B and PSA-B scale scores.

All free-responses for each Story-b are structured to fit in the two scales PAC-B (Problem Affect-Cognitions) and PSA-B (Problem-Solving Actions) using a *coding* of responses (see rater's manual for the coding of the SPST-B in Appendix D) with 3 scoring levels as follows:

Problem Affect-Cognitions (I would think and feel)	**Problem-Solving Actions** (I would do)
0 POINT - This level involves emotional arousal, insulted feelings, impulsive, or distorted cognitions.	0 POINT- This level involves the application of avoidance, impulsive, or ir-rational negative strategies to resolve problems.
1 POINT - This level refers to positive beliefs/ expectations/thinkings such as: admitting a problem exists, viewing it as a challenge and perceiving a problem from an "empathic" or "forgivable / tolerable" perspectives.	1 POINT - This level refers to "acceptable" positive solutions which involve emotion-focused coping strategies or tolerating a problem rather than resolving it thoroughly through evaluation of consequences and alternatives.
2 POINT - This reflects rational positive beliefs/ expectations/cognitions such as: understanding why a problem occurs, recognizing self-responsibility to resolve it as soon as possible, and how to keep it under self-control.	2 POINT - This level refers to effective, deliberate, adaptive and rational positive strategies to resolve a problem as soon and as well as possible.

A manual for the coding of the competence of subjects' responses to each situation was developed according to procedures suggested by D'Zurilla and his colleagues (1969, 1995). For example, the scores for Story # 5 (b) were as follows:

Story # 5 (b):

"You like dressing well and you like a fashionable way of dressing. However, your parents don't like the way you dress and always nag you about it".

    What would you think or feel?   What would you do?

Problem affect-cognitions	Problem-solving actions
(I would think or feel)	(I would do)

0 ---Subject feels upset, thinks parents are too old to understand a youth's needs or don't care. Examples: "My friends dress the same way, but their parents don't object" or "Parents are too old to see its beauty."

1 ---Subject feels sad that parents don't understand a youth's needs, but doesn't want to upset them. Examples: "These clothes are suitable for me, but not for my parents" or "The dress is colourful and fashionable, thus my parents don't like it."

2 ---Subject thinks that parents have personal reasons to object and that is why they don't like it, or thinks about how he/she can explain feelings to parents. Examples: "Is it true that the dress is not good or not suitable for me?" or "If the dress is good/beautiful/ suitable, how can I explain my feelings or persuade parents to change their minds?"

0 ---Subject ignores or objects to the parent's attitudes and acts as he/she likes. Examples: "I still wear what I like" or "I get angry with my parents"

1 ---Subject gives up what his/her parents don't like or only wears it when parents are absent. Examples: "I obey my parents and wouldn't wear those dresses" or "I only wear it in suitable places such as at parties or dances"

2 ---Subject asks parents the reason for the aversion and finds a good chance to explain. If parents still keep their ideas and object, the subject accepts, and looks for another chance to convince. Examples: "I ask my parents why they don't like those clothes and why they are not suitable" or "I assess if the clothes are well matched for me. If so, I attempt to convince my parents, or ask another adult to persuade my parents."

The Teacher Rating Scale of Interpersonal Problem Solving (TRSIPS)

In addition to the SPST, the Teacher Rating Scale of Interpersonal Problem Solving (TRSIPS) was developed for use by teachers to assess interpersonal difficulties in adolescents. The TRSIPS is a teacher report inventory of an adolescent's problem-solving behaviour. The scale is a multi-dimensional measure that was completed by classroom teachers in the SPST validity study. The TRSIPS includes 40 items, divided into five subscales: (a) *Interpersonal Problem Behaviour* (IPB); (b) *Negative Problem-Solving Behaviour* (NPSB); (c) *Rational Problem-solving Behaviour* (RPSB); (d) *Impulsive Behaviour* (IB); and (e) *Avoidance Behaviour* (AB). Items of the TRSIPS are statements that are rated on a 3-point scale ranging from 0 = *not true at all* to 2 = *often true*.

The IPB subscale was designed to assess a variety of adolescent disruptive behaviours where the adolescents' problem-solving ability is hypothesized to be deficient. The subscale includes 12 items that identify interpersonal problems across a variety of disruptive behaviours or psychological disorders (eg. having problems making or keeping friends, getting in many fights, having disruptive behaviours, etc.).

The NPSB subscale was designed to be associated with the negative dimensions of the problem-solving process. The subscale consists of six items that involve a set of negative problem-solving strategies or activities such as acting without stopping to think, blaming others for mistakes, having negative attitudes and inappropriate behaviours in conflict situations.

The RPSB subscale includes six items that reflect rational or adaptive strategies of the social problem-solving process such as thinking about likely consequences before making decisions, thinking of alternative solutions and consequences when solving interpersonal problems, and identifying and resolving problems from the perspectives of others.

The IB subscale consists of six items which relate to impulsive or provocative behaviours such as easily getting angry in playing with others, being impulsive, or having temper tantrums or being hot tempered.

The AB subscale has six items that involve withdrawal behavioural strategies such as avoidance or showing reserved behaviours in social settings, withdrawal when frustrated, avoidance or being afraid of facing problematic situations.

Item construction

In order to construct items that represented and matched the five target dimensions of the TRSIPS, the following procedures were adapted from the guidelines of D'Zurilla and his colleagues (D'Zurilla & Maydeu-Olivares, 1995; D'Zurilla et al., 2002, 2004): (a) Item generation and item collection (identifying as many items as possible); (b) Item development (development of procedures to screen the items and retain the most representative ones); and (c) Item validation (examining and checking the items against the relevant domain).

An initial procedure was to generate items. The modified five-dimensional model was given to five psychology lecturer and PhD students. They were asked to write from six to ten behaviors that cover each dimension. The behaviors mentioned by the respondents were scrutinized by researchers for ensuring their relevance with each corresponding dimension. Additionally, three focus groups were conducted with school teachers, parents, and adolescents to identify interpersonal difficulties (problems) that occur in interpersonal relationships between an adolescent with his/her peers (same sex and opposite sex), parents, teachers, and other adults (e.g., doesn't get along well with other students or teachers, having problems making or keeping friends, getting in troubles, having disruptive behaviors or psychological disorders, threatening people with physical violence or acts like a bully, showing inappropriate behaviors when dealing with conflict with others, abusing people verbally). Formal written permission for recording discussion was sought from all participants. Researchers worked as facilitators and carefully monitored the focus groups sessions. The researchers carefully scrutinized rational problem-solving behaviors and irrelevant/ inappropriate/ impulsive behaviors were collected to obtain an appropriate pool of negative/ positive problem-solving behaviors. These negative/ positive problem-solving behaviors were finalized and transformed into statements and appropriate response format. The next procedure was to collect items from various sources to reflect the five relevant dimensions of the TRSIPS (Conner, 1990; D'Zurilla et al., 1996; Gresham & Elliott, 1990; Heppner & Peterson, 1982; Nguyen & Nguyen, 2017, 2019). The preliminary item pool of the TRSIPS contained over 200 items.

To develop items that matched the five target dimensions of the TRSIPS, screening procedures were conducted to eliminate redundancy narrowed this item pool down to 78 items. This was achieved by condensing similar items into a single item, and by excluding items that seemed less related to the relevant target dimensions. Then these items were written in a uniform format. The next step, the items were subjected to an informal content validity examining procedure in which four school psychologists were asked independently to rate the items within each subscale using a 4-point scale ranging from 0 (= Item does not address this subscale at all) to 3 (= Item addresses this subscale very much). This step eliminated 28 items and retained 50 items that had a mean rating of ≥ 2.

Try-out study of the 50 item-scale was carried out with 40 adolescents (20 girls and 20 boys) of age range 14-18 in order to check internal consistency and the difficulty in language comprehension and understanding level. After try-out, six items were modified, and tend items were discarded based on inappropriateness. Some difficult words were altered with suitable synonyms. The finalized 40 items were then retained to form the last version of the TRSIPS.

The TRSIPS includes 40 items, divided into five subscales: (a) Interpersonal Problem Behavior (IPB); (b) Negative Problem Solving Behavior (NPSB); (c) Rational Problem Solving Behavior (RPSB); (d) Impulsive Behavior (IB); and (e) Avoidance Behavior (AB). Items of the tool are rated on a 3-point scale (0 = not true at all; 1 = sometimes true; 2 = often true).

The IPB subscale was designed to assess a variety of adolescent disruptive behaviors where the adolescent's problem solving ability is hypothesized to be deficient. The subscale includes 8 items that identify interpersonal problems across a variety of disruptive behaviors or psychological disorders (e.g., having problems making or keeping friends, having disruptive behaviors). The NPSB subscale was designed to be associated with the negative dimensions of the problem-solving process. The subscale has eight items that involve a set of negative problem-solving strategies or activities such as acting without stopping to think, blaming others for mistakes, having negative attitudes, and inappropriate behaviors in conflict situations. The RPSB subscale includes eight items that reflect rational or adaptive strategies of the social problem-solving process such as thinking about likely consequences before making decisions, thinking of alternative solutions and consequences when solving interpersonal problems, and identifying and resolving problems from the perspectives of others. The IB subscale consists of eight items which relate to impulsive or provocative behaviors such as easily getting angry in playing with others, being impulsive, or having temper tantrums or being hot-tempered. The AB subscale has eight items that involve withdrawal behavioral strategies such as avoidance or showing reserved behaviors in social settings, withdrawal when frustrated, avoidance or being afraid of facing problematic situations.

Below are some examples of TRSIPS items that have a loading on each of five dimensions. These items describe a high school student with disruptive behaviours. Based on each item classroom teacher rates the student's problems and problem-solving skill at one of the levels (0 1 2) below:

0 = Not true at all   1 = Sometimes true   2 = Often true

Subscales	Behaviours	Levels		
Interpersonal Problem Behavior	Has problems making or keeping friends	0	1	2
	Doesn't get along well with other students	0	1	2
	Gets into more trouble than other students the same age	0	1	2
	Makes fun of or teases other students	0	1	2
Negative Problem Solving Behavior	Acts without stopping to think	0	1	2
	Denies having done wrong or blames other students for mistakes he/she has made	0	1	2
	Has a poor understanding of the attitudes, feelings, and perspectives of others when he/she goes about problem solving	0	1	2
	Has a negative attitude and inappropriate behaviors in conflict situations	0	1	2
Rational Problem Solving Behavior	Thinks about likely consequences before making decisions	0	1	2
	Tries to see problems from the perspective of others	0	1	2
	Has good self-control when in conflict with other students	0	1	2

	Approaches problems from different angles in order to find an effective solution	0	1	2
Impulsive Behavior	Has temper tantrums or is hot-tempered	0	1	2
	Easily gets angry in playing with other students	0	1	2
	Is explosive or anti-social	0	1	2
	Threatens people with physical violence or acts like a bully	0	1	2
Avoidance Behavior	Displays avoidance or reserved behaviors in social settings	0	1	2
	Avoids or is afraid of facing problematic situations which he/she is responsible for	0	1	2
	Isolates him/herself from other students	0	1	2
	Shows avoidance or withdrawal behaviors when frustrated	0	1	2

Test Scoring

The score of each subscale of TRSIPS is calculated individually. However, a total score of TRSIPS can be calculated by adding the scores of the RPSB, NPSB, IB, and AB in the following way as an overall unweighted interpersonal problem-solving index:

TRSIPS = RPSB + (16 - NPSB) + (16 - IB) + (12 - AB)

To obtain this index, the NPSB, IB, AB subscales are reversed-scored by subtracting the actual scores of these subscales from the maximum scores. Here is an example of a specific case:

Subscales	Items		Total score
IPB	Items # 1 2 20 23 24 25 29		9
	Scores: 1 1 2 1 2 1 1		
NPSB	Items # 3 5 9 12 14 16 19 31		11
	Scores: 2 1 1 2 1 1 2 1		
RPSB	Items # 15 30 33 35 37 39		4
	Scores: 1 0 1 0 1 1		
IB	Items # 6 10 11 17 22 27 34 38		9
	Scores: 1 1 0 1 2 1 1 2		

AB	Items # 8 13 18 26 28 40	9
	Scores: 1 2 2 1 1 2	

The subject's scores on the five subscales of the TRSIPS are: IPB = 9; NPSB = 11; RPSB = 4; IB = 9; AB = 9.

TRSIPS = RPSB + (16 - NPSB) + (16 - IB) + (12 - AB) = 4 + (16 - 11) + (16 - 9) + (12 - 9) = 19.

In summary, the SPST employed a combined cross-situational and cognitive-behaviour-analytic approach to construct its items. The SPST also used a combined multiple-choice and free-response format. Based on the modified multidimensional model of social problem solving, the instrument was organized into sub-subscales/subscales/scales that assessed constructive and dysfunctional dimensions of the social problem-solving process. For the purpose of the SPST validation study, an additional measure - the TRSIPS - was designed. It would be predicted that these two measures have significant correlations. The correlations are discussed in the next chapter.

Hypotheses and Predictions

The content design of the SPST was based on empirically supported theory and was adapted from guidelines proposed by D'Zurilla and his colleagues (1969, 1986, 1995, 1996). Thus, it is logical to hypothesize that the SPST would be a reliable and valid measure of adolescent interpersonal problem solving. It was expected that:

(1) A significant correlation should be found between test and re-test scores, which supports the test-retest reliability of the SPST;

(2) Intersubscale correlations of the SPST should be significant and positive. It means that the scores of sub-subscales/scales assessing problem-affect cognitions (orientation) should be significantly and positively correlated with those of sub-subscales/scales assessing problem-solving actions (problem-solving skills) which supports the hypothesis that how people think or feel can affect what they do as in the modified problem-solving model outlined.

(3) Internal correlations between the SPST-A and SPST-B scores should be significant and positive. It means that the SPST-A score should be significantly and positively correlated with the SPST-B score which supports the homogeneity of the SPST;

(4) Internal correlations for the SPST-A and its subscales as well as the SPST-B and its scales should be significant (positive or negative). This shows the multidimensionality

of social problem solving as in the modified model outlined and thus would support the construct validity of the SPST. This means that the correlations among the Negative Problem Solving, Impulsivity Style, and Withdrawal Style subscales assessing dysfunctional dimensions, as well as the correlations between the Positive Problem Solving and Rational Problem Solving subscales assessing constructive dimensions should be significantly positive. In contrast, the correlations between the subscales assessing dysfunctional dimensions and the subscales assessing constructive dimensions should be significantly negative. Also, the correlation between the Problem Affect-Cognitions (PAC-B) and Problem-Solving Actions (PSA-B) should be significantly positive.

(5) Alpha coefficients for the SPST-A and its subscales as well as the SPST-B and its scales should be adequate, so that they can be classified as homogeneous and consistent.

(6) There should be significant positive correlations between the Social Problem Solving Scale (SPST) and D'Zurilla et al. (1996)'s Social Problem Solving Inventory-Revised (SPSI-R) scores as substantial evidence of the concurrent validity of the SPST;

(7) There should be significant positive correlations between the Social Problem Solving Scale (SPST) and Teacher Rating Scale of Interpersonal Problem Solving (TRSIPS) scores in order to support the external validity of the SPST;

(8) The SPST should have an ability to discriminate between different adolescent populations. In other words, disruptive adolescents should have significantly different scores from non-problematic adolescents and problem adolescents should score lower on the SPST-A and the SPST-B than regular adolescents. Similarly, metropolitan adolescents would be predicted to have higher mean scores on the SPST subscales/scales or items (problematic situations) than rural adolescents. Also, different age groups and male-female groups would be predicted to have significantly different mean scores on the SPST subscales or items.

Evidence concerning the above hypotheses and predictions is presented in the following two chapters.

Chapter 5:

RELIABILITY AND VALIDITY

As presented in last chapter, the design and development of the Social Problem Solving Scale (SPST) and the Teacher Rating Scale of Interpersonal Problem Solving (TRSIPS) were based on a modified multidimensional model of social problem solving and employed a combined cross-situational and cognitive-behaviour-analytic approach. A consequent requirement was to administer the SPST and TRSIPS to high school student samples to determine whether these instruments are reliable and valid so as to measure what they is proposed to measure. This chapter presents methods, predictions and results of investigating the reliability and validity of these instruments.

Methods

Subjects

A review of sampling and administrative methods suggest that the norm of a measure is important for its usefulness in practice and thus the SPST and TRSIPS should be administered to subjects in various categories, such as diagnostic groups, for the purpose of evaluating its psychometric properties. Thus, two Vietnamese regular and disruptive high school student samples were included in this study.

The SPST was administered to two samples of Vietnamese high school students: regular students (referred to as "normal" students) and students who had been diagnosed as having psychological and behavioural problems (referred to as "disruptive" or "problem" students). A total of 416 high school students participated in this research.

The first sample consisted of 248 regular school students (50.4% male and 49.6% female) at four regular high schools in rural and metropolitan Hanoi. Participants ranged in age from 14 to 19 years with the majority of them aged 15-18 years. The mean age was 16.21 years old (SD=1.39). All grades (8 through 12) were represented. In order to have a representative sample, classes from these grades were randomly selected. Thus, at each high school, one class was chosen for each year.

The second sample was drawn from 203 high school students with psychological and behavioural problems. According to Blankenship & Lilly's definition (1981), behavioural problems exist when there is a deviation from age-appropriate behavioural norms, and these problems may include unco-operativeness, truancy, attention-seeking, excessive talking, aggression, vandalism, and stealing (Beazley, 1984). Cooperman and Bloom (1986) define chronically disruptive behaviour as a consistent and persistent pattern of conduct which is in defiance of school rules.

The 203 "problem" students were members of 59 classes in two high schools: one was a semi-private, special high school where the majority of problem students from metropolitan Hanoi were placed. They were placed there from regular high schools due to their disturbed behaviour. The other was a regular high school in the suburb of Hanoi city in which classroom teachers identified the most 'disruptive' or most 'troublesome' students. These students typically showed behaviours that disturbed others such as fighting, talking (too much) in class rooms, getting into more trouble than other students, or having difficulties with making and keeping friends. The mean age was 17.41 years old (SD= .98). Five grades (8 through 12) were represented. Once the students had been selected, the classroom teachers were asked to complete the Conners' Teacher Ratings Scale (CTR-28) for each student (Conners, 2000). Only students who had standard scores above 65 on two scales (the Conduct Problem & Hyperactivity scales) were retained. Of the original sample identified, 168 "disruptive or problem" students met the criteria and thus were included in this study.

The TRSIPS was designed and administered to test the validity of the SPST. The major aim of this scale was to identify adolescent interpersonal problems and to assess adolescent problem-solving behaviour (both adaptive and dysfunctional) from the perspective of classroom teachers. Thus, the TRSIPS was administered to only the "disruptive/problem" high school student sample. Due to some classroom teachers leaving, some students were not rated, and thus 133 of 168 disruptive students were rated by the classroom teachers.

Measures

The Conners' Teacher Rating Scale (CTRS-28)

The Conners' Teacher Rating Scale (CTRS-28) was used as a screening measure to assess student disruptivity. The instrument has been shown to be a valid screen for children's behavioural disorders (Stein & O'Donnel, 1985; Taylor & Sandberg, 1984; Conners, 1990). The CTRS-28 consists of a 28 item, four-point Likert scale, which provides standardized scores for four categories (scales): Conduct Problem (e.g., temper outbursts, quarrelsomes, uncooperative with teacher), Hyperactivity (e.g., restless, makes inappropriate noises), Inattentive-passivity (e.g., immature, daydreams), and a 10-item Hyperactivity Index. The measure is suitable for children aged 3-18 years. The CTRS's psychometric properties have been well researched (Cohen, Beker, & Campell 1989; Stein & O'Donnel, 1985; Taylor & Sandberg, 1984). For example, Edelbrock, Greenbaum, and Conover (1985) found that the instrument had a high test-retest reliability (r =.94) as well as high concurrent validity.

The Social Problem-Solving Inventory-Revised (SPSI-R)

The Social Problem-Solving Inventory-Revised (SPSI-R) was used to assess the concurrent validity of the SPST. The SPSI-R was originally derived from the Social Problem Solving Inventory (SPSI) (D'Zurilla & Nezu, 1990), a 70-item measure of social problem solving based on the prescriptive model developed by D'Zurilla and Goldfried (1971). The SPSI includes two main scales, the Problem Orientation Scale and Problem Solving Skills Scale. The Problem Orientation Scale consists of three subscales: Cognition, Emotion, and Behavior. The Problem-Solving Skills Scale consists of four subscales: Problem Definition and Formulation, Generation of Alternative Solutions, Decision Making, and Solution Implementation and Verification. A factor-analytic study of the SPSI conducted by Maydeu-Olivares and D'Zurilla (1996) revealed five factors: Positive Problem Orientation, Negative Problem Orientation, Rational Problem Solving, Impulsivity/Carelessness Style, and Avoidance Style. On the basis of the factor analysis, the measure was revised, reducing it to 52-items. The SPSI-R was then divided in five subscales: Positive Problem Orientation (PPO); Negative problem Orientation (NPO); Rational Problem Solving (RPS); Impusivity/Carelessness Style (ICS); Avoidance Style (AS).

The SPSI-R is a self-report measure of social problem solving ability. Items are self-statements depicting either positive or negative responses to real-life problem-situations. Each item is rated on a 5-point scale ranging from *not at all true of me* (0) to *extremely true of me* (4).

Both the SPSI and SPSI-R have been shown to have adequate reliability and validity with adults and adolescents (D'Zurilla & Nezu, 1990; D'Zurilla, Nezu A. & Maydeu-Olivares, 1996; Sadowski, Moore, & Kelly, 1994). According to D'Zurilla and Nezu (1990), test-retest reliabilities over an average 3-week period for the Problem Orientation Scale (POS), the Problem-Solving Skills Scale (PSSS) and the total SPSI score ranged from .83 to .88. The test-retest reliabilities for subscales were from .73 to .86. Internal consistencies for the POS, PSSS and SPSI were .94, .92, and .94. Alpha coefficients for the subscales ranged from .65 to .90. With regard to criterion validity, the SPSI scores have been found to be related to internal locus-of-control, psychological stress, frequency of personal problem, general severity of psychological symptoms, and academic achievements in college student samples (D'Zurilla & Nezu, 1990; D'Zurilla & Sheedy, 1991, 1992).

Test-retest (3 week) reliabilities for the scales of the SPSI-R in two samples (college and nursing students) were from .68 to .91. Internal consistencies for the scales of SPST-R in four different samples (2 college student samples, middle-aged adults, and elderly adults) ranged from .69 to .95. Coefficient alphas for the SPSI-R scales were .76 (Positive Problem Solving), .91 (Negative Problem Orientation), .92 (Rational Problem Solving), .83 (Impulsivity/Carelessness Style), and .88 (Avoidance Style) (D'Zurilla, et al., 1996). The validity of the SPSI-R was supported by significant correlations between its scales and different measures of psychological distress in college students, such as the Reynolds Adolescent Depression Scale (RADS; Reynolds, 1986), Social Skills Rating Scale (SSRS; Gresham & Elliot, 1990), Beck Depression Inventory (BDI; Beck et al., 1961), and State-Trait Anxiety Inventory-Trait scale (STAI; Spielberger et al., 1970).

The Teacher Rating Scale of Interpersonal Problem Solving (TRSIPS)

The TRSIPS, as indicated earlier, was also administered to test the validity of the SPST. The major aim of this instrument was to identify adolescent interpersonal problems, and to assess adolescent problem-solving behaviour (both adaptive and dysfunctional) from the perspective of classroom teachers. The scale was also designed on the modified five-dimensional model of social problem solving as noted previously. However, the positive problem-solving dimension was replaced by an interpersonal problem dimension. The replacement aimed to test the convergent validity of the SPST to determine whether an adolescent's social problem-solving deficits involve the adolescent's interpersonal difficulties. As described earlier in chapter 4, the TRSIPS is an inventory that functions as a teacher's report of an adolescent's problem-solving behaviour. The TRSIPS included 40 items, divided into five subscales: (a) *Interpersonal Problem Behaviour* (IPB); (b) *Negative Problem-Solving Behaviour* (NPSB); (c) *Rational Problem-Solving Behaviour* (RPSB); (d) *Impulsive Behaviour* (IB); and (e) *Avoidance Behaviour* (AB). Items of the TRSIPS were rated on a 3-point scale ranging from 0 = *not true at all* to 2 = *often true*. Reliability and validity data for the TRSIPS are presented in this study (p. 85-90).

Administrative procedures

The SPST was designed to be administered individually or to groups. While 248 regular students completed the SPST in small groups in their classrooms (under the supervision of teachers, psychologists or the author), the problem students completed the SPST individually in the staff room or other rooms under the author's supervision[11]. Students were spaced in such seating such that work was completed independently.

As indicated previously in the SPST pilot administration, it would take a "normal" adolescent over one hour to complete the 12 items of the SPST-A (Stories-a) and 12 items of the SPST-B (Stories-b). The testing time is a concern for a clinical assessment. Hence, in order to reduce the testing time, the SPST was divided into: Form A including all 12 items of the SPST-A, but including 7 items of the SPST-B (ie., Items # 1, # 3, # 5, # 7, # 9, # 10.1, and # 11) and Form B consisting of all 12 items of the SPST-A, yet having 7 items of the SPST-B (ie., Items # 2, # 4, # 6, # 8, # 9, # 10.2, and # 12) (see Appendices B and C). Both these forms were administered to the regular and problem school student samples.

The interval between test-retest administrations was 2 weeks. On the first administration, Form A was administered to half the subjects and Form B to other half. These forms, as noted earlier, are assumed to be parallel-forms. They have the same Stories-a, but different Stories-b. On the second administration, Form B was given to those who took Form A in the first test, and Form A was administered to those who took Form B previously.

As indicated earlier, the TRSIPS was administered to test the validity of the SPST. The major aim of this measure was to identify adolescent interpersonal problems and to assess adolescent problem-solving behaviour (both adaptive and dysfunctional) from the perspective of classroom teachers. Thus, the TRSIPS scale was administered to only the "disruptive" high school student sample. Due to some classroom teachers leaving, some students were not rated, and thus 133 of 168 disruptive students were rated by the classroom teachers.

---

[11] These psychologists and teachers were trained in the use of the SPSS

Predictions of the SPST and TRSIPS Results

Factor Analysis of the SPST Scales

The factor analytic technique was used to test the multidimensional model which underpins the scale construction. The Principle Component Analysis includes computation of the correlation matrix (to determine the appropriateness of the factor model), factor extraction (to determine the number of common factors) and rotation (to make the factor structure more interpretable). *Matrix of intercorrelations for the SPST subscales*: an intercorrelation matrix analysis of the scores of the combined sample (regular and problem high school students) was conducted to report the intercorrelations of the SPST and to reveal information about the reliability and validity of the measure. As indicated previously, the structure of the SPST includes the Social Problem Solving Scale in Part A (SPST-A) and Social Problem Solving Scale in Part B (SPST-B). The SPST-A was structured into five subscales: Positive Problem solving (PPS), Negative Problem Solving (NPS), Rational Problem Solving (RPS), Impulsivity Style (IS), and Withdrawal Style (WS) which assess five dimensions of social problem solving. These subscales can be further divided into ten sub-subscales: Positive Orientation (PO), Negative Orientation (NO), Rational Orientation (RO), Impulsivity Orientation (IO), Withdrawal Orientation (WO), Positive Problem-Solving Skills (PPSS), Negative Problem-Solving Skills (NPSS), Rational Problem-Solving Skills (RPSS), Impulsivity Problem-Solving Style (IPSS), and Withdrawal Problem-Solving Style (WPSS) which assess *problem affect cognitive* level and *problem-solving action* level of each problem-solving dimension. The SPST-A can be condensed into two main scales which allow assessment of two main problem-solving processes: Problem Affect-Cognitions (PAC-A) and Problem-Solving Actions (PSA-A). The SPST-B was organized into two scales: the PAC-B which assesses overall problem affect-cognitions and PSA-B which assesses overall problem-solving actions.

It was expected that the SPST-A intercorrelations among the constructive components and those among the dysfunctional components would be positive, whereas the intercorrelations between constructive and dysfunctional components would be negative. Similarly, the correlations between the sub-subscales of the SPST-A which assess problem affect-cognitions and the sub-subscales which assess problem-solving actions were expected to be positive and significant. The SPST-B intercorrelation was expected to be positive because the PAC-B and PSA-B scales are constructive or facilitative dimensions. It was predicted that the SPST-A would be positively associated with the SPST-B because a higher SPST-A score as well as a higher SPST-B score reflects greater social problem-solving skills.

Factor extraction: It was predicted that the factor analysis procedure would reduce the number of psychological dimensions from 5, which is the total number of subscales on the SPST-A, to 2 common factors extracted to represent a constructive and dysfunctional problem-solving model as outlined. Similarly, the procedure was expected to extract a general factor for the SPST-B scales because the PAC-B and PSA-B scales are constructive components.

Rotation: Factor rotations applied to the original factor matrices were to simplify the interpretation of the obtained factors of the SPST. It was proposed to use uncorrelated factors (Varimax Rotation) for the SPST-A because uncorrelated factors were expected.

Matrix of intercorrelations for the TRSIPS subscales: an intercorrelation matrix analysis of the scores of the problem high school sample was conducted to report the intercorrelations of the TRSIPS and to reveal information about the reliability and validity of the measure.

Reliability estimates

A good test is one that is sufficiently reliable to measure what it was designed to measure (Aiken & Groth-Marnat, 2006) and common properties for the reliability of a test are *consistency* and *stability* (Friedenberg, 1995). According to experts in psychological testing (Aiken & Groth-Marnat, 2006; Friedenberg, 1995; Murphy & Davidshofer, 1994), there are several methods of estimating the reliability of a test including internal consistency, parallel forms, and test-retest reliability. Each of these methods takes into account somewhat different conditions that may affect test scores and hence the test's reliability. In order to determine whether or not the SPST is sufficiently reliable, the following methods were used: *internal consistency* and *test-retest* reliability.

Internal consistency reliability refers to the fact that all items on the same scale consistently or reliably measure the same dimension (Conners, 2000; Murphy & Davidshofer, 1994). Internal consistency can be assessed with an overall summary (the alpha coefficient) or with a series of item-total correlations. Test-retest reliability refers to the temporal stability of the ratings by determining whether a second administration of the test yields substantially the same results as an earlier administration (Conners, 2000).

Validity estimates

Reliability is a necessary but not a sufficient condition for validity. Traditionally, the validity of a test has been defined as the extent to which the test correctly measures the construct (or constructs) that it is supposed to measure (Aiken & Groth-Marnat, 2006; Conners, 2000). However, it would be insufficient to imply that a test has only one validity. In contrast, a test may have many different validities and thus validity is perhaps better perceived as the "scientific inquiry into test score meaning" (Messick, 1989).

The American Psychological Association's Technical Recommendations for Psychological Tests and Diagnostic Techniques (1985) recognized four different ways of defining validity: (1) content validity, (2) construct validity, (3) predictive validity, and (4) concurrent validity. Today, it is recognized that these facets represent four different strategies for validating the inferences that are made on the basis of test scores (American Psychological Association's Standards for Educational and Psychological Testing, 1985, cited in Murphy & Davidshofer, 1994). Nevertheless, as Murphy and Davidshofer (1994) indicated, both content and construct validation strategies are involved in determining whether a test provides a valid measure of a specific attribute, whereas both predictive and concurrent approaches investigate the validity of predictions or decisions that are based on the test scores. With this in mind, the validity of the SPST and TRSIPS was evaluated using several different strategies as follows:

Content validity. The basic procedure for evaluating content validity, as Murphy and Davidshofer (1994) suggested, consists of three steps: (1) describe the content domain, (2) determine the areas of the content domain that are measured by each of the test items and (3) compare the structure of the test with the structure of the content domain. Obviously, the process of describing and assessing a test's content validity need not wait until the test has been constructed. In general, the procedure has been detailed and completed in earlier chapters. However, in this chapter, the findings of the internal correlations among the variables of the SPST and TRSIPS will provide further information about the content validity of the SPST and TRSIPS.

Construct validity. The construct validity of a psychological test refers to the extent to which the test is a measure of a specific construct. Construct validity is not determined in a single way or by one investigation, whereas it would be fair to say that any type of data (from identifying the behaviours that relate to the construct to be measured to determining the relations between it and other constructs) or statistics might be useful in examining construct validity (Murphy & Davidshofer, 1994). As suggested by Aiken and Groth-Marnat (2006), among the sources of evidence for the construct validity of a test are: experts' judgments, studies of the test relationships, an analysis of the internal consistency of the test, correlations of the new measure with other tests, and questioning examinees or raters about their responses to a test in order to reveal the specific mental processes referring to those responses.

Although various methods might be used to assess construct validity, three most common methods were employed: (1) correlating scores on the new test with scores on other tests; (2) using correlation matrix analyses to examine the expected relationships among sub-sub-scales/subscales/scales and to determine whether these relationships do indeed exist; and (3) assessing the internal consistency of the new test to investigate the construct validity of the measure.

The construct validity of SPST was assessed by examining the correlations between the SPST-A and teachers' behavioural reports - Teacher Rating Scale of Interpersonal Problem Solving (TRSIPS). The TRSIPS, as described previously, has a similar structure to the SPST-A with the exception of the Interpersonal Problem Behaviour (IPB) subscale. It was predicted that the IPB score of the TRSIPS would be negatively associated with the SPST-A and SPST-B scores. It was expected that the Negative Problem-Solving Behaviour (NPSB), Impulsive Behaviour (IB) and Avoidance Behaviour (AB) subscales of the TRSIPS would be positively associated with the Negative Problem Solving (NPS), Impulsivity Style (IS), and Withdrawal Style (WS) subscales of the SPST-A and negatively associated with the Rational Problem Solving (RPS) subscale. The TRSIPS total score would be expected to be positively correlated with the SPST-A total score and the SPST-B total score because a higher score on any of these measures indicates greater social problem-solving abilities.

Concurrent Validity. Concurrent validity studies provide a technique for determining criterion validity of a test by comparing the correlation between test scores and a *current* criterion measure (Friedenberg, 1995). Concurrent validation procedures are employed whenever a test is administered to subjects in various categories (such as diagnostic groups) for the purpose of determining whether the average scores of different groups are significantly different (Aiken & Groth-Marnat, 2006). In this study, concurrent validity was examined by calculating Pearson correlation coefficients between the SPST-A and another criterion social problem solving measure - Social Problem-Solving Inventory-Revised (SPSI-R) (D'Zurilla et al., 1996) in both regular and disruptive adolescent groups. As noted previously, both the SPSI-R and the SPST were based on a five-dimensional model of social problem solving developed by D'Zurilla and his colleagues. However, they employed different approaches The SPSI-R is a process measure using self-statements, whereas the SPST is an outcome measure using cross-problematic situations.

It was predicted that the SPST-A would be positively associated with the SPSI-R because a higher score on any of the two measures indicates greater social problem-solving abilities or skills. It was expected that the Rational Problem Solving (RPS) scale of the SPSI-R (constructive component) would be positively correlated with the Rational Problem Solving (RPS) subscale of SPST-A (constructive component) and negatively correlated with the Negative Problem Solving (NPS), Impulsivity Style (IS), and Withdrawal Style (WS) subscales of the SPST-A (dysfunctional components). In addition, it was expected that significant differences between different groups (such as regular and disruptive adolescent groups; rural and metropolitan groups) on the SPST scores would be found.

Reliability and Validity of the TRSIPS

The reliability of TRSIPS was provided by calculating Cronbach's coefficient alpha. Results of investigating the reliability coefficients (Cronbach's alpha) for the TRSIPS and its subscales are reported in Table 1. The coefficient alpha for the TRSIPS was .89. Reliability coefficients for the five IPB, NPSB, RPSB, IB, and AB subscales were .82, .77, .77, .82, .65, respectively. These results indicated that the TRSIPS scale has acceptable internal consistency.

Table 1

Reliabilities for the TRSIPS and Its Subscales

	Internal Consistency (alpha)
	Problem High School Student Sample (N=133)
IPB	.82
NPSB	.77
RPSB	.77
IB	.82
AB	.65
TRSIPS	.89

Notes: IPB = Interpersonal Problem Behaviour; NPSB = Negative Problem-Solving Behaviour; RPSB = Rational Problem-Solving Behaviour; IB = Impulsive Behaviour; AB = Avoidance Behaviour; TRSIPS = Teacher Rating Scale of Interpersonal Problem Solving.

The construct validity of the TRSIPS was supported by analysizing the intercorrelations among the TRSIPS subscales that were reported in Tables 2 and 3. As noted previously, the structure of the TRSIPS included five components, the IPB assessing interpersonal problem behaviour would be predicted to negatively correlate with the RPSB which assesses rational problem-solving behaviour, yet positively associate with the dysfunctional components (i.e., the NPSB, IB, and AB subscales). The correlations between the constructive component (i.e., the RPSB) and the dysfunctional components should be significantly negative or not be significant. The RPSB subscale would be expected to associate positively with the TRSIPS total scale. While the NPSB, IB, and AB subscales would be expected to associate negatively with the TRSIPS. The analyses of the intercorrelations (presented in Table 2) indicated that most of the inter-subscale correlations were significantly positive (or negative) as predicted. As expected, the

IPB score was negatively correlated with the RPSB subscale score (-.13), but positively associated with the NPSB, IB, and AB subscale scores (.37, .40, and .47, P < .01). The correlations between the RPSB subscale score (constructive component) and the NPSB and IB subscale scores (dysfunctional components) were significant and negative (-.25, -.32, P < .01) as predicted.

Table 2

Intercorrelations among the Subscale Scores and the TRSIPS Total Score in a Disruptive High School Student Sample (N = 133)

	IPB	NPSB	RPSB	IB	AB
IPB	-				
NPSB	.37**	-			
RPSB	-.13	-.25**	-		
IB	.40**	.65**	-.32**	-	
AB	.47**	.30**	-.12	.19*	-
TRSIPS	-.50**	-.83**	.53**	-.85**	-.53**

Notes: IPB = Interpersonal Problem Behavior; NPSB = Negative Problem-Solving Behavior; RPSB = Rational Problem-Solving Behavior; IB = Impulsive Behavior; AB = Avoidance Behavior; TRSIPS = Teacher Rating Scale of Interpersonal Problem Solving.
*P < .05; **P < .01.

To examine construct validity, a two-stage procedure was utilized conducting both exploratory and confirmatory factor analysis. Exploratory factor analysis (EFA) was performed on the data for the first sample that consists of 73 disruptive students of a semi-private, special high school, using maximum likelihood extraction (MLE) technique, to explore the emerging factor structure of the data. Confirmatory factor analysis was reexamined on the second sample to compare the theory-driven a-priori five-factor model with any model which emerged through EFA. A set of criteria were used to define the number of factors to retain in this analysis including: the definition of the number of variables which have significant factor loadings on factors and examination of whether the factors can be interpreted in a meaningful way with respect to the social problem-solving theory (Yong & Pearce, 2013).

Consideration of the resulting EFA models, it became apparent that five items in the TRSIPS (items: 4, 7, 21, 32, 36) were not able to meaningfully integrate into factors. The items had their low factor loadings (< 0.3) or cross loadings for multiple factors. On examination of the item meanings, there were sufficient evidence to suggest that with this particular sample the interpretation of the items may differ. These items were therefore taken out of the scale for the purpose of further analyses (these items would be needed to prepare for next pilot research). EFA was thus conducted on 35 of the TRSIPS items. According to the eigenvalues greater than 1.0 rule, ten factors were extracted. However, a reexamination of the factor loadings illustrated that the factors were un-interpretable, and some of the factors did not have any high loadings. In addition, the scree plot suggested that fewer factors would be most appropriate. The confirmatory factor analysis (CFA) was thus reexamined on the data for full sample (N=133) using Principal Axis Factoring (PAF) technique. The results of CFA for 35 items of the TRSIPS (reported in Table 3) indicate clear and exclusive five factors solution reflecting the theory driven five-factor model of interpersonal problem solving of adolescents. It became apparent that 7 items of the IPB subscale, 8 items of the NPSB subscale, 6 items of the RPSB subscale, 8 items of the IB subscale, and 6 items of the WB subscale were meaningfully integrated into factor 1 (loadings ranged from .333 to .767), factor 2 (loadings ranged from .438 to .654), factor 3 (loadings ranged from .469 to .707), factor 4 (loadings ranged from .348 to .796), factor 5 (loadings ranged from .372 to .571), respectively.

Table 3

Factor Loadings for the Theory Driven Five-Factor Model of the TRSIPS Subscale Scores in a Disruptive High School Student Sample (N = 133)

Item #	IPB	NPSB	RPSB	IB	AB
29	.767				
2	.730				
1	.701				
25	.699				
23	.665				
24	.587				
20	.333				
12		.654			
31		.604			
16		.596			

19	.570			
3	.524			
5	.494			
9	.490			
14	.438			
33		.707		
30		.707		
37		.669		
35		.541		
39		.536		
15		.469		
34			.796	
11			.774	
17			.737	
27			.637	
10			.546	
6			.485	
22			.482	
38			.348	
18				.571
8				.518
13				.502
40				.489
26				.453
28				.372

Notes: IPB = Interpersonal Problem Behavior; NPSB = Negative Problem-Solving Behavior; RPSB = Rational Problem-Solving Behavior; IB = Impulsive Behavior; AB = Avoidance Behavior.

The concurrent validity of the TRSIPS was examined by calculating Pearson correlation coefficients between the TRSIPS and another social problem solving measure - Social Problem Solving Test – Part A (SPST-A) (Nguyen & Nguyen, 2017). The SPST-A is an outcome measure of interpersonal problem-solving competence in adolescents. The tool was organized into five subscales: (1) positive problem solving (PPS), (2) negative problem solving (NPS), (3) rational problem solving (RPS), (4) impulsivity style (IS), and (5) withdrawal style (WS). The preliminary psychometric evaluation of the SPST-A indicated that the tool was a reliable and valid measure of social problem solving ability for Vietnamese adolescents (Nguyen & Nguyen, 2018). Results of correlational analyses are presented in Table 4. Although the TRSIPS (a process measure) and the SPST-A (an outcome measure) used different measurement methods, their scales and subscales scores showed significant positive correlations. As predicted, the IPB, NPSB, and IB subscales scores of the TRSIPS were significantly positive correlated with the IS subscale score of the SPST-A (.24 to .30, P < .01). The correlation between the RPSB subscale score of the TRSIPS and the RPS subscale score of the SPST-A was significantly positive as expected (.22, P < .01). The correlation between the TRSIPS and the SPST-A total scores was significantly positive (.40, P < .01). The highest amount of common variance that the TRSIPS and the SPST-A share was 16%. These results indicated that the concurrent validity of the TRSIPS was acceptable.

Table 4

Correlations between the TRSIPS Scores and the SPST-A Scores in
a Disruptive High School Student Sample (N = 102)

	IPB	NPSB	RPSB	IB	AB	TRSIPS
PPS	-.12*	-.13*	.19**	-.08	-.19**	.20**
NPS	.09	.11*	-.01	.11*	-.01	-.09
RPS	-.24**	-.31**	.22**	-.22**	-.36**	.41**
IS	.24**	.30**	-.19**	.30**	.13*	-.35**
WS	.13*	.06	-.18**	.12*	-.01	-.12*
SPST-A	-.27**	-.31**	.27**	-.28**	-.23**	.40**

Notes: IPB = Interpersonal Problem Behavior; NPSB = Negative Problem-Solving Behavior; RPSB = Rational Problem-Solving Behavior; IB = Impulsive Behavior; AB = Avoidance Behavior; TRSIPS = Teacher Rating Scale of Interpersonal Problem Solving Competence; PPS = Positive Problem Solving; NPS = Negative Problem Solving; RPS = Rational Problem Solving; IS = Impulsivity Style; WS = Withdrawal Style; SPST-A = Social Problem Solving Test for Stories-a.
*P<.05; **P<.01.

Reliability and Validity of the SPST

The purpose of this section is to present the results of the reliability and validity studies of the SPST in two samples of Vietnamese high school students: regular students ("normal" students) and students who had been diagnosed as having psychological and behavioural problems ("disruptive" students). An intercorrelation matrix analysis was computed to examine the expected relationships among sub-subscales/subscales/scales of the SPST and to determine whether these relationships do indeed exist. This may reveal considerable information about the reliability and validity of the measure. The reliability of the SPST was evaluated by investigating internal consistency and test-retest reliability coefficients. The validity of the SPST was assessed by examining the relationship between the SPST and other measures of social problem solving, i.e. the TRSIPS and the SPSI-R developed by D'Zurilla et al. (1996).

Factoring the correlation matrices

An intercorrelation matrix analysis was performed on the SPST-A data for the combined sample. The correlation matrix (reported in Table 5) indicates that a considerable number of correlations exceed .3, the Bartlett Test of Sphericity is significant and thus the matrix is suitable for factoring.

The original factor matrix displays two factors extracted with their associated eigenvalues of 2.15 and 1.48 (other factors have eigenvalues below 1.00). The factor scree plot also suggests that there are two general factors. The Withdrawal Style subscale has high loadings on more than one factor and thus the orthogonal (varimax rotation) procedure was applied to make interpretation of the output easier.

Table 5

Matrix of Intercorrelations for SPST-A Subscales for the Combined Regular and Problem High School Student Sample (N = 409)

Subscales	PPS	NPS	RPS	IS	WS
PPS	-				
NPS	-.02	-			
RPS	.49**	-.20**	-		
IS	-.19**	.62**	-.29**	-	
WS	.15*	.42**	-.02	.48**	-

Table 6

Original and Rotated Factor Matrices for the SPST-A Produced by the Principal Axis
Factoring technique and Varimax Rotation of Correlation Matrix

	Original (unrotated) factor matrix		Rotated factor matrix		Communality
	I	II	I'	II'	
Subscales					
IS	.87688		.83064		.77405
NPS	.80234		.82954		.69992
WS	.63452	.51341	.78816		.66619
PPS		.82725		.87292	.76720
RPS	-.49774	.68428		.82730	.71599

Notes: Factor loadings < .3 have not been printed; PPS = Positive Problem Solving; NPS = Negative
Problem Solving; RPS = Rational Problem Solving; IS = Impulsivity Style; WS = Withdrawal Style.

The loadings in the rotated factor matrix apparently determined two common factors for the
SPST-A data (see Table 6). The percentage of variance explained by the two factors is 72.5%.
Factor I comprises 3 subscales of the SPST-A (ie. Impulsivity Style, Negative Problem Solving
and Withdrawal Style) with factor loadings ranging from .79 to .83. The factor may be well
labeled negative or dysfunctional problem-solving. The Positive Problem Solving and Rational
Problem Solving subscales have high loadings (.87 and .83) on factor II. An appropriate name
for the factor II is Positive or Constructive problem-solving.

A correlation matrix analysis of the SPST-B and SPST-A data for the combined sample is
reported in Table 7. The correlation between the PAC-B and PSA-B is .41. The Principle Component Analysis extracted a single factor (with an eigenvalue of 1.42) for the PAC-B and PSA-
B scales. 70.7% of the variance is accounted for by that factor. The correlation between the
PAC-A and PSA-A scales is .71 and a single factor with an eigenvalue of 1.71 was extracted
which accounts for 85.5% of the variance.

The results of factor analysis for the PAC-B, PSA-B, PAC-A and PSA-A scales (reported in Table 8) indicate that these scales has a common factor with an eigenvalue of 2.40. The factor scree splot also suggest a single factor for these scales (see Appendix F). 60% of the variance is accounted for by this factor.

Table 7

Matrix of Intercorrelations for the SPST-A and SPST-B Scales for the Combined Regular and Problem High School Student Sample (N = 409)

Scales	PAC-B	PSA-B	PAC-A	PSA-A
PAC-B	-			
PSA-B	.41**	-		
PAC-A	.36**	.46**	-	
PSA-A	.36**	.46**	.71**	-

Notes: PAC-A = Problem Affect-Cognitions for Stories-a; PSA-A = Problem-Solving Actions for Stories-a; PAC-B = Problem Affect-Cognitions for Stories-b; PSA-B = Problem-Solving Actions for Stories-b.
*p < .05; **p < .01.

Table 8

Original (Unrotated) Factor Matrices for the SPST Scales Produced by the Principal Axis Factoring Technique (N = 409)

Scales	Original (unrotated) factor matrix I	Communality
PAC-B	.65372	.42735
PSA-B	.74667	.55751
PAC-A	.83976	.70519
PSA-A	.84251	.70892

Notes: PAC-A = Problem Affect-Cognitions for Stories-a; PSA-A = Problem-Solving Actions for Stories-a; PAC-B = Problem Affect-Cognitions for Stories-b; PSA-B = Problem-Solving Actions for Stories-b.

Intercorrelations of the SPST

The intercorrelations of the SPST for the regular and problem high school student groups as independent samples are reported in Tables 9, 10, 11, 12, 13 and 14. Tables 9 and 10 describe intercorrelations among the ten sub-subscales of SPST-A for normal and disruptive high school student samples. As predicted, all intersubscale correlations between five sub-subscales which assess problem affect-cognitions and five sub-subscales which assess problem-solving actions in both regular and problem high school student samples were significantly positive. That is, the Positive Orientation (PO), Negative Orientation (NO), Rational Orientation (RO), Impulsive Orientation (IO), and Withdrawal Orientation (WO) scores were positively correlated with the Positive Problem-Solving Skills (PPSS), Negative Problem-Solving Skills (NPSS), Rational Problem-Solving Skills (RPSS), Impulsivity Problem-Solving Style (IPSS), and Withdrawal Problem-Solving Style (WPSS) (in the order presented in Table 9 and Table 10), and ranged from a low .38 to a moderate .67. The largest amount of common variance that the RO and RPSS in the problem sample share is 45%. Thus, none of them is high enough to suggest that any of the sub-subscales may be redundant.

As expected, the PO and RO scores were positively correlated with the PPSS and RPSS scores (constructive facets), yet negatively or not significantly correlated with the NPSS, IPSS, and WPSS scores (dysfunctional facets). Conversely, the NO, IO, and WO scores were positively associated with the NPSS, IPSS, and WPSS scores, but negatively or not significantly correlated to the PPSS and RPSS scores as predicted.

The internal correlations for the RPS subscale were strongest. The results indicated that internal correlations for all five subscales of the SPST-A were significant and moderate. The results indicated that adolescents' problem affect-cognitions were significantly correlated with the adolescents' problem-solving actions (strategies).

Table 9

Intercorrelations Among the sub-subscales of the SPST-A

in the Regular High School Student Sample (N = 245)

	PO	NO	RO	IO	WO	PPSS	NPSS	RPSS	IPSS	WPSS
PO	-									
NO	.01	-								
RO	.30**	-.02	-							
IO	-.09	.54**	-.07	-						
WO	.06	.28**	-.11*	.53**	-					
PPSS	.38**	.07	.17*	.01	.31**	-				
NPSS	-.07	.46**	.22**	.38**	.31**	.15*	-			
RPSS	.46**	-.13*	.58**	-.24**	-.08	.26**	-.27**	-		
IPSS	-.29**	.45**	-.29**	.47**	.27**	-.01	.56**	-.27**	-	
WPSS	-.17*	.40**	-.16*	.39**	.54**	.23**	.43**	-.27**	.41**	-

Note: PO = Positive Orientation, NO = Negative Orientation, RO = Rational Orientation, IO = Impulsive Orientation, WO = Withdrawal Orientation, PPSS = Positive Problem-Solving Skills, NPSS = Negative Problem-Solving Skills, RPSS = Rational Problem-Solving Skills, IPSS = Impulsivity Problem-Solving Style, WPSS = Withdrawal Problem-Solving Style.
$*p < .05; **p < .01$.

Table 10

Intercorrelations Among the sub-subscales of the SPST-A

in the Problem High School Student Sample (N = 164)

	PO	NO	RO	IO	WO	PPSS	NPSS	RPSS	IPSS	WPSS
PO	-									
NO	-.06	-								
RO	.43**	-.11	-							
IO	-.11	.54**	-.17*	-						
WO	.08	.32**	.04	.48**	-					
PPSS	.49**	-.03	.42**	-.25**	-.12	-				
NPSS	-.15*	.41**	-.10	.41**	.36**	.01	-			
RPSS	.49**	-.16*	.67**	-.19*	-.14*	.47**	-.08	-		
IPSS	-.23**	.43**	-.34**	.61**	.26**	-.28**	.46**	-.38**	-	
WPSS	-.01	.23**	.00	.23**	.54**	.15*	.37**	.06	.27**	-

Note: PO = Positive Orientation, NO = Negative Orientation, RO = Rational Orientation, IO = Impulsive Orientation, WO = Withdrawal Orientation, PPSS = Positive Problem-Solving Skills, NPSS = Negative Problem-Solving Skills, RPSS = Rational Problem-Solving Skills, IPSS = Impulsivity Problem-Solving Style, WPSS = Withdrawal Problem-Solving Style.
*p < .05; **p < .01.

Intercorrelations among the five subscales of the SPST-A in both regular and problem student samples are reported in Tables 11 and 12. As predicted, both the correlations between the Positive Problem Solving (PPS) and Rational Problem Solving (RPS) subscales (constructive components) and those among the Negative Problem Solving (NPS), Impulsivity Style (IS), and Withdrawal Style (WS) subcales (dysfunctional components) were significantly positive, whereas the correlations between the constructive components and the dysfunctional components were negatively or not significantly positively correlated. The results supported the internal validity of the SPST-A. The degrees of the relationship between the subscale scores and the SPST-A total scores ranged from a low (.35) to a high (.94) indicating that all subscales could contribute significantly to the SPST-A total score.

Table 11

Intercorrelations among the Subscales and Scales of the SPST-A

in the Regular High School Student Sample (N = 245)

	PPS	NPS	RPS	IS	WS	PAC-A	PSA-A	SPST-A
PPS	-							
NPS	.05	-						
RPS	.39**	-.21**	-					
IS	-.11*	.64**	-.29**	-				
WS	.16*	.46**	-.17*	.55**	-			
PAC-A	.24**	-.65**	.53**	-.83**	-.71**	-		
PSA-A	.43**	-.68**	.63**	-.68**	-.49**	.70**	-	
SPST-A	.35**	-.72**	.62**	-.83**	-.66**	.94**	.90**	-

Note: PPS = Positive Problem Solving; NPS = Negative Problem Solving; RPS = Rational Problem Solving; IS = Impulsivity Style; WS = Withdrawal Style; PAC-A = Problem Affect-Cognitions for Stories-a; PSA-A = Problem-Solving Actions for Stories-a; SPST-A = Social Problem-Solving Test for Stories-a.

*p < .05; **p < .01.

Table 12

Intercorrelations among the Subscales and Scales of the SPST-A

in the Problem High School Student Sample (N = 164)

	PPS	NPS	RPS	IS	WS	PAC-A	PSA-A	SPST-A
PPS	-							
NPS	.08	-						
RPS	.58**	-.15*	-					
IS	-.27**	.61**	-.31**	-				
WS	-.11	.44**	-.08	.41**	-			
PAC-A	.50**	-.67**	.54**	-.80**	-.51**	-		
PSA-A	.60**	-.60**	.66**	-.73**	-.36**	.74**	-	
SPST-A	.59**	-.68**	.64**	-.82**	-.47**	.94**	.92**	-

Note: PPS = Positive Problem Solving; NPS = Negative Problem Solving; RPS = Rational Problem Solving; IS = Impulsivity Style; WS = Withdrawal Style; PAC-A = Problem Affect-Cognitions for Stories-a; PSA-A = Problem-Solving Actions for Stories-a; SPST-A = Social Problem-Solving Test for Stories-a.

*p < .05; **p < .01.

Intercorrelations for the SPST-B in the regular and problem student samples are presented in Tables 13 and 14. As expected, the interscale correlations between the PAC-B and PSA-B scores were significantly positive, and ranged from a low (.35) to a moderate (.58). The correlations between the PAC-B and PSA-B scale scores and the SPST-B total score were high, from .79 to .89. These results indicated that the interscale correlations of the SPST-B were significant, and that the scale scores could contribute significantly to SPST-B total score.

Table 13

Intercorrelations between the PAC-B and PSA-B Scores and the SPST-B
Total Score in a Regular High School Student Sample (N = 245)

	PAC-B	PSA-B
PAC-B	-	
PSA-B	.35**	-
SPST-B	.79**	.85**

Notes: PAC-B = Problem Affect-Cognitions for Stories-b; PSA-B = Problem-Solving Actions for Stories-b. SPST-B = Social Problem Solving Test for Stories-b.
*p<.05; **p<.01

Table 14

Intercorrelations between the PAC-B and PSA-B Scores and the SPST-B
Total Score in a Problem High School Student Sample (N = 164)

	PAC-B	PSA-B
PAC-B	-	
PSA-B	.58**	-
SPST-B	.89**	.89**

Notes: PAC-B = Problem Affect-Cognitions for Stories-b; PSA-B = Problem-Solving Actions for Stories-b; SPST-B = Social Problem Solving Test for Stories-b.
*p <.05; **p <.01

Internal correlations between the SPST-A and the SPST-B among the subscales and scales are presented in Tables 15, 16, 17, and 18. Although the SPST-A and the SPST-B were structured differently and used different formats (see chapter 4), the Problem Affect-Cognitions (PAC-B) and Problem-Solving Actions (PSA-B) scales were significantly and positively correlated with the SPST-A subscales (i.e., Positive Problem Solving and Rational Problem Solving) which assess constructive components, but negatively associated with the subscales (ie., Negative Problem Solving, Impulsivity Style, and Withdrawal Style) which assess dysfunctional components (see Tables 15 and 16). The Negative Problem Solving, Impulsivity Style, and Withdrawal Style subscales of the SPST-A were negatively correlated with the SPST-B (-.17 to -.40), whereas the Rational Problem Solving and Positive Problem Solving subscales of the SPST-A were positively correlated with the SPST-B (.20 to .43) as predicted.

Table 15

Intercorrelations between the SPST-A Subscales and the SPST-B Scales in a Regular (Non-problematic) High School Student Sample (N = 245)

	PAC-B	PSA-B	SPST-B
PPS	.16*	.16*	.20**
NPS	-.13*	-.29**	-.26**
RPS	.27**	.43**	.43**
IS	-.20**	-.24**	-.27**
WS	-.16*	-.24**	-.25**

Notes: PAC-B = Problem Affect-Cognitions for Stories-b; PSA-B = Problem-Solving Actions for Stories-b; SPST-B = Social Problem Solving Test for Stories-b; PPS = Positive Problem Solving; NPS = Negative Problem Solving; RPS = Rational Problem Solving; IS = Impulsivity Style; WS = Withdrawal Style.
*p <.05; **p <.01.

Table16

Intercorrelations between the SPST-A Subscale Scores and the SPST-B Scale Scores in a
Problem High School Student Sample (N = 164)

	PAC-B	PSA-B	SPST-B
PPS	.24**	.30**	.31**
NPS	-.24**	-.33**	-.32**
RPS	.29**	.47**	.43**
IS	-.34**	-.37**	-.40**
WS	-.04	-.26**	-.17*

Notes: PAC-B = Problem Affect-Cognitions for Stories-b; PSA-B = Problem-Solving Actions for Stories-b; SPST-B = Social Problem Solving Test for Stories-b; PPS = Positive Problem Solving; NPS =
Negative Problem Solving; RPS = Rational Problem Solving; IS = Impulsivity Style; WS = Withdrawal
Style.
*p <.05; **p <.01.

Interscale correlations between the PAC-A and PSA-A scales of the SPST-A were from .70 to
.74 (see Tables 17 and 18). The correlations between the PAC-B and PSA-B scales ranged
from .35 to .58. The correlations between the PAC-A and PSA-A scale scores and the SPST-
A total score were .90 to .94, respectively. The correlations between the PAC-A and PSA-A
scales of SPST-A and the PAC-B and PSA-B scales of SPST-B were from .23 to .55. These
results reflect the multidimensionality of the SPST and provided substantial evidence for the
internal validity of the instrument.

Most importantly, SPST-A total scores were significantly correlated with SPST-B total scores
in both the regular and disruptive student samples. The degree of the relationships ranged
within a moderate level from .44 to .51. Thus, they not only integrate into a homogeneous
measure (the SPST), but can be used "separately" as two independent problem-solving
measures for different uses in clinical settings.

Table 17

Intercorrelations between the SPST-A and the SPST-B (Among the Scale and Total Scores) in a Regular High School Student Sample (N = 245)

	PAC-A	PSA-A	PAC-B	PSA-B	SPST-A
PAC-A	-				
PSA-A	.70**	-			
PAC-B	.29**	.23**	-		
PSA-B	.36**	.43**	.35**	-	
SPST-A	.94**	.90**	.29**	.42**	-
SPST-B	.40**	.41**	.79**	.85**	.44**

Notes: PAC-A = Problem Affect-Cognitions for Stories-a; PSA-A = Problem-Solving Actions for Stories-a; PAC-B = Problem Affect-Cognitions for Stories-b; PSA-B = Problem-Solving Actions for Stories-b; SPST-A = Social Problem Solving Test for Stories-a; SPST-B = Social Problem Solving Test for Stories-b.
*p <.05; **p <.01.

Table 18

Intercorrelations between the SPST-A and the SPST-B (among the Scale and Total Scores) in a Problem High School Student Sample (N = 164)

	PAC-A	PSA-A	PAC-B	PSA-B	SPST-A
PAC-A	-				
PSA-A	.74**	-			
PAC-B	.29**	.41**	-		
PSA-B	.47**	.55**	.58**	-	
SPST-A	.94**	.92**	.37**	.54**	-
SPST-B	.43**	.53**	.89**	.89**	.51**

Notes: PAC-A = Problem Affect-Cognitions for Stories-a; PSA-A = Problem-Solving Actions for Stories-a; PAC-B = Problem Affect-Cognitions for Stories-b; PSA-B = Problem-Solving Actions for Stories-b; SPST-A = Social Problem Solving Test for Stories-a; SPST-B = Social Problem Solving Test for Stories-b.
*p <.05; **p <.01.

Reliability of the SPST

Internal Consistency. Internal consistency can be measured by specific methods such as Cronbach's alpha, the split-half method, and the Kuder-Richardson method. Results of investigating the reliability coefficients (Cronbach's alpha) for the SPST-A and its subscales are reported in Table 19. The SPST-A achieved coefficient alphas of .92 and .91 for normal and disruptive student samples. Alpha reliability coefficients for the Problem Affect-Cognitions (PAC-A) and Problem-Solving Actions (PSA-A) scales of SPST-A were from .80 to .89. Reliability coefficients for the Positive Problem Solving (PPS), Negative Problem Solving (NPS), Rational Problem Solving (RPS), Impulsivity Style (IS), and Withdrawal Style (WS) subscales of the SPST-A ranged from .61 to .84. In general, the reliability coefficients were high for the PSA-A scale and the SPST-A and moderate for the five subscales. The results indicated that the reliability coefficients for the SPST-A and its subscales were adequate.

Table 19

Reliabilities for the SPST-A and Its Subcales

	Internal Consistency (alpha)	
	Regular student sample (N = 245)	Problem student sample (N = 164)
SubScales		
PPS	.61	.72
NPS	.69	.70
RPS	.74	.80
IS	.79	.84
WS	.75	.70
Scales		
PAC-A	.80	.80
PSA-A	.89	.88
SPST-A	.92	.91

Notes: PPS = Positive Problem Solving; NPS = Negative Problem Solving; RPS = Rational Problem Solving; IS = Impulsivity Style; WS = Withdrawal Style; PAC-A = Problem Affect-Cognitions for Stories-a; PSA-A = Problem-Solving Actions for Stories-a; SPST-A = Social Problem Solving Test for Stories-a.

Alpha reliability coefficients for the SPST-B and its scales in regular and disruptive high school student samples are presented in Table 20. The SPST-B showed moderate internal consistency coefficients (.74 to .78). Reliability coefficients for the Problem Affect-Cognitions (PAC-B) and Problem-Solving Actions (PSA-B) scales of the SPST-B were also moderate, and ranged from .64 to .68. The results indicated that the reliability coefficients for SPST-B and its scales were significant and moderate. Alpha coefficients for the SPST (i.e., coefficient alpha for the combination of the PAC-B, PSA-B, PAC-A, and PSA-A scales) in a regular adolescent group (N = 72) and a problem adolescent group (N = 66) ranged from .72 to .80 and were significant and moderate.

Table 20

Reliabilities for the SPST-B Scales

	Internal Consistency (alpha)	
Scales	Regular high school student sample (N=72)	Problem high school student sample (N=66)
PAC-B	.68	.66
PSA-B	.68	.64
SPST-B	.74	.78

Notes: PAC-B = Problem Affect-Cognitions for Stories-b; PSA-B = Problem-Solving Actions for Stories-b; SPST-B = Social Problem Solving Test for Stories-b.

Internal consistency also can be assessed with a series of items-total correlations. The correlations between the item scores and the SPST-A total score in the regular and problem student samples as reported in Table 21 were significantly high, and ranged from .47 to .71. The results demonstrated that all item scores could contribute significantly to the SPST-A total score.

In summary, these results indicated that the SPST-A and its subscales, as well as the SPST-B and its scales, could be considered homogeneous and consistent. Consequently, the SPST as a whole could be considered homogeneous and consistent.

Table 21

Correlations between the Item Scores and the SPST-A Total Score
in Regular and Problem High School Student Samples

	Regular Sample (N = 245)	Problem Sample (N = 164)
Stories-a		
# 1	.52	.47
# 2	.49	.56
# 3	.52	.47
# 4	.58	.56
# 5	.52	.59
# 6	.62	.66
# 7	.63	.64
# 8	.67	.63
# 9	.63	.71
# 10	.66	.62
# 11	.52	.48
# 12	.57	.56

Notes: All correlations are significant at p <.01.

Stability. In order to confirm the stability of the SPST, test-retest reliabilities were assessed. The test-retest reliability results are presented in Table 22. Test-retest reliability coefficients for the SPST-A total scores for the normal and disruptive high school samples were .76 and .87, respectively. The test-retest reliabilities for the PAC-A and PSA-A scale scores ranged from .71 to .86. Test-retest correlation coefficients for the PPS, NPS, RPS, IS, and WS subscales ranged from .52 to .89. These results indicated that the SPST-A is a relatively stable measure over a first and second administration separated by a 2-week interval.

Table 22

Test-Retest Reliabilities for the SPST-A and Its Subscales

	Regular High School Students (N=71)	Problem High School Students (N=65)
SubScales		
PPS	.71	.73
NPS	.81	.69
RPS	.69	.71
IS	.89	.52
WS	.75	.70
Scales		
PAC-A	.86	.73
PSA-A	.81	.71
SPST-A	.87	.76

Notes: PPS = Positive Problem Solving; NPS = Negative Problem Solving; RPS = Rational Problem Solving; IS = Impulsivity Style; WS = Withdrawal Style; PAC-A = Problem Affect-Cognitions for Stories-a; PSA-A = Problem-Solving Actions for Stories-a; SPST-A = Social Problem Solving Test for Stories-a. All correlations are significant at p <.01.

Validity of the SPST

Content validity. As indicated previously, the content validity of a measure can be evaluated by describing the content domain, determining the areas of the content domain, and comparing the structure of the test with the structure of the content domain. In general, these procedures have been detailed and discussed in earlier chapters. For example, the content validity of the SPST is established by showing that the interpersonal problematic situations sampled by the measure are a representative sample of adolescent interpersonal difficulties (see chapter 3 and

4). The SPST consists of 24 interpersonal problematic situations which have been validated from the original pool of close to 500 problems, and they have been demonstrated to be representative situations of a variety of adolescent interpersonal problem categories.

The boundaries and the contents of the domain which the SPST aims to measure are clearly described as five particular domains of the social problem-solving process (see chapter 4). The response items for each of the situations were generated by adolescents. Comparing the structure of the SPST-A, which includes five subscales, with the structure of the five content domains, no evidence indicated that the test items fall outside the boundaries of the particular domains. In addition, the correlations between the items and SPST-A total scores as reported in Table 21 show that the magnitude of these correlations was from .47 to. 71.

Further examination of the intercorrelations between the sub-subscale scores and the SPST-A total score (presented in Tables 23 and 24) revealed that the sub-subscale scores were highly correlated with the SPST-A subscale scores. The degree of these correlations ranged from .77 to .92. Thus, it seems clear that the SPST-A subscales measure what they are supposed to measure.

Correlations between the subscale scores and SPST-A total score (reported in Tables 11 and 12, p. 96-98) were from a low .35 to a high .94. Also, the correlations between the scale scores and the SPST-B total score (reported in Tables 13 and 14, p. 99) were high, from .80 to .89. The correlations between the SPST-A and SPST-B scores ranged from .44 to .51. These results provide further substantial evidence for the content validity of the SPST and support the conclusion that it measures what it is supposed to measure.

Table 23

Correlations between the Sub-subscale and Subscale Scores and the SPST-A Total Score in a Regular High School Student Sample (N = 245)

	PPS	NPS	RPS	IS	WS	SPST-A
PO	.83					.44
PPSS	.83					.15*
NO		.86				-.60
NPSS		.85				-.64
RO			.91			.50
RPSS			.86			.62
IO				.92		-.71
IPSS				.77		-.73
WO					.91	-.54
WPSS					.84	-.63

Notes: PPS = Positive Problem Solving; NPS = Negative Problem Solving; RPS = Rational Problem Solving; IS = Impulsivity Style; WS = Withdrawal Style; SPST-A = Social Problem Solving Test for Stories-a; PO = Positive Orientation; PPSS = Positive Problem-Solving Skills; NO = Negative Orientation; NPSS = Negative Problem-Solving Skills; RO = Rational Orientation; RPSS = Rational Problem-Solving Skills; IO = Impulsive Orientation; IPSS = Impulsivity Problem-Solving Style; WO = Withdrawal Orientation; WPSS = Withdrawal Problem-Solving Style.
All correlations are significant at $p < .01$, exception of: *$p < .05$.

Table 24

Correlations between the Sub-subscale and Subscale Scores and the SPST-A Total Score in a
Problem High School Student Sample (N = 164)

	PPS	NPS	RPS	IS	WS	SPST-A
PO	.87					.52
PPSS	.85					.49
NO		.84				-.58
NPSS		.84				-.57
RO			.91			.58
RPSS			.92			.60
IO				.92		-.72
IPSS				.87		-.76
WO					.91	-.44
WPSS					.84	-.39

Notes: PPS = Positive Problem Solving; NPS = Negative Problem Solving; RPS = Rational Problem
Solving; IS = Impulsivity Style; WS = Withdrawal Style; SPST-A = Social Problem Solving Test for
Stories-a; PO = Positive Orientation; PPSS = Positive Problem-Solving Skills; NO = Negative Orien-
tation; NPSS = Negative Problem-Solving Skills; RO = Rational Orientation; RPSS = Rational Prob-
lem-Solving Skills; IO = Impulsive Orientation; IPSS = Impulsivity Problem-Solving Style; WO =
Withdrawal Orientation; WPSS = Withdrawal Problem-Solving Style.
All correlations are significant at p <.01.

Construct validity. The construct validity of the SPST was assessed by examining the correlations between the SPST and teacher's behavioural reports - Teacher Rating Scale of Interpersonal Problem Solving (TRSIPS). The TRSIPS, as described previously, has a similar structure
to the structure of the SPST-A with the exception of the Interpersonal Problem Behaviour (IPB)
subscale.

The data are reported in Tables 25 and 26. As predicted, both the SPST-A and SPST-B were
negatively correlated with the Interpersonal Problem Behaviour (IPB). The SPST-A total score
was significantly and positively associated with the TRSIPS total score as expected. Similarly,

the SPST-B total score was positively correlated with the TRSIPS total score. The results suggest that an adolescent's poor problem-solving skills relate to his/her interpersonal problems as noted by teachers.

Although not all subscale correlations were strongly negative or positive as expected, the correlations between the Negative Problem-Solving Behaviour (NPSB) and Impulsive Behaviour (IB) subscales of the TRSIPS (dysfunctional components) and the Impulsivity Style (IS) subscale of the SPST-A (dysfunctional components) were significantly positive as predicted. The correlation between the Rational Problem Solving (RPS) and the Rational Problem-Solving Behaviour (RPSB) scores was significantly positive, whereas the RPS score (constructive component) was negatively correlated to the Negative Problem-Solving Behaviour, Impulsive Behaviour and Avoidance Behaviour scores (dysfunctional components) as expected.

Also as expected, the TRSIPS total score was positively correlated with the Rational Problem Solving and Positive Problem Solving scores, but negatively (or not significantly) associated with the Impulsivity Style, Negative Problem Solving, and Withdrawal Style scores. As predicted, the SPST-A total score was negatively correlated with the NPSB, IB, AB scores (dysfunctional components), but positively correlated with the RPSB score (constructive component). These results indicate that there is substantial evidence of the construct validity of SPST and suggest that the instrument is a valid measure.

Another common method of studying construct validity involves the mathematical technique known as correlation matrix analyses. This method provides information about the expected relationships among variables and helps determine whether this parttern of relationships does indeed exist (Murphy & Davidshofer, 1994). The results of the SPST intercorrelation analyses are presented in Tables 11, 12, 13, 14, 15, 16, 17, and 18 (p. 97-103). As noted previously, most of the expected relationships did indeed exist and occurred as predicted. For example, the SPST-A total scores were positively correlated with the SPST-B total scores as predicted. The Rational Problem Solving score was positively associated with both the SPST-A and SPST-B total scores, but negatively associated with the Negative Problem Solving (NPS), Impulsivity Style (IS), and Withdrawal Style (WS) subscale scores as expected. Inversely, the NPS, IS, and WS subscale scores were negatively correlated with both the SPST-A and SPST-B total scores as predicted. The results indicated that both the SPST-A and the SPST-B reflected the multidimensional nature of the construct of social problem solving. Consequently, the findings provided further support for the construct validity of the SPST.

As indicated by Aiken and Groth-Marnat (2006), among other sources of evidence for the construct validity of a measure is an analysis of the internal consistency. The results of investigating the internal consistency of the SPST are reported in Tables 19 and 20 (p. 104-105). Alpha coefficients for the SPST-A total score were high ($r \geq .91$). Alpha coefficients for the SPST-B total score were moderate ($r \geq .74$). Coefficient alphas for the SPST-A subscales and the SPST-B scales were from a moderate (.61) to a high (.89). The results also showed that the construct validity of the SPST was adequate and provide further evidence that it is a valid measure of interpersonal problem solving.

Concurrent Validity. The concurrent validity of the SPST-A was examined by calculating Pearson correlation coefficients between the SPST-A and another social problem solving measure - the TRSIPS. The results of investigating the concurrent validity of the SPST-A and SPST-B were reported in Tables 25 and 26.

Table 25

Correlations between the SPST-A and the TRSIPS (among Subscale and Total Scores) In a Problem High School Student Sample (N = 102)

	IPB	NPSB	RPSB	IB	AB	TRSIPS
PPS	-.12	-.13	.19*	-.08	-.19*	.20*
NPS	.09	.11	-.01	.11	-.01	-.09
RPS	-.24**	-.31**	.22**	-.22**	-.36**	.41**
IS	.24**	.30**	-.19*	.30**	.13	-.35**
WS	.13	.06	-.18*	.12	-.01	-.12
SPST-A	-.27**	-.31**	.27**	-.28**	-.23**	.40**

Note: PPS = Positive Problem Solving; NPS = Negative Problem Solving; RPS = Rational Problem Solving; IS = Impulsivity Style; WS = Withdrawal Style; PAC-A = Problem Affect-Cognitions for Stories-a; PSA-A = Problem-Solving Actions for Stories-a; SPST-A = Social Problem-Solving Test for Stories-a.

*p < .05; **p < .01.

Table 26

Correlations between the SPST-B and the TRSIPS (among Subscale and Total Scores)

In a Problem High School Student Sample (N = 102)

	IPB	NPSB	RPSB	IB	AB	TRSIPS
PAC-B	-.22**	-.20*	.20**	-.21*	-.20*	.30**
PSA-B	-.21**	-.24**	.22**	-.22**	-.01	.25**
SPST-B	-.17*	-.19*	.24**	-.17*	-.11	.26**

The concurrent validity of the SPST-A was also examined by calculating Pearson correlation coefficients between the SPST-A and another criterion social problem solving measure - the Social Problem-Solving Inventory-Revised (SPSI-R) (D'Zurilla et al., 1996).

The results of correlational analyses are presented in Tables 27 and 28. Although the SPST-A and the SPSI-R used different measurement methods, their scale and subscale scores showed significant positive correlations. As predicted, the Negative Problem Orientation, Impulsivity/Carelessness Style, and Avoidance Style subscale scores of the SPSI-R were positively correlated with the Negative Problem Solving, and Impulsivity Style subscale scores of the SPST-A (.22 to .50). The correlations between the Rational Problem Solving scores of the SPST-A and the Rational Problem Solving scale scores of the SPSI-R for both normal and disruptive high school student samples were positive as expected, and were most significant (.49 to. 51). The correlations between the SPST-A and the SPSI-R total scores ranged from .52 to .61. None of these correlations is high enough to suggest that any of the subscales may be redundant. The highest amount of common variance that the SPST-A and the SPSI-R share is 37%. These results indicated that the concurrent validity of the SPST-A was adequate, but not high enough to make it be redundant or indistinguishable from the SPSI-R.

Table 27

Correlations between the SPST-A and the SPSI-R (among Subscale and Total Scores)

In a Regular High School Student Sample (N = 83)

	PPO	NPO	RPS*	ICS	AS	SPSI-R
PPS	.04	-.09	.27**	.05	.07	
NPS	-.21*	.36**	-.20*	.37**	.50**	
RPS	.34**	-.16	.51**	-.24*	-.32**	
IS	-.40**	.46**	-.42**	.35**	.48**	
WS	-.25**	.46**	-.16	.17	.22*	
SPST-A						.61**

Note: PPO = Positive Problem Orientation; NPS = Negative Problem Orientation; RPS* = Rational Problem Solving of the SPSI-R; ICS = Impulsivity/Carelessness Style; AS = Avoidance Style; SPSI-R = Social Problem-Solving Inventory-Revised; PPS = Positive Problem Solving; NPS = Negative Problem Solving; RPS = Rational Problem Solving; IS = Impulsivity Style; WS = Withdrawal Style; SPST-A = Social Problem-Solving Test for Stories-a.
*p < .05; **p < .01.

Table 28

Correlations between the SPST-A and the SPSI-R (among Subscale and Total scores)

In a Problem High School Student Sample (N = 52)

	PPO	NPO	RPS*	ICS	AS	SPSI-R
PPS	.35**	.05	.34**	.02	-.14	
NPS	-.35*	.42**	-.05	.32**	.40**	
RPS	.31**	-.12	.49**	-.05	-.18	
IS	-.33**	.22*	-.20*	.24*	.31**	
WS	-.08	.46**	-.23*	.34**	.42**	
SPST-A						.52**

Note: PPO = Positive Problem Orientation; NPS = Negative Problem Orientation; RPS* = Rational Problem Solving of the SPSI-R; ICS = Impulsivity/Carelessness Style; AS = Avoidance Style; SPSI-R = Social Problem-Solving Inventory-Revised; PPS = Positive Problem Solving; NPS = Negative Problem Solving; RPS = Rational Problem Solving; IS = Impulsivity Style; WS = Withdrawal Style; SPST-A = Social Problem-Solving Test for Stories-a.
*p < .05; **p < .01.

Cross-validation. Cross-validation involves administering the test to a second independent sample of subjects to examine whether the test retains its validity (the validity generalization) across different samples (Aiken & Groth-Marnat, 2006; Murphy & Davidshofer, 1994). It was assumed that the 127 regular high school students who were administered Form A and 118 regular students who took Form B were two independent samples because the 245 students in the regular sample were randomly assigned to odd or even numbers to take Form A or Form B respectively. Similarly, in the "problem" sample, 87 problem high school students who took Form A and 77 problem students who took Form B were two independent samples. As described previously, Form A and Form B have the same SPST-A (only the order of Stories-a is different). Hence, comparisons between these samples provide information about the validity generalization of SPST-A.

An analysis of variance method (ONE WAY-ANOVA) was employed. The mean scores of split samples on the SPST-A subscales were reported in Tables 29 and 30. The mean scores of these split regular samples on all sub-subscales of the SPST-A were not significantly different ($p < .05$). Similarly, the mean scores of the split problem samples did not differentiate significantly ($p < .05$). In contrast, the mean scores of the regular and problem samples (reported in Tables 31 and 32) were found to be significantly different on a majority of sub-subscales of the SPST-A (i.e., Positive Orientation, Negative Problem-Solving Skills, Rational Orientation, Rational Problem-Solving Skills, and Impulsivity Problem-Solving Style). The results in general supported the validity generalization of SPST-A which can be said to result in stable classification functions with comparative proportions of adolescents correctly classified.

Table 29

Means and Standard Deviations for the Sub-subscales/Subscales of the SPST-A in Split Regular High School Student Samples

	First split sample (N = 127)		Second split sample (N = 118)		F	P
	Mean	SD	Mean	SD	Ratio	
PO	17.61	2.74	17.22	2.91	1.14	.286
PPSS	15.47	2.81	15.28	2.85	.284	.595
PPS	33.08	4.55	32.50	4.85	.93	.336
NO	10.76	3.16	10.14	3.13	2.38	.124
NPSS	7.07	3.22	6.94	3.08	.10	.747
NPS	17.83	5.29	17.08	5.47	1.19	.277
RO	17.93	3.31	18.55	3.18	2.24	.136
RPSS	19.16	2.71	19.42	2.64	.61	.437
RPS	37.09	5.38	37.97	5.14	1.74	.189
IO	11.00	4.31	10.49	4.06	.90	.344
IPSS	3.36	2.51	3.15	2.53	.42	.516
IS	14.36	5.83	13.64	5.80	.93	.335
WO	8.92	3.71	8.47	3.69	.92	.338
WPSS	6.45	3.05	5.97	2.66	1.67	.197
WS	15.37	6.07	14.44	5.45	1.58	.209
SPST-A	166.60	17.80	169.31	17.06	1.47	.226

Notes: PO = Positive Orientation; PPSS = Positive Problem-Solving Skills; PPS = Positive Problem Solving; NO = Negative Orientation; NPSS = Negative Problem-Solving Skills; NPS = Negative Problem Solving; RO = Rational Orientation; RPSS = Rational Problem-Solving Skills; RPS = Rational Problem Solving; IO = Impulsive Orientation; IPSS = Impulsivity Problem-Solving Style; IS = Impulsivity Style; WO = Withdrawal Orientation; WPSS = Withdrawal Problem-Solving Style; WS = Withdrawal Style; SPST-A = Social Problem Solving Scale for Stories-a.

Table 30

Means and Standard Deviations for the Sub-subscales/Subscales of the SPST-A in Split
Problem High School Student Samples

	First split sample (N = 87) Mean	SD	Second split sample (N = 77) Mean	SD	F Ratio	P
PO	16.75	3.69	17.36	3.32	1.25	.265
PPSS	14.70	3.12	15.03	3.49	.40	.530
PPS	31.44	5.95	32.39	5.81	1.05	.308
NO	11.29	3.37	10.92	3.12	.55	.461
NPSS	7.92	3.39	7.27	3.04	1.64	.203
NPS	19.22	5.78	18.19	5.04	1.44	.231
RO	16.72	3.67	16.95	3.44	.16	.689
RPSS	17.80	3.76	18.01	3.71	.13	.722
RPS	34.53	6.78	34.96	6.56	.17	.680
IO	10.07	4.31	10.16	4.23	.02	.897
IPSS	4.09	3.45	3.97	3.07	.05	.818
IS	14.16	6.99	14.13	6.56	.00	.977
WO	7.56	3.46	7.58	3.25	.00	.968
WPSS	5.36	2.69	5.73	2.44	.85	.359
WS	12.92	5.46	13.31	4.95	.23	.632
SPST-A	163.68	19.42	165.71	19.58	.45	.505

Notes: PO = Positive Orientation; PPSS = Positive Problem-Solving Skills; PPS = Positive Problem
Solving; NO = Negative Orientation; NPSS = Negative Problem-Solving Skills; NPS = Negative Problem Solving; RO = Rational Orientation; RPSS = Rational Problem-Solving Skills; RPS = Rational
Problem Solving; IO = Impulsive Orientation; IPSS = Impulsivity Problem-Solving Style; IS = Impulsivity Style; WO = Withdrawal Orientation; WPSS = Withdrawal Problem-Solving Style; WS = Withdrawal Style; SPST-A = Social Problem Solving Scale for Stories-a.

Group Discrimination. According to Aiken and Groth-Marnat (2006), concurrent validation procedures are employed whenever a test is administered to people in various categories (such as diagnostic groups) for the purpose of determining whether the average scores of different types of people are significantly different. If the average score differs significantly from category to category, then the measure may be used as another, perhaps more efficient, means of grouping people into the various categories.

Using this approach, the SPST was administered to regular and problem adolescent groups to determine whether the average scores of these groups were significantly different. An analysis of variance method (ONE WAY-ANOVA)[12] was employed to complete the task. The results are reported in Tables 31 and 32. Significant differences between the mean scores of the regular and problem adolescent groups were found on the sub-subscales: Positive Orientation (PO), Negative Problem-Solving Skills (NPSS), Rational Orientation (RO), Rational Problem-Solving Skills (RPSS), and Impulsivity Problem-Solving Style (IPSS), $(p < .01)$. Similarly, significant differences were found on the Negative Problem Solving (NPS) and Rational Problem Solving (RPS) subscale scores $(p < .01)$. The total SPST-A mean scores of the two groups differed significantly $(p < .01)$. Also, the total SPST-B mean scores of these groups were significantly different from each other $(p < .01)$.

---

[12] One way ANOVA was employed because the regular and problem high school student samples are independent samples.

Table 31

Means and Standard Deviations for the Sub-subscales of the SPST-A in Regular and Problem
High School Student Samples

	Regular sample (N = 149)		Problem sample (N = 164)		F	P
	Mean	SD	Mean	SD	Ratio	
PO	17.94	2.58	17.04	3.53	6.57	.011
PPSS	15.00	2.69	14.85	3.29	.18	.669
NO	10.44	3.06	11.12	3.25	3.60	.059
NPSS	6.21	2.85	7.61	3.24	16.55	.000
RO	19.18	2.85	16.83	3.55	41.13	.000
RPSS	19.79	2.33	17.19	3.72	28.23	.000
IO	10.81	4.34	10.11	4.26	2.08	.150
IPSS	2.79	2.19	4.04	3.27	15.54	.000
WO	8.15	3.62	7.57	3.35	2.12	.146
WPSS	5.58	2.44	5.53	2.58	.04	.445

Notes: PO = Positive Orientation; PPSS = Positive Problem-Solving Skills; NO = Negative Orientation; NPSS = Negative Problem-Solving Skills; RO = Rational Orientation; RPSS = Rational Problem-
Solving Skills; IO = Impulsive Orientation; IPSS = Impulsivity Problem-Solving Style; WO = Withdrawal Orientation; WPSS = Withdrawal Problem-Solving Style.

Table 32

Means and Standard Deviations for the Subscales, the SPST-A and the SPST-B in Regular and Problem High School Student Samples

	Regular sample (N = 149)		Problem sample (N = 164)		F	P
	Mean	SD	Mean	SD	Ratio	
PPS	32.93	4.40	31.89	5.88	3..14	.077
NPS	16.65	5.15	18.74	5.45	12.07	.001
RPS	38.97	4.58	34.73	6.66	42.26	.000
IS	13.60	5.83	14.15	6.77	.59	.445
WS	13.73	5.22	13.10	5.22	1.13	.289
SPST-A	171.93	15.96	164.63	19.46	13.00	.000
SPST-B	17.23	4.89	13.13	5.18	51.78	.000

Notes: PPS = Positive Problem Solving; NPS = Negative Problem Solving; RPS = Rational Problem Solving; IS = Impulsivity Style; WS = Withdrawal Style; SPST-A = Social Problem Solving Scale for Stories-a; SPST-B = Social Problem Solving Scale for Stories-b.

It was hypothesized that regular and problem groups would respond differently to each item of the SPST-A. A comparison of the mean scores of all 12 items (problematic situations) on all 5 subscales of the SPST-A for the regular and problem student groups (reported in Table 33, 34, 35, 36 and 37) showed that there were significant differences (p <.05) on the all 12 items. Significant differences between the two groups on Positive Problem Solving scores were found for 5 items (i.e., Items # 3, # 6, # 8, # 9, and # 10), yet differences on the Rational Problem Solving score were found for 9 items (i.e., Items # 3, # 4, # 5, # 6, # 7, # 8, # 9, # 10, and # 11). While the Negative Problem Solving score of the two groups differed significantly on 5 items (i.e., Items # 1, # 6, # 7, # 9, and # 11). The Impulsivity Style score differentiated significantly for 2 items (i.e., Items # 5, # 8) and the Withdrawal Style score differed significantly on 6 items (i.e., Items # 2, # 3, # 4, # 10, # 11, and # 12). The results indicated that the Rational Problem Solving subscale is most able to discriminate between regular and problem adolescents and that all these situations would be able to discriminate between regular and problem adolescent groups.

Table 33

Analysis of Variance for the PPS in Regular and Problem
High School Student Samples

	Positive Problem Solving (PPS)					
	Regular sample (N = 149)		Problem sample (N = 164)		F	P
	Mean	SD	Mean	SD	Ratio	
Stories-a						
# 1	2.43	.95	2.44	.99	.01	.931
# 2	2.09	1.03	2.30	1.15	2.92	.088
# 3	2.11	.81	1.91	.90	3.97	.047
# 4	2.48	.95	2.68	1.05	3.10	.079
# 5	3.03	.94	2.81	1.11	3.67	.056
# 6	3.23	.77	2.82	.99	17.00	.000
# 7	2.56	1.17	2.78	1.11	2.99	.084
# 8	3.29	.74	3.04	.95	6.46	.011
# 9	2.84	.82	2.38	1.02	18.53	.000
# 10	3.60	.57	3.43	.69	5.65	.018
# 11	3.19	.71	3.07	.87	1.28	.182
# 12	2.09	1.15	2.22	1.11	1.07	.302

Table 34

Analysis of Variance for the NPS in Regular and Problem
High School Student Samples

Negative Problem Solving (NPS)						
Regular sample (N = 149)			Problem sample (N = 164)		F	P
	Mean	SD	Mean	SD	Ratio	
Stories-a						
# 1	1.13	1.03	1.50	1.20	8.32	.004
# 2	1.30	.79	1.49	1.01	3.24	.072
# 3	.79	.82	.90	.91	1.25	.264
# 4	2.32	1.07	2.38	1.12	.26	.613
# 5	1.31	.79	1.36	.98	.25	.615
# 6	1.40	.96	1.72	.95	8.93	.003
# 7	1.59	1.01	1.88	1.16	5.64	.018
# 8	1.84	1.04	1.98	.98	1.43	.233
# 9	.75	.82	1.05	1.02	8.26	.004
# 10	.75	.83	.91	.94	2.43	.119
# 11	.46	.78	.71	1.00	6.05	.014
# 12	3.01	.86	2.86	.91	2.35	.126

Table 35

Analysis of Variance for the RPS in Regular and Problem
High School Student Samples

Rational Problem Solving (RPS)						
Regular sample (N = 149)			Problem sample (N = 164)		F	P
	Mean	SD	Mean	SD	Ratio	
Stories-a						
# 1	2.90	1.08	2.77	1.13	1.00	.317
# 2	2.66	1.01	2.53	1.17	1.16	.283
# 3	3.42	.75	2.84	1.02	32.40	.000
# 4	3.56	.65	3.04	.82	39.13	.000
# 5	3.02	.94	2.64	.89	13.44	.000
# 6	3.30	.88	2.96	.98	10.26	.002
# 7	3.68	.62	3.35	.95	13.00	.000
# 8	3.28	.85	2.70	1.13	25.47	.000
# 9	3.48	.81	3.07	1.07	14.26	.000
# 10	3.44	.74	3.07	.98	14.07	.000
# 11	3.37	.75	2.92	.91	22.32	.000
# 12	2.87	1.07	2.84	1.12	.04	.845

Table 36

Analysis of Variance for the IS in Regular and Problem

High School Student Samples

	Impulsivity Style (IS)					
	Regular sample (N = 149)		Problem sample (N = 164)		F	P
	Mean	SD	Mean	SD	Ratio	
Stories-a						
# 1	.81	.82	.85	.96	.17	.678
# 2	1.54	.76	1.61	1.07	.39	.532
# 3	.34	.60	.46	.82	2.10	.148
# 4	.87	.79	.83	.92	.14	.709
# 5	1.14	1.00	.87	.99	5.73	.017
# 6	1.13	.97	1.04	.99	.77	.380
# 7	1.57	1.02	1.73	1.16	1.68	.195
# 8	1.58	.84	1.82	1.04	4.96	.027
# 9	.38	.66	.43	.78	.48	.487
# 10	.89	.90	.93	.99	.14	.708
# 11	2.08	1.00	2.21	1.20	1.02	.313
# 12	1.26	.92	1.33	1.14	.33	.567

Table 37

Analysis of Variance for the WS in Regular and Problem
High School Student Samples

Withdrawal Style (WS)						
Regular sample (N = 149)			Problem sample (N = 164)		F	P
	Mean	SD	Mean	SD	Ratio	
Stories-a						
# 1	2.01	1.03	1.91	1.17	.62	.432
# 2	1.70	.93	1.45	1.05	5.10	.025
# 3	1.05	1.02	.76	.95	6.86	.009
# 4	.48	.83	.77	1.05	7.04	.008
# 5	1.54	.81	1.51	.93	.14	.705
# 6	1.56	.89	1.52	.96	.04	.841
# 7	.55	.80	.48	.83	.55	.459
# 8	1.03	.95	1.13	1.05	.78	.337
# 9	.21	.53	.34	.70	3.19	.075
# 10	1.05	1.02	1.30	1.15	3.96	.047
# 11	1.28	1.10	.95	.96	8.06	.005
# 12	1.24	1.09	.92	1.04	7.08	.008

A comparison of the SPST-A mean scores for the regular and problem student groups on all 12 items (problematic situations) in Part A (Stories-a) is reported in Table 38. Significant differences between the two groups were found for Items # 3, # 4, # 6, # 8, # 9, # 10, and # 11 (p ≤.04). The results suggest that these items would be most able to discriminate between normal and disruptive adolescent groups.

Table 38

Analysis of Variance for the SPST-A in Regular and Problem

High School Student Samples

	Regular sample (N = 149)		Problem sample (N = 164)		F	P
	Mean	SD	Mean	SD	Ratio	
Stories-a						
# 1	13.38	2.12	12.95	2.59	2.48	.116
# 2	12.20	2.75	12.28	3.51	.05	.825
# 3	15.32	2.02	14.62	2.37	7.85	.005
# 4	14.38	2.08	13.74	2.57	5.78	.017
# 5	14.06	2.36	13.71	2.85	1.36	.245
# 6	14.44	2.74	13.48	2.67	9.89	.002
# 7	14.52	2.23	14.03	2.85	2.86	.091
# 8	14.11	2.39	12.81	2.58	21.08	.000
# 9	16.97	2.12	15.62	3.08	20.05	.000
# 10	16.35	2.07	15.37	2.51	14.09	.000
# 11	14.75	3.35	14.13	2.83	4.36	.038
# 12	11.44	2.99	11.95	2.95	2.34	.127

Similarly, the mean scores of the regular and problem groups on all 12 items in Part B (Stories-b) on 2 scales (i.e., Problem Affect-Cognitions and Problem-Solving Actions) were computed and reported in Tables 39, 40 and 41. Significant differences between the two groups (p ≤.05) were found on either one scale (such as Items # 1, # 2, # 3, # 7, # 8, # 10.1, and # 12), or on two scales (such as Items # 4, # 5 # 6, # 9, # 10.2, and # 11). The results indicated that all Stories-b can discriminate between normal and disruptive groups.

Table 39

Analysis of Variance for the PAC-B in Regular and Problem

High School Student Samples

	Problem Affect-Cognitions (PAC-B)							
	Regular group (N = 149)			Problem group (N = 164)				
	N	Mean	SD	N	Mean	SD	F	P
Stories-b								
# 1	112	.79	.77	117	.73	.76	.45	.502
# 2	109	.41	.74	114	.45	.65	.74	.711
# 3	112	1.23	.86	117	1.15	.81	.51	.477
# 4	109	1.18	.87	114	.91	.91	5.16	.024
# 5	112	1.17	.71	117	.80	.67	16.09	.000
# 6	109	1.20	.69	114	.89	.75	10.16	.002
# 7	112	.81	.80	117	.73	.77	.68	.409
# 8	109	.92	.75	114	.89	.68	.06	.813
# 9	149	.95	.69	164	.66	.69	13.18	.000
# 10.1	148	.51	.83	164	.49	.77	.08	.777
# 10.2	109	1.45	.88	114	1.19	.94	4.61	.033
# 11	112	1.05	.77	117	.85	.66	4.42	.037
# 12	109	.51	.77	114	.58	.82	.39	.530

Table 40

Analysis of Variance for the PSA-B in Regular and Problem
High School Student Samples

Problem Solving-Actions (PSA-B)

	Regular group (N = 149)			Problem group (N = 164)				
	N	Mean	SD	N	Mean	SD	F	P
Stories-b								
# 1	112	1.22	.58	117	1.01	.65	6.93	.009
# 2	109	1.14	.63	113	.79	.60	17.84	.000
# 3	112	1.61	.69	117	1.26	.79	12.78	.000
# 4	109	1.50	.72	113	1.12	.84	13.25	.000
# 5	112	1.13	.65	117	.91	.62	6.79	.010
# 6	109	1.54	.55	113	1.20	.63	17.99	.000
# 7	112	1.13	.74	117	.91	.77	4.45	.036
# 8	109	1.53	.57	113	1.18	.63	19.34	.000
# 9	149	1.24	.74	164	.80	.69	29.12	.000
# 10.1	148	1.26	.87	164	.84	.89	17.85	.000
# 10.2	109	1.89	.39	113	1.67	.70	8.06	.005
# 11	112	1.33	.75	117	.78	.70	33.33	.000
# 12	109	1.20	.51	112	.88	.69	16.19	.000

The SPST-B mean scores of the regular and problem student groups were found to be significantly different ($p \leq .04$) in 9 of the 12 items (see Table 41). The results indicated that Items # 1, # 2, # 3, # 4, # 5, # 6, # 9, # 10.1, # 10.2, and # 11 are better able to discriminate between normal and disruptive groups and that the SPST-B seemed to be more sensitive than the SPST-A in identifying differences in interpersonal-problem-solving skills between these groups.

In sum, the findings of the regular and disruptive student differences indicated that the SPST was able to assess interpersonal problem-solving deficits and pin-point specific areas of deficiency in high school students with interpersonal behaviour disorders. Moreover, they suggested that assessment by a single summary score is not as informative as a profile of assessments in each situation. Hence, each pair of situations (including one Story-a and one Story-b) could be scored individually to be used as "a mini-test" or a short cut measure to identify adolescent interpersonal problem-solving deficiencies in a specific relationship.

Table 41

Analysis of Variance for the SPST-B in Regular and Problem
High School Student Samples

	Regular sample			Problem sample			F	P
	N	Mean	SD	N	Mean	SD	Ratio	
Stories-b								
# 1	78	2.18	1.10	88	1.73	1.19	6.39	.012
# 2	71	1.73	1.08	76	1.24	.99	8.40	.004
# 3	78	2.94	1.13	88	2.39	1.35	7.95	.005
# 4	71	2.69	1.33	76	1.95	1.51	9.96	.002
# 5	78	2.36	1.09	88	1.73	1.08	13.99	.000
# 6	71	2.80	.94	76	2.12	.97	19.01	.000
# 7	78	1.85	1.29	88	1.55	1.34	2.16	.143
# 8	71	2.52	.83	76	2.24	1.02	3.43	.066
# 9	149	2.19	1.21	164	1.47	1.13	30.09	.000
# 10.1	148	1.78	1.34	163	1.33	1.36	8.69	.003
# 10.2	71	3.35	1.06	74	2.92	1.43	4.27	.040
# 11	78	2.50	1.14	88	1.67	1.07	23.46	.000
# 12	71	1.77	1.03	74	1.42	1.29	3.34	.069

Other group differences. The analysis of variance method (ONE WAY-ANOVA) was employed to assess the ability of the SPST to discriminate between age groups, rural-metropolitan groups, and male-female groups in the regular high school student sample. For each, differences on total scores and individual item scores are reported.

It was proposed that adolescents at a higher age would have a higher score on the SPST. A comparison of the mean scores of the adolescents aged 15-16 and 17-18 are reported in Tables 42 and 43. The mean scores of the two groups were found to be significantly different on the Positive Orientation (PO), Positive Problem-Solving Skills, Rational Orientation (RO), Withdrawal Orientation (WO), and Withdrawal Problem-Solving Style (WPSS) sub-subscales ($p < .05$). Similarly, significant differences between the two groups were found on the Rational Problem Solving (RPS) and Withdrawal Style (WS) scores ($p < .01$). However, the mean scores for the two age groups the Negative Problem Solving (NPS) and Impulsivity Style (IS) subscales did not differ significantly. The total SPST-B scores between the two groups differentiated significantly ($p < .01$), but the total SPST-A scores did not. The higher age group had higher mean scores on the RPS subscale and on the SPST-B, but lower mean score on the WS subscale when compared to the younger age group.

Table 42

Means and Standard Deviations for the Sub-subscales of the SPST-A in aged 15-16 and 17-18 Regular High School Groups

| | Aged 15-16 group (N = 97) | | Aged 17-18 group (N = 99) | | F | P |
	Mean	SD	Mean	SD	Ratio	
PO	17.00	2.87	18.02	2.62	6.76	.010
PPSS	15.80	2.97	14.80	2.65	6.28	.013
NO	9.95	3.22	10.52	3.10	1.57	.211
NPSS	6.92	3.51	6.57	2.77	.65	.423
RO	17.69	3.40	18.95	3.08	7.38	.007
RPSS	19.02	2.76	19.73	2.46	3.59	.060
IO	10.36	4.13	10.09	4.25	.81	.370
IPSS	3.00	2.33	2.98	2.31	.00	.951
WO	9.25	3.85	7.98	3.40	5.97	.015
WPSS	6.52	3.13	5.64	2.48	4.77	.030

Notes: PO = Positive Orientation; PPSS = Positive Problem-Solving Skills; NO = Negative Orientation; NPSS = Negative Problem-Solving Skills; RO = Rational Orientation; RPSS = Rational Problem-Solving Skills; IO = Impulsive Orientation; IPSS = Impulsivity Problem-Solving Style; WO = Withdrawal Orientation; WPSS = Withdrawal Problem-Solving Style.

Table 43

Means and Standard Deviations for the Subscale, the SPST-A and the SPST-B in Aged 15-16 and 17-18 Regular High School Groups

	Aged 15-16 group (N = 97)		Aged 17-18 group (N = 99)		F	P
	Mean	SD	Mean	SD	Ratio	
PPS	32.80	5.05	32.82	4.31	.00	.983
NPS	16.88	5.49	17.08	5.20	.07	.789
RPS	36.71	5.49	38.68	4.99	6.88	.009
IS	13.36	5.53	13.88	5.83	.41	.524
WS	15.76	6.18	13.62	4.92	7.25	.008
SPST-A	167.52	17.72	170.92	16.35	1.95	.164
SPST-B	14.76	4.93	17.23	5.12	11.82	.001

Notes: PPS = Positive Problem Solving; NPS = Negative Problem Solving; RPS = Rational Problem Solving; IS = Impulsivity Style; WS = Withdrawal Style; SPST-A = Social Problem Solving Scale for Stories-a; SPST-B = Social Problem Solving Scale for Stories-b.

Mean scores of students aged 15-16 and 17-18 on each item of the SPST-A and the SPST-B are reported in Tables 44 and 45. The SPST-A mean scores between the age groups were found to be significantly different (p <.05) in the Stories-a # 3, # 8, and # 10. The SPST-B mean scores of the two groups differed significantly on Stories-b # 2, # 6, # 9, and # 10.1 (p < .05).

Table 44

Analysis of Variance for the SPST-A in Aged 15-16
and 17-18 Regular High School Groups

	Aged 15-16 group (N = 97)		Aged 17-18 group (N = 99)		F	P
	Mean	SD	Mean	SD	Ratio	
Stories-a						
# 1	12.74	2.39	13.14	2.21	1.47	.226
# 2	12.19	2.76	12.28	2.73	.06	.805
# 3	14.43	2.44	15.15	2.38	4.35	.038
# 4	13.94	2.25	14.10	2.39	.24	.624
# 5	14.13	2.30	13.95	2.37	.31	.581
# 6	14.81	2.49	14.15	2.80	3.07	.081
# 7	14.03	2.49	14.47	2.07	1.84	.177
# 8	13.30	2.80	14.14	2.19	5.52	.020
# 9	16.47	2.39	16.90	2.05	1.79	.183
# 10	15.50	2.67	16.29	2.02	5.45	.021
# 11	14.15	2.56	14.77	2.22	3.17	.077
# 12	12.08	2.89	11.57	3.16	1.43	.233

Table 45

Analysis of Variance for the SPST-B in Aged 15-16

and 17-18 Regular High School Groups

	Aged 15-16 group			Aged 17-18 group			F	P
	N	Mean	SD	N	Mean	SD	Ratio	
Stories-b								
# 1	52	1.85	1.11	53	2.13	1.13	1.72	.193
# 2	45	1.31	1.02	46	1.78	1.11	4.44	.038
# 3	52	2.60	1.40	53	3.00	1.00	2.89	.092
# 4	45	2.29	1.39	46	2.78	1.33	2.99	.087
# 5	52	2.23	1.08	53	2.19	1.11	.04	.844
# 6	45	2.47	.94	46	2.87	.93	4.19	.043
# 7	52	1.88	1.23	53	1.81	1.32	.09	.768
# 8	45	2.27	1.12	46	2.37	.85	.24	.621
# 9	97	1.43	1.19	99	2.28	1.21	24.53	.000
# 10.1	97	1.43	1.27	98	1.85	1.33	4.94	.027
# 10.2	45	3.09	1.22	46	3.35	.95	1.28	.261
# 11	52	2.08	1.22	52	2.48	1.06	3.26	.073
# 12	45	1.93	.91	46	1.76	1.12	.65	.423

The results of analysis of variance for the rural and metropolitan groups are reported in Tables 46 and 47. Due to differences of age and size between the two groups in the regular student sample, a comparison included only subjects who aged from 15 to 17 years. Significant differences between the two groups were found on the Positive Orientation (PO), Positive Problem-Solving Skills (PPSS), Negative Problem-Solving Skills (NPSS), Rational Orientation (RO), Rational Problem-Solving Skills (RPSS), Withdrawal Problem-Solving Skills (WPSS) scores ($p < .05$). Mean scores for the Rational Problem Solving (RPS) and Withdrawal Style (WS) subscales differentiated significantly ($p < .01$) between the two groups, whereas the Positive Problem Solving (PPS), Negative Problem Solving (NPS), and Impulsivity Style (IS) mean scores did not. Both the total SPST-A and the total SPST-B mean scores for the two groups were found to be significantly different ($p < .01$). The metropolitan adolescents scored higher on the RPS subscale, but lower on the WS subscale when compared to the rural adolescents. Also, the city group had higher mean scores on the SPST-A and SPST-B when compared to the country group.

Table 46

Means and Standard Deviations for the Sub-subscales of the SPST-A
in Rural and Metropolitan Groups

	Rural group (N = 47)		Metropolitan group (N = 104)		F	P
	Mean	SD	Mean	SD	Ratio	
PO	16.32	2.99	17.79	2.77	8.62	.004
PPSS	16.25	3.07	15.10	2.72	6.40	.021
NO	9.74	3.45	10.38	3.15	1.26	.263
NPSS	8.32	3.57	6.29	2.94	13.48	.000
RO	15.89	3.46	18.68	2.76	28.15	.000
RPSS	18.30	3.02	19.47	2.49	6.27	.013
IO	10.06	3.65	11.00	4.62	1.50	.222
IPSS	3.57	2.55	2.84	2.25	3.20	.075
WO	9.70	3.51	8.56	3.88	2.97	.086
WPSS	7.45	3.59	5.71	2.39	12.30	.001

Notes: PO = Positive Orientation; PPSS = Positive Problem-Solving Skills; NO = Negative Orientation; NPSS = Negative Problem-Solving Skills; RO = Rational Orientation; RPSS = Rational Problem-
Solving Skills; IO = Impulsive Orientation; IPSS = Impulsivity Problem-Solving Style; WO = Withdrawal Orientation; WPSS = Withdrawal Problem-Solving Style.

Table 47

Means and Standard Deviations for the Subscales, the SPST-A
and the SPST-B in Rural and Metropolitan Groups

	Rural group (N = 47)		Metropolitan group (N = 104)		F	P
	Mean	SD	Mean	SD	Ratio	
PPS	32.57	5.39	32.88	4.69	.13	.720
NPS	18.06	5.84	16.67	5.20	2.14	.145
RPS	34.19	5.81	38.15	4.65	10.03	.000
IS	13.64	5.46	13.84	6.10	.04	.849
WS	17.15	6.28	14.27	5.49	8.13	.005
SPST-A	161.91	19.08	170.26	16.62	7.43	.007
SPST-B	12.79	4.78	16.41	4.74	18.85	.000

Notes: PPS = Positive Problem Solving; NPS = Negative Problem Solving; RPS = Rational Problem Solving; IS = Impulsivity Style; WS = Withdrawal Style; SPST-A = Social Problem Solving Scale for Stories-a; SPST-B = Social Problem Solving Scale for Stories-b.

A comparison of the mean scores of the rural and metropolitan groups on each item of the SPST-A and the SPST-B is reported in Tables 48 and 49. The SPST-A mean scores of the two groups were found to be significantly different on Items # 1, # 3, # 4, # 8, # 9, # 10, # 11, and # 12 (p ≤ .05). The SPST-B mean scores of the two groups differed significantly on Items # 1, # 3, # 5, # 8, # 9, # 10.2, and # 11 (p ≤ .05). The metropolitan group had higher scores on 7 of 12 items in Stories-a and 7 of 12 items in Stories-b while the rural group had higher score on 1 of 12 items in Stories-a.

Table 48

Analysis of Variance for the SPST-A in Rural

and Metropolitan Regular High School Groups

	Rural sample (N = 47)		Metropolitan sample (N = 104)		F	P
	Mean	SD	Mean	SD	Ratio	
Stories-a						
# 1	11.77	2.52	13.26	2.21	12.06	.000
# 2	12.29	2.84	11.96	2.80	.46	.497
# 3	13.21	2.84	15.20	1.93	25.22	.000
# 4	13.17	2.53	14.30	2.11	8.13	.005
# 5	13.93	2.30	13.99	2.55	.02	.901
# 6	14.53	2.38	14.45	2.94	.03	.870
# 7	13.74	2.45	14.28	2.21	1.77	.185
# 8	12.79	2.80	13.90	2.59	5.73	.018
# 9	15.83	2.35	16.77	2.12	5.91	.016
# 10	14.38	2.69	16.25	2.15	20.74	.000
# 11	13.65	2.56	14.65	2.31	5.61	.019
# 12	13.19	2.86	11.24	3.17	13.08	.000

137

Table 49

Analysis of Variance for the SPST-B in Rural

and Metropolitan Regular High School Groups

	Rural group (N = 47)			Metropolitan group (N = 104)			F	P
	N	Mean	SD	N	Mean	SD	Ratio	
Stories-b								
# 1	25	1.44	1.13	56	2.12	0.99	7.60	.007
# 2	22	1.13	1.08	48	1.60	1.09	2.80	.099
# 3	25	2.24	1.36	56	2.89	1.19	4.77	.032
# 4	22	2.18	1.50	48	2.58	1.30	1.30	.258
# 5	25	1.84	1.07	56	2.36	1.10	3.88	.050
# 6	22	2.18	.96	48	2.64	.91	3.79	.056
# 7	25	1.92	1.26	56	1.66	1.27	.73	.397
# 8	22	1.82	1.26	48	2.42	.85	5.49	.022
# 9	47	1.00	1.02	104	2.04	1.23	25.52	.000
# 10.1	47	1.28	1.19	104	1.56	1.24	1.71	.193
# 10.2	22	2.73	1.28	48	3.40	1.03	5.47	.022
# 11	24	1.75	1.07	56	2.45	1.16	6.33	.014
# 12	22	2.05	.95	48	1.73	.94	1.70	.196

The results of analysis of variance for the male and female regular high school student groups are reported in Tables 50 and 51. Significant differences between the two groups were found on the Impulsivity Problem-Solving Style (IPSS) and Withdrawal Orientation (WO) scores (p < .05). Mean scores for the Negative Problem Solving (NPS) and Withdrawal Style (WS) sub-scales between the two groups differentiated significantly (p < .05), whereas the Rational Problem Solving (RPS), Positive Problem Solving (PPS), and Impulsivity Style (IS) mean scores did not. The total SPST-B mean scores between the two groups were found to be significantly different (p < .01), but the total SPST-A mean scores were not. The boys had higher score on the IPSS, but had lower score on the WO when compared to the girls. The girls scored higher on the SPST-B when compared to the boys.

Table 50

Means and Standard Deviations for the Sub-subscales of the SPST-A

in Male and Female Regular High School Groups

	Male group (N = 118)		Female group (N = 122)		F	P
	Mean	SD	Mean	SD	Ratio	
PO	17.57	3.14	17.22	2.53	.89	.346
PPSS	15.61	3.00	15.16	2.67	1.48	.224
NO	10.80	3.31	10.10	2.98	2.95	.087
NPSS	7.41	3.35	6.63	2.92	3.66	.056
RO	18.11	3.29	18.28	3.20	.16	.688
RPSS	19.33	2.93	19.18	2.41	.19	.664
IO	10.26	4.34	11.21	4.04	3.09	.080
IPSS	3.62	2.78	2.95	2.21	4.26	.040
WO	8.18	3.65	9.28	3.72	5.27	.022
WPSS	6.07	3.02	6.43	2.75	.88	.347

Notes: PO = Positive Orientation; PPSS = Positive Problem-Solving Skills; NO = Negative Orientation; NPSS = Negative Problem-Solving Skills; RO = Rational Orientation; RPSS = Rational Problem-
Solving Skills; IO = Impulsive Orientation; IPSS = Impulsivity Problem-Solving Style; WO = Withdrawal Orientation; WPSS = Withdrawal Problem-Solving Style.

Table 51

Mean and Standard Deviations for the Subscale, the SPST-A and
the SPST-B in Male and Female Regular High School Groups

| | Male group (N = 118) | | Female group (N = 122) | | F | P |
	Mean	SD	Mean	SD	Ratio	
PPS	33.18	5.23	32.38	4.17	1.69	.194
NPS	18.20	5.76	16.73	4.97	4.51	.034
RPS	37.44	5.55	37.46	4.96	.00	.978
IS	13.88	6.27	14.16	5.40	.14	.708
WS	14.26	5.82	15.70	5.70	3.76	.053
SPST-A	168.27	19.18	167.25	15.71	.21	.650
SPST-B	14.81	5.29	16.45	4.46	6.81	.009

Notes: PPS = Positive Problem Solving; NPS = Negative Problem Solving; RPS = Rational Problem
Solving; IS = Impulsivity Style; WS = Withdrawal Style; SPST-A = Social Problem Solving Scale for
Stories-a; SPST-B = Social Problem Solving Scale for Stories-b.

A comparison of the mean scores of the male-female groups on each item of the SPST-A and the SPST-B is reported in Tables 52 and 53. The total SPST-A mean scores of the two groups were found to be significantly different on Items # 3 and # 5 (p ≤ .05). The SPST-B mean scores of the two groups differed significantly on Items # 3, # 5, # 8, and # 9 (p ≤ .05). The adolescent boys had higher mean scores on 2 of 12 items in Stories-a, but had lower mean scores on 4 of 12 items in Stories-b when compared to the girls.

Table 52

Analysis of Variance for the SPST-A in Male

and Female Regular High School Groups

	Male group (N = 118)		Female group (N = 122)		F	P
	Mean	SD	Mean	SD	Ratio	
Stories-a						
# 1	12.62	2.25	12.94	1.09	.298	.298
# 2	11.94	2.82	12.09	2.75	.17	.667
# 3	15.04	2.46	14.33	2.44	5.07	.025
# 4	14.29	2.45	13.75	2.17	3.31	.070
# 5	14.49	2.49	13.73	2.23	6.24	.013
# 6	14.37	2.78	14.41	2.53	.01	.914
# 7	14.11	2,53	14.10	2.21	.00	.971
# 8	13.64	2.75	13.59	2.41	.02	.891
# 9	16.40	2.65	16.70	1.78	1.06	.304
# 10	15.41	2.90	15.80	2.41	1.28	.259
# 11	14.41	2.55	14.17	2.44	.54	.461
# 12	11.78	2.87	11.66	3.25	.08	.770

Table 53

Analysis of Variance for the SPST-B in Male

and Female Regular High School Groups

	Male group			Female group			F	P
	N	Mean	SD	N	Mean	SD	Ratio	
Stories-b								
# 1	63	2.05	1.18	63	1.97	1.03	.16	.689
# 2	55	1.35	1.07	59	1.51	1.06	.67	.416
# 3	63	2.65	1.22	63	3.08	1.15	4.10	.045
# 4	55	2.44	1.34	59	2.31	1.49	.24	.623
# 5	63	1.84	1.00	63	2.35	1.08	7.48	.007
# 6	55	2.55	.88	59	2.73	.96	1.12	.291
# 7	63	1.65	1.26	63	1.89	1.27	1.12	.293
# 8	55	2.09	1.06	59	2.54	.86	6.30	.014
# 9	118	1.59	1.33	122	2.05	1.19	8.14	.005
# 10.1	117	1.37	1.36	121	1.64	1.24	2.70	.102
# 10.2	54	3.09	1.23	59	3.31	1.04	0.99	.322
# 11	62	2.29	1.21	63	2.14	1.08	.52	.472
# 12	54	2.00	1.12	59	1.81	1.07	.82	.368

Summary of Results

(1) Results of factor analysis of the SPST-A subscales in the combined regular and problem student sample indicated that there were two common factors which support the constructive and dysfuntional problem-solving model used in the scale construction. Results of factor analysis of the SPST-B scales in the combined sample indicated that there was a general factor which support the assumption that what adolescents think and feel affects what they do.

(2) Results of analysing the correlation coefficients between the variables of the SPST-A and the SPST-B in the regular and problem student groups as two independent samples indicated that there were significant correlations between the variables which assess problem affect-cognitions (problem orientations) and the variables which assess problem-solving actions (strategies). The results showed that what an adolescent thinks and feels is related to his/her social problem-solving strategies. The SPST-A subscale scores were significantly associated (positive or negative) with the SPST-B scale scores as predicted. Also, the correlation between the SPST-A total score and the SPST-B total score was significantly positive in both the two samples. The results provided strong support for the internal validity of the SPST.

(3) Results of computing the internal consistency (alpha) of SPST-A and SPST-B in regular and problem high school student samples showed that internal consistency reliabilities for subscales and scales of the SPST-A as well as the scales of the SPST-B were adequate. Consequently, the SPST could be classified as a homogeneous and consistent measure. The results also indicated substantial evidence for the construct validity of the SPST.

(4) Results of comparing the correlation between the first and second administrations over a two week period indicated that the test-retest reliabilities for the subscales and SPST-A total were sufficient. Thus, the SPST-A is relatively stable between the first and second administrations over a 2-week interval.

(5) Results of investigating the correlation coefficients between the score of each situation and the SPST-A total score in both regular and problem samples revealed that the magnitude of all the relationships was above .45. The results further supported the internal consistency reliability and the content validity of the SPST.

(6) Results of comparing the correlation coefficients between the SPST-A and the SPSI-R indicated that the SPST-A subscale scores were significantly correlated with the SPSI-R scale scores, and that the correlations were positive among constructive (or dysfunctional) components, but negative between constructive and dysfunctional components. The correlations between the SPST-A total scores and the SPSI-R total scores in both regular and problem high school student

samples were significantly positive. It means that the higher scores on the SPST-A and the SPSI-R reflect greater social problem-solving abilities. The results supported the concurrent validity of the SPST-A.

(7) Results of comparing the correlation coefficients between the SPST (i.e., SPST-A and SPST-B) and the TRSIPS indicated that the SPST subscale scores and the TRSIPS subscale scores were significantly correlated and that the correlations were positive or negative as expected. Both the SPST-A and SPST-B total scores were negatively correlated with the Interpersonal Problem Behaviour (IPB) subscale score. The TRSIPS total score was significantly and positively associated with the SPST-A total score. Also, the TRSIPS total score and the SPST-B total score were significantly and positively correlated. The results provided evidence for the construct and concurrent validity of the SPST.

(8) Results of comparing the mean scores of the regular and problem high school student groups indicated that the two groups differentiated significantly on five sub-subscales of the SPST-A. The SPST-A mean scores between the two groups were significantly different. Also, the SPST-B mean scores between the two groups differed significantly. Results of comparing the mean scores of the two split halves of the regular high school student sample and the two split halves of the problem high school student sample indicated that no significant difference between these split half samples on any sub-subscales of the SPST-A was found. The results indicated that the SPST are able to discriminate between normal and disruptive adolescent groups and retain its validity across samples.

(9) A comparison of the means of the regular and problem groups on all 12 items (problematic situations) in Part A (Stories-a) on 5 subscales showed that there were significant differences (on at least one subscale) on all the 12 items. The SPST-A means of the two groups were significantly different on 7 of the 12 items. Similarly, all 12 items in Part B (Stories-b) were found to be significantly different on at least one scale. The SPST-B mean scores of 9 of the 12 items were significantly different between the two groups. The results indicated that the SPST can identify cognition-skill deficits of social problem solving in disruptive adolescents.

(10) Results of investigating the ability of the SPST to discriminate between age groups, rural-metropolitan groups, and male-female groups within the regular high school student sample indicated that there were significant differences between these groups on some subscales and on some items. The SPST-B mean scores differed significantly between the age groups, rural-metropolitan groups, and male-female groups. The SPST-A mean scores differed significantly between the rural-metropolitan groups, but did not discriminate between the age groups and did

not differentiate significantly between the male-female groups. The results showed that the SPST-B is better able than the SPST-A to discriminate between all these adolescent groups.

Chapter 6:

DISCUSSION AND CONCLUSIONS

The purpose of this study was to develop a reliable and valid measure of social problem solving ability for adolescents based on the model of five social problem solving dimensions recently developed by D'Zurilla et al. (1996). Based on the assumption that how people think or feel can considerably affect what they do, the model was modified in order to include five problem solving dimensions (i.e., positive problem solving, negative problem solving, rational problem solving, the impulsivity style, and the withdrawal styles). Each dimension was further divided into two levels: *affect-cognition* (the level involves what the problem-solver thinks and feels) and *action* (the level involves what the problem-solver does). The development of Social Problem Solving Scale (SPST) was based on the modified problem solving model to assess adolescents' problem solving abilities in dealing with interpersonal problems.

This chapter presents a discussion involving an evaluation of psychometric properties of the SPST, conclusions and implications for practice and research directions in the future.

Psychometric Properties of the SPST

The crucial aim in evaluating the psychometric properties of the SPST was to determine whether the instrument is sufficiently reliable and valid to measure what it is supposed to measure. The SPST includes two groups of items: Stories-a (SPST-A) and Stories-b (SPST-B). The SPST-A was structured into five subscales (i.e., Positive Problem Solving; Negative Problem Solving; Rational Problem Solving; Impulsivity Style; and Withdrawal Style) to assess the five social problem-solving dimensions according to the modified model outlined. Each subscale can be broken down into two sub-subscales to assess two relatively separate processes (i.e., problem affect-cognitions and problem-solving actions) within the problem-solving dimension.

The present factor analytic results of the scores on the SPST-A subscales for the combined sample support a two factor model. The two factors are labeled as dysfunctional problem-solving (factor I) and constructive problem-solving (factor II). The Positive Problem Solving and Rational Problem Solving subscales have high loadings on the constructive problem-solving factor, whereas the Negative Problem Solving, Impulsivity Style and Withdraw Style subscales have high loadings on the dysfunctional problem-solving factor. Therefore, the Positive Problem Solving and Rational Problem Solving subscales are best viewed as different processes in term of the quality of solution (responses) within constructive problem-solving. Also, the Negative Problem Solving, Impulsivity Style and Withdraw Style subscales are best viewed as variations of negative responses within dysfunctional problem-solving. The results indicated that the SPST-A subscales measure distinct components (constructive and dysfunctional) of social problem solving and that positive problem solving and rational problem solving dimensions should load together on a facilitative factor, while negative problem solving, impulsivity style, and withdrawal style dimensions should load together on a inhibitive factor. This demonstrated that the SPST-A subscales measure "what they were designed to measure".

As indicated by test designers (Ailken & Groth-Marnat, 1994; Murphy & Davidshofer, 1994), the square of the loading of a given subtest on a factor is the proportion of the total variance of the subtest scores that can be accounted for by that factor. The loadings of the Positive Problem Solving and Rational Problem Solving subscales are .87 and .83, respectively. Thus, 76% and 68% of the variance of these subscale scores can be accounted for by the Positive/Constructive factor. Similarly, the loadings of the Negative Problem Solving, Impulsivity Style and Withdraw Style subscales are .83, .83 and .79, repectively, and thus from 62% to 68% of the variance of the subscale scores is accounted for by the dysfunctional factor. The results indicated that the SPST-A subscales can pinpoint specific areas of interpersonal problem-solving deficits which provides a useful basis for intervention and treatment programs.

The factor analytic results of the scores on the SPST-B scales for the combined regular and problem high school student sample indicated that the Problem Affect-Cognitions for Stories-b (PAC-B) and Problem-Solving Actions for Stories-b (PSA-B) have a general factor which supports a single construct as outlined. These scales have loadings of over .84. Namely over 70% of the variance of the SPST-B scale scores can be accounted for by the common factor. The findings indicated that adolescents' problem affect-cognitions and problem-solving actions were significantly correlated.

The factor analytic results of the scores on the Problem Affect-Cognitions for Stories-a (PAC-A) and Problem-Solving Actions for Stories-a (PSA-A) scales for the combined sample indicated that the SPST-A scales have a common factor which supports a single construct as predicted. The SPST-A scales have loadings of over .92 and over 85% of the variance of the SPST-A scale scores can be accounted for by the common factor. The results also demonstrated that adolescents' problem affect-cognitions significantly correlated with their problem-solving actions.

The factor analytic results of the scores on the PAC-A, PSA-A, PAC-B, PSA-B scales indicated that the SPST-A and SPST-B scales have a common factor with an eigenvalue of 2.40

and then 60% of the variance of the SPST scale scores can be accounted for by the common factor. This demonstrated that the SPST-A and SPST-B scales measure variables of interpersonal problem solving abilities, measure "what they would be expected to measure".

As predicted, the results of factor analysis of the scores on the SPST-A and SPST-B scales strongly supported the assumption that what people think and feel affects what they do, and that an adolescent's problem affect-cognitions strongly relate to the adolescent's problem-solving strategies. The results are especially important in the context of the development of a clinical tool because an intervention strategy based on the scale scores need to address thoughts and feelings about the interpersonal problem as well as providing adolescents with training in rational problem solving skills.

The results are consistent with several previous studies in children and adults which have shown that situational cognitive schemas can influence problem-solving strategies (Lochman & Lampron, 1986) and that one's social goals (i.e., social affect-cognitions) may be an important factor in the choice of social problem-solving strategies employed (Lochman, Wayland, & White, 1993; Rubin & Krasnor, 1986; Smith & Lazarus, 1990). Bandura and Wood (1989) also found that people with optimistic self-appraisals (positive orientations) of problem-solving capability tend to perform efficiently in complex problem-solving situations, whereas those who have pessimistic expectancies (negative orientations) tend to be more erratic and inefficient in their problem-solving strategies.

The investigation of the internal correlations for the SPST-A and its subscales as well as the SPST-B and its scales in the regular and problem student groups as independent samples indicated that the internal correlations of the SPST reflected the intercorrelational structure of the theoretical multidimensional model of social problem solving used in the construction of the scales.

As predicted, correlations between the Positive Problem Solving (PPS) and Rational Problem Solving (RPS) subscales (which were designed to assess the constructive dimensions of the social problem-solving process) and those between the Negative Problem Solving (NPS), Impulsivity Style (IS), and Withdrawal Style (WS) subscales (which were designed to assess the dysfunctional dimensions of social problem-solving process) were significant and positive (.39 to. 64). The highest amount of variance that any two subscales shared was 41% (between negative problem solving and impulsivity style in the regular student sample). Thus, none of these correlations is high enough as to suggest that any of the subscales may be redundant. In contrast, correlations between the subscales assessing constructive dimensions (i.e., the PPS and RPS) and the subscales assessing dysfunctional dimensions (i.e., the IS, NPS, and WS) were negative or not significant as expected. These results indicated that the SPST-A subscales are relatively independent and measure distinct components (constructive and dysfunctional) of social problem solving and attest to the multidimensionality of the SPST-A. In addition, the correlations between the item scores (situation) and the SPST-A total score were found to be significantly high (.47 to .71). These results indicate that the SPST-A is a homogeneous and consistent measure.

The correlations between the Problem Affect-Cognitions (PAC-B) that assess an adolescent's problem affect-cognitions and the Problem-Solving Actions (PSA-B) that assesses the adolescent's problem-solving strategies was significantly positive (.35 to .58), as expected. The largest amount of variance that the two subscales share is 32% which is not high enough to suggest that any of the scales may be redundant. The results showed that the SPST-B scales are relatively independent and measure distinct processes (problem affect-cognitions and problem-solving actions) of social problem solving. The SPST-B findings are consistent with the SPST-A findings which reflected the assumption that what people think and feel affects what they do. Again, the SPST-B findings showed that an adolescent's problem affect-cognitions considerably relate to the adolescent's problem-solving strategies.

Similarly, the correlations between the SPST-A and SPST-B scores were significantly positive (.44 to .51) as predicted. The highest amount of variance that the SPST-A and the SPST-B share is only 26%. Thus, neither of the measures is redundant. The results indicated that the SPST-A and the SPST-B may be considered relatively independent measures and that they approach a person's social problem-solving abilities from different perspectives and attest to the SPST tapping and detecting various dimensions or processes of social problem solving. This is useful for clinical assessment because researchers (D'Zurilla & Sheedy, 1991) suggested that a measure assessing orientation and skill components separately is important for research on social problem solving. The findings provide substantial evidence for both the reliability and validity of the instrument.

The findings of this study showed that internal consistency coefficients (Cronbach's alphas) for the SPST-A and its subscales in both the regular and problem adolescent samples were adequate. Alpha reliability coefficient for the SPST-A was high (.91 to .92). Two main scales of the SPST-A (i.e., Problem Affect-Cognitions and Problem-Solving Actions) showed high internal consistency coefficients (.80 to. 89). All five subscales of the SPST-A (i.e., Positive Problem Solving, Rational Problem Solving, Negative Problem Solving, Impulsivity Style, and Withdrawal Style) showed moderate to high internal consistency coefficients (.61 to .84). These results indicated that the SPST-A and its subscales are homogeneous and consistent measures which are sufficiently reliable to measure various dimensions of social problem solving.

The SPST-B showed moderate internal consistency coefficients (.74 to .78) in both the regular and problem adolescent samples. Alpha reliability coefficients for the two scales of the SPST-B in the regular and problem student samples were moderate (.64 to .68). The results indicated that the reliability coefficients for the SPST-B and its scales were adequate. Hence, the SPST-B and its scales may be accepted as homogeneous and consistent measures.

Results of test-retest reliabilities over an average 2-week period for the SPST-A in both the regular and problem adolescent samples showed that the test-retest correlations were from moderate to high (.76 to .87). Test-retest reliabilities for all five subscales and two main scales of the SPST-A were from moderate (.52) to high (.89). The results indicated that the SPST-A is a relatively stable measure between a first-second ardministration over a 2-week interval. In addition, a comparison of the mean scores of 4 split samples (ie., a comparison of the mean scores of the SPST-A and its subscales between Form A and Form B from the regular adolescent sample and problem adolescent sample) revealed that there were no significant differences between the two split regular samples as well as the two split problem samples. The results further supported the stability of the SPST-A.

In sum, the findings of the study demonstrated that the consistency and stability of the SPST were adequate. Hence, the SPST appears to be sufficiently reliable to measure the various dimensions of interpersonal problem solving which it was designed to measure.

As presented in chapter 5, the findings of this study also strongly supported the validity of the SPST. The content validity of the SPST was significant and adequate - its items (i.e., problematic situations in Stories-a and Stories-b) were demonstrated to be a representative sample of problematic situations categorized and validated from a large pool of adolescent social problems.

The cross validity of the SPST-A was supported with strong evidence that there were no significant differences in all 12 items (situations) in Stories-a between the split halves of the regular high school student sample. Also, no significant differences in all the 12 items between the split halves of the disruptive high school student sample were found. In contrast, when comparing the mean scores between the regular and disruptive samples, significant differences on five sub-subscales of the SPST-A were found. Similarly, significant differences between the two samples were found on 7 of the 12 items in Stories-a and on 9 of the 12 items in Stories-b. The results indicated that the SPST-A may retain its validity across comparative samples.

Substantial evidence of the construct validity of the instrument was provided with the findings of the intercorrelation matrix analyses which showed that the expected relationships among all sub-subscales/subscales/scales of the SPST did indeed exist. Most important evidence for the construct validity of the SPST was provided by the significant relationship between the SPST subscale scores and the TRSIPS subscales scores because the two instruments have been developed from the same model of social problem solving (see Chapter 4). Thus, the significant correlations between them indicate, as anticipated, that they measure the same construct. The TRSIPS is a teacher report inventory of an adolescent's problem-solving behaviour. Low scores on the Interpersonal Problem Behaviour (IPB), Negative Problem-Solving Behaviour (NPSB), Impulsive Behaviour (IB), and Avoidance Behaviour (AB) subscales of the TRSIPS are indicative of behaviours typically associated with effective problem solving. Whereas high scores on the Rational Problem-Solving Behaviour (RPSB) subscale and the TRSIPS as a whole are indicative of effective problem solving.

Although the two instruments employed different methods, the results of analysing the relationship between the SPST and TRSIPS scores revealed that there were significant and negative correlations between social problem solving as assessed by the SPST-A and interpersonal problem behaviour measured by the IPB subscale of TRSIPS as predicted. Also, the SPST-B score was negatively associated with the IPB score as expected. The results suggested that subjects who scored low on the SPST-A and/or the SPST-B were those who had more interpersonal problem behaviours as reviewed by teachers.

The correlation between the SPST-A total score and the TRSIPS total score was significantly positive (.40) as expected. Similarly, the correlation between the SPST-B total score and the TRSIPS total score was significantly positive (.26) as predicted. The results suggested that subjects who had low scores on the SPST-A and the SPST-B were also those who were identified by classroom teachers as students with ineffective problem-solving behaviours. The RPSB subscale score of the TRSIPS was significantly and positively correlated with the RPS and PPS subscale scores of the SPST-A, whereas the RPSB score was negatively associated with the IS and WS subscale scores of SPST-A as expected. The RPSB score was significantly and positively correlated with the PAC-B and PSA-B scale scores of SPST-B as predicted. However, the highest amount of common variance that any two subscales/scales of the measures shared was 17%. Thus, none of them are high enough to suggest that either one is redundant with any of these other measures. The results indicated that adolescents with higher social problem-solving abilities reported fewer difficulties in interpersonal problems. The findings indicated substantial evidence for the convergent validity of the SPST.

In addition, even more convincing support for the concurrent validity of SPST-A was provided by calculating Pearson correlation coefficients to detemine the degree of relationship between the SPST-A total score, SPST-A subscale scores and criterion scores on the Social Problem-Solving Inventory-Revised (SPSI-R; D'Zurilla et al., 1996) for the regular and problem high school samples. The scoring procedures of the SPST-A and the SPSI-R are similar, that is, high scores on the subscales of the SPST-A and high scores on the scales of the SPSI-R assessing dysfunctional dimensions of social problem solving are indicative of poor problem-solving skills, whereas high scores on the subscales and scales of the measures assessing constructive dimensions of social problem solving are indicative of effective problem-solving skills. These findings showed that there were significantly positive correlations between SPST-A total scores and the SPSI-R total scores in both the regular and problem samples as expected. The results suggested that subjects who displayed low scores on the SPST-A were also those who had low scores on the SPSI-R which reflect their poor social problem-solving abilities or skills. The subscale scores of the SPST-A were also found to be significantly correlated with the scale scores of the SPSI-R as predicted. However, the highest amount of common variance that any two subscales/scales of the measures share is 37%. Again, none of them are so high as to suggest that either one is redundant with any of these other measures.

The scores of each subject on all sub-subscales/subscales/scales of the SPST (i.e., an individual's SPST-A total score and SPST-A subscale scores as well as the individual's SPST-B total score and SPST-B scale scores) in both the problem and regular student samples were analysed to detect and determine whether there were any kind of individual deficits of social problem solving (e.g., lower scores on the constructive dimensions, but higher score on the dysfunctional dimensions). The results of analysing the scores of problem students (who have had behavioural problems and were assessed/classified by classroom teachers as the most "disruptive" or most "troublesome" students) showed that 131 of the 167 problem students (78.44%) were found to have lower or higher scores of at least one SD on one or more subscales (or scales) of the SPST. In contrast, in the normal high school student sample, there were only 19.73% falling in the extreme range. The results suggested that the predictive validity of the SPST was significant.

The ability of the SPST to discriminate between various groups of adolescents such as regular-disruptive groups, rural-metropolitan groups, age groups, and male-female groups was demonstrated. The sensitivity of the SPST to discriminate interpersonal problem-solving ability between normal adolescents and adolescents with behavioural problems was investigated by comparing the mean scores on all sub-subscales/subscales/scales of the SPST between the regular and problem student populations. The results showed that the disruptive adolescents had significantly lower mean scores on the PO, RO, and RPSS sub-subscales (which assess constructive facets of the social problem-solving process), yet had significantly higher mean scores on the NPSS and IPSS sub-subscales (which measure dysfunctional facets of the social problem-solving process) when compared to the regular (nondisruptive) adolescents. When compared to the nondisruptive adolescents, the disruptive adolescents had a significantly lower mean score on the RPS subscale assessing the rational problem-solving dimension, but had a significantly higher mean score on the NPS subscale assessing the negative problem-solving dimension. Both the regular and problem groups displayed equivalent mean scores on the PPSS (assessing positive problem-solving skills) and the WPSS (assessing the withdrawal problem-solving style). The results indicated that the disruptive adolescents had substantial deficits of social problem solving, as assessed by the SPST. The problem adolescents were most deficient of effective and rational problem-solving strategies, but used more irritable problem-solving strategies than withdrawn. The results indicated that the SPST has the ability to discriminate between regular and problem adolescents and can pinpoint specific areas of cognition and skill deficits in problem adolescents which provides a useful basis for intervention and treatment programs.

The mean score of the SPST-A in the nondisruptive adolescent group was significantly higher than that in the disruptive adolescent group. Also, the mean score of the SPST-B in the regular adolescent pattern was significantly higher than that in the problem adolescent group. The findings of the present research were consistent with the results of previous studies in the area of social problem solving in adolescence (Sadowski, Moore, and Kelley, 1994). Sadowski et al. (1994) conducted a study involving normal and clinical adolescent samples and found that the mean scores on the Social Problem-Solving Inventory-Revised (SPSI-R) for normal and emotionally disturbed adolescent groups were significantly different. The "clinical" adolescents had considerably lower mean scores on the scales assessing constructive dimensions of the social problem-solving process and on the whole SPSI-R scale, yet had significantly higher mean scores on the scales assessing dysfunctional dimensions, when compared with the normal adolescents. In sum, the ability of the SPST to discriminate between normal and disruptive adolescent groups was substantial and significant.

The SPST not only has the ability to differentiate between regular and disruptive adolescents and pin-point performance deficiencies of social problem solving among problem adolescents, but it provides specific indices of situational contexts in which the subject's problem-solving behaviour proves to be difficult, and the subject's knowledge (as the extent to which it is supposed to be deficient or sufficient) of problem affect-cognitions (orientation), as well as use of possible alternative problem-solving strategies in various dimensions of social problem solving. For example, results of analysing the subjects' responses to problematic situations revealed that there were significant differences in problem-solving strategies employed between the regular and problem adolescent groups. Problem-solving strategies used by the problem adolescents were more negative and more impulsive than those chosen by the normal adolescents. The normal adolescents selected and offered more effective and adaptive solutions than the disruptive adolescents. However, the present findings revealed that problem adolescents performed at equivalent or close rates (i.e., are not significantly different as expected) on factors assessing negative, impulsive and avoidance cognitions (dysfunctional orientations), when compared with regular adolescents. Also, when compared to the normal adolescents, the problem adolescents performed at equivalent levels on the factors assessing positive problem solving strategies (acceptable solutions) or withdrawal (negative) problem-solving strategies while the regular adolescents showed considerably more positive and rational cognitions (constructive orientations). The results showed that the SPST representing the multidimensional nature of social problem solving and using the cognitive-behaviour-analytic approach would be useful for clinical assessments in adolescence.

The analyses of the free-responses showing problem affect-cognitions (PAC-B) and problem-solving actions (PSA-B) revealed that there were significant differences in the quality and quantity of responses between the regular and problem adolescent groups. The free-responses performed by the disruptive adolescents were considerably fewer and less competent. These responses were less deliberate/empathic, and were more negative and more impulsive than those of the normal adolescents. The disruptive adolescents displayed significantly fewer effective problem-solving strategies than the normal adolescents. The results suggested that normal adolescents may possess a broader range or a better quality of social problem-solving abilities or skills. The findings identified by the SPST-B strongly supported the findings identified by the SPST-A. Hence, the results not only support the reliability and validity of the measure, but also indicate its usefulness in assessment and research.

In sum, the findings of this study involving normal-disruptive adolescents supported the notion that a wide and varied array of cognition and skill deficits may be related to disruptive adolescents. There emerged a portrait of their cognition-skill deficits showing deficiencies in both positive, rational cognitions and rational, adaptive strategies to solve problematic situations. Thus, disruptive adolescents are most likely to use negative strategies or impulsivity style when they encounter interpersonal problems. The findings also suggested that both disruptive and nondisruptive adolescents may possess dysfunctional problem affect-cognitions (i.e., negative, withdrawal, and impulsive orientations), but that nondisruptive adolescents may better control or manage affect-cognitive conflicts so as to avoid choosing negative or impulsive problem-solving strategies. Instead, they tend towards effective, adaptive problem-solving strategies.

These findings provided empirical support for previous predictions that social goals (conceptualized as a cognitive construct) influence interpersonal problem-solving strategies (Rubin & Krasnor, 1986; Schmidt, Ollendick, & Stanowicz, 1988), and that differences between socially competent and socially incompetent children may be due not only to prosocial goals they lack or dysfunctional social goals they possess, but also to how the children manage goal conflicts and coordinate multiple goals (Dodge, Asher, & Parkhurst, 1989).

A further analysis of the SPST-A mean score and the SPST-B mean score examining each item (situation) in Stories-a and Stories-b showed that there were significant differences between the normal and disruptive adolescent groups. For example, the disruptive adolescents had significantly lower SPST-A mean scores on 7 of the 12 items in Stories-a (such as Items # 3, # 4, # 6, # 8, # 9, # 10, and # 11). Also, the disruptive adolescents displayed significantly lower SPST-B mean scores in 9 of the 12 items in Stories-b (such as Items # 1, # 2, # 3, # 4, # 5, # 6, # 9, # 10.1, # 10.2, and # 11). The results revealed that ineffective or unadaptive problem-solving strategies of the disruptive students were not found in all situations. Instead, they were most evident in some particular situations. The results suggested that both normal and disruptive adolescents are likely to solve some problematic situations effectively, yet be ineffective in others. Moreover, a normal (or disruptive) adolescent may be deficient in one situation (or a set of situations), whereas another adolescent is deficient in a second situation (or another set of situations) and the situational contexts for these deficiencies vary across adolescents. Hence, it is proposed that adolescents' social behaviours, when they go about problem-solving in interpersonal problematic situations, are best understood as responses to specific situations or tasks. This would be consistent with the predictions from previous findings (Dodge et al, 1985; Freedman et al., 1978; Lochman & Lampron; 1986). For example, Dodge et al. (1985) suggested that "one child may be deficient in one situation, whereas another child is deficient in a second situation" (p. 352) and that "children's responding (and teachers' ratings of children's behaviour) in social settings has both an overall coherence as well as marked cross-situational variation" (p. 351).

A comparison of the SPST-A subscale mean scores between the normal and disruptive adolescent groups on each of 12 items in part A (Stories-a) demonstrated that significant differences on at least one subscale were found on all 12 items. The RPS mean scores of the disruptive group were found to be significantly lower on 9 of the 12 items when compared to the normal group. Also, the PPS mean scores of the disruptive group were significantly lower than those of the normal group on 5 of the 12 items, while the NPS mean scores of the disruptive group were significantly higher than those of the normal group on 5 of the 12 items. The results further indicated that the disruptive adolescents had considerable deficiency in effective, rational problem solving strategies, thus they would be likely to use negative problem-solving strategies when they go about problem solving. However, when compared with the normal group, the IS mean scores of the disruptive group was significantly higher in 1 of 12 items, yet significantly lower on 1 of the 12 items. A comparison of the WS mean scores between the two groups showed similarly "muddy" findings. The results further supported the conclusions already noted, that is, both normal and disruptive adolescents may respond ineffectively in some problematic situations; a problem adolescent may be deficient in one situation, whereas a normal adolescent may be deficient in a second situation. These results further demonstrated that both the normal and disruptive adolescents might possess dysfunctional problem-solving skills in some situations. However, the results also indicated that all 12 items of the SPST-A make considerable contributions to the ability of the SPST-A to discriminate between normal and disruptive adolescents.

A comparison of the PAC-B and PSA-B mean scores between the normal and disruptive adolescent groups showed that significant differences on at least one scale were found for all 12 items of the SPST-B (Stories-b). When compared with the normal group, the disruptive group had lower PAC-B mean scores on 6 of the 12 items, while the disruptive group had lower PSA-B mean scores than the normal group on all the 12 items. The results indicated that the disruptive adolescents had more serious deficiencies of effective, rational problem-solving strategies than problem affect-cognitive deficit (it is possible that another group of disruptive adolescents would display a pattern of deficient responding different from the disruptive group) and thus the SPST assessing orientation and skill components separately is useful for research on social problem solving. The results indicated that all 12 items of the SPST-B would be able to discriminate between normal and disruptive adolescents. The findings of the SPST-B item analyses are consistent with the findings identified by the SPST-A item analyses. These findings also support the need to assess the social problem-solving abilities of disruptive adolescents in each situation because a profile of assessments in each situation may be more informative than a single summary score. The clinical assessment of disruptive adolescents could benefit from taking a profile approach to identifying cognition-skill deficits of social problem solving in adolescence (Dodge et al., 1985).

More evidence of the discriminate ability of the SPST was provided by comparison of the mean scores of rural-metropolitan groups, age groups, and male-female groups within the regular high school sample. A comparison of the mean scores of rural and metropolitan patterns found that there were significant differences between their performance on a majority of subscales of the SPST-A and the SPST-B. The two groups also displayed significant differences on the SPST-A mean score and the SPST-B mean score. The metropolitan group had higher scores on the factors assessing the rational problem-solving dimension and had higher scores on the whole SPST-A and the whole SPST-B, yet had lower scores on the factors assessing negative problem-solving skills and the withdrawal style. However, no significant difference was found on the factor assessing the impulsive problem-solving style. The rural group had significantly higher scores on the factor measuring positive problem-solving skills (acceptable solutions). The results suggested that rural adolescents may have deficiencies in the quality of their solutions when they go about problem solving. This may reflect the assumption that due to the limitation of social experience, or lack of effective or deliberate cognitions and rational problem-solving skills, and thus rural adolescents are most able to employ negative problem-solving strategies or the withdrawal style when they encounter interpersonal problems.

A comparison of the mean scores between the rural and metropolitan groups on all 12 items in Stories-a showed that the metropolitan group had significantly higher scores on 7 of the 12 items (such as Items-a # 1, # 3, # 5, # 8, # 9, # 10, and # 11), yet had lower scores on 1 of the 12 items (i.e., Item # 12). Similarly, the metropolitan group had significantly better scores on 7 of the 12 items of the SPST-B (such as Items # 1, # 3, # 5, # 8, # 9, # 10.2, and # 11). The results suggested that both rural and metropolitan adolescent groups may solve some problematic situations effectively, yet be ineffective in others. In general, metropolitan adolescents may possess a broader range of social competence (or social experience/skills). Thus they are better able to go about effective problem solving when they encounter a variety of social problems. However, rural adolescents may be better able to go about problem solving in some particular problems (such as conflicts generated by co-playing friends). The results suggested that assessment of adolescent social problem-solving abilities or skills using cross-situational method would be useful to detect specific deficits and identify social contexts inhibiting skills.

A comparison of the mean scores of the adolescents aged 15-16 and 17-18 (within the metropolitan student population) showed that there were significant differences on 5 of 10 sub-subscales of the SPST-A. The SPST-B mean scores between the two age groups differed significantly, but the SPST-A mean scores did not. The more senior adolescents earned higher scores on the subscale measuring the rational problem solving, and had lower scores on the subscale measuring the withdrawal when compared to the younger adolescents. Compared to the younger adolescents, the seniors had a significantly higher SPST-B mean score. However, both the senior and younger groups scored similarly on the subscales measuring the negative problem solving and the impulsivity components. The findings supported the assumption that as children grow up they gain more social experience and skills so as to deal with their interpersonal problems.

A comparison of the mean scores of the age groups on all 12 items in Part A (Stories-a) and 12 items in Part B (Stories-b) revealed that the students aged 17-18 scored significantly higher on 3 of the 12 items in Part A (such as Items # 3, # 8, and # 10) and 4 of the 12 items in Part B (i.e., Items # 2, # 6, # 9, and # 10.1). The results suggested that seniors do not solve problems better than younger adolescents in all social situations. However, they may offer more effective, adaptive problem-solving strategies in some particular situations (such as problems in relationships with teachers, younger children, or friends of the opposite sex) where they may possess a broader range of social experience and skills.

A comparison of the mean scores between the male and female populations (within the normal sample) revealed significant differences on very few sub-subscales of the SPST-A. The male group had a higher mean score on the impulsive Problem-Solving Style, but had a lower mean score on the factor assessing the Withdrawal Orientation when compared to the female group. The male group also scored significantly higher on the subscale assessing Negative Problem-Solving Skills when compared to the female group. The two groups scored similarly on the other subscales of the SPST-A.

The SPST-A mean scores of the two male and female groups were not significantly different, but the SPST-B mean scores differed significantly. The female group scored significantly higher on the SPST-B, when compared to the male group. The findings suggest that female adolescents may employ less impulsive problem-solving styles, but be more likely to use the avoidance style, when they encounter their interpersonal problems, while adolescent boys tend to employ more negative problem-solving strategies than adolescent girls when they go about problem solving. The findings also suggested that adolescent girls may be more sensitive than

adolescent boys in their social problems (e.g., more empathic, better in controlling their negative feeling) when they go about problem solving. Thus, adolescent girls may have a better
overall performance quality of social problem solving than adolescent boys when they deal
with their interpersonal problems. These findings appear to be consistent with the findings of
previous studies. For example, Offer and Boxer (1991) reported that adolescent girls were more
empathic than adolescent boys, and that adolescent girls were more concerned with the other
person, and that they would not hurt another person "just for the heck of it".

A comparison of the mean scores of the two groups on all 12 items in part A (Stories-a) and
12 items in Part B (Stories-b) revealed that the female group scored significantly higher on 4
of the 12 items in Part B (such as Items # 3, # 5, # 8, and # 9 which refer to provocative
situations with teachers), but had lower mean scores on 2 of the 12 items in Part A (such as
Items # 3 and # 5). The "muddy" results suggested that Vietnamese female adolescents may
solve problems better than male adolescents in some social problems which involve provocative situations and problems with teachers, while male adolescents may solve problems better
in other situations which refer to problematic situations with opposite sex friends and conflicts
with parents. That is, there are contextual factors which mediate differences between male and
female social problem-solving behaviour.

In summary, the findings of this study provided strong evidence for the reliability and validity
of the SPST. These findings indicated that the development of the SPST using the combined
cross-situational and cognitive-behaviour- analytic approach was useful for clinical assessments and research purposes. The results of administrating the SPST to the two Vietnamese
regular and disruptive high school student samples demonstrated that the SPST may identify
and discriminate weaknesses and strengths of social problem-solving processes between different groups and individuals. The SPST is able to identify deficiencies in the quality and
quantity of problem affect-cognitions and problem-solving strategies in disruptive adolescents.
The deficiencies in quality are most apparent, with disruptive adolescents generating significantly fewer effective, rational, adaptive problem-solving strategies (responses) when they encounter potential interpersonal problematic situations. The cognition-skill deficits of disruptive
adolescents are also most evident in particular problem situations. Thus, a profile of assessments in each situation using the SPST would be useful for intervention and treatment or training programs because it could identify both the component deficits of social problem solving
and the situational contexts in which effective social problem-solving behaviours are least
likely to be demonstrated.

Conclusion and Implications for Practice
and Future Research

The preliminary psychometric evaluation demonstrates that the SPST appears to be a reliable and valid measure of social problem-solving processes in adolescence that is likely to be useful for both research and clinical practice. The SPST offers a performance measure of social problem solving that is based on an empirically supported, multidimensional theoretical model of social problem solving, and utilizes the combined cross-situational and cognitive-behaviour-analytic approach. Another advantage of the SPST is the combination of multiple-choice and free-response formats in the measure which help to pin-point specific cognition and skill deficits of an adolescent's and detect or tap a broad range of the adolescent's social problem solving abilities, hence increasing the reliability and validity of the measure as well as its usefulness in practice.

The findings of the present research have indicated that the SPST has multidimensionality (which reflects the multidimensional nature of social problem solving), and that the SPST-A can effectively assess an adolescent's ability to recognize an effective strategy (i.e., rational, adaptive solution), and identify the adolescent's performance quality across various dimensions (both constructive or dysfunctional) of interpersonal problem solving abilities or skills. On the other hand, the SPST-B was found to be better able to evaluate the two social problem-solving processes: problem affect-cognitive orientation and problem-solving strategies or skills, which the adolescent may possess. In addition, the SPST-A can provide specific indices of an individual's knowledge of problem affect-cognitions which underlies the choice of problem-solving strategies employed, or social contexts in which problematic situations persist. The SPST-B can tap or detect a wide range of an individual's social goals and problem-solving skills which he/she may possess. Hence, in order to assess an adolescent's social problem-solving abilities in educational or clinical settings, the adolescent should complete both the SPST-A, including all 12 structured items (problematic situations), and the SPST-B, including 12 free-response items. However, for purposes of research or designing intervention training programs, the SPST-A and the SPST-B can be used as two separate measures of social problem solving.

As the findings indicated, both the SPST-A and the SPST-B are able to discriminate between normal and disruptive adolescents. However, the SPST-B was demonstrated to be better able to distinguish problem-solving abilities between different groups or individuals. In addition, as the findings suggested, each pair of situations (including one Story a and one Story b) is relatively independent, and thus each could be used as a "mini-test" or as a short-cut measure to identify adolescent interpersonal problem-solving deficiencies in a particular interpersonal relationship or situation. For example, Items (a pair of situations) # 3, 4, 6, 9, and # 10 were found to be best able to distinguish between normal and disruptive adolescents, whereas Items # 1, 3, 8, 9, 10 and # 11 were best able to distinguish between rural and metropolitan adolescent groups, and Item # 10 was best able to discriminate between younger and older adolescents.

In sum, these initial results indicate that the SPST is a potentially reliable and valid measure of social problem solving ability for Vietnamese adolescents, and that the instrument has the ability to pinpoint specific deficient areas of an adolescent's social problem solving and indicate weaknesses and strengths of the adolescent's social problem-solving abilities or skills, as well as particular social contexts where problem-solving behaviour may prove difficult. Hence, the measure can provide a useful basis for intervention training programs.

As the SPST is still in the early stages of development, there are some points that need to be mentioned. Firstly, caution is recommended pertaining to stable reliability because a 2-week interval is considered to be short to evaluate test-retest reliability. Secondly, generalization to other samples is limited as the SPST were administered to regular and disruptive Vietnamese high school student samples, but not to an English-speaking adolescent sample. Thus, there is a need for the continuation of norming and standardizing the measure on different populations, including a representative sample of Vietnamese adolescents from all social groups, and those given other diagnostic labels such as aggressive, delinquent, and depressive. Also, there is a need for the investigating new items (problematic situations) that represent problems in adolescent relationships with other adults and siblings (such as sibling conflict situations).

In summary, future research could investigate the reliability and validity of the SPST in a variety of adolescent comparison groups (including English-speaking adolescent comparison groups) such as non-aggressive and aggressive, non-delinquent and delinquent, and non-depressive and depressive adolescents. An investigation of the psychometric properties of the SPST given to these comparison groups under controlled conditions would be of considerable value in widening the use of the SPST in practice. It would also be beneficial to compare the SPST with measures of coping, self-awareness and self-control or measures of social conflict resolution skills, such as the Social Skills Rating Scale (SSRS; Gresham & Elliot, 1990) and the Problem-Solving Measure for Conflict (PSM-C; Allen et al., 1976). In addition, future research could evaluate the utility of the SPST for assessing intervention efficacy or as a measure of treatment outcome in social problem solving skills training programs.

REFERENCES

Achenbach, T., & Edelbrock, C. (1983). *Manual for the child behavior checklist and revised child behavior profile.* Burlington, VT: University of Vermont Department of Psychiatry.

Ailken, L. R., & Groth-Marnat. G. (2006). *Psychological testing and assessment, 12th Ed.* Pearson Education (US). Boston, MA, United States.

Allen, G. J., Chinsky, J. M., Larcen, S. W., Lochman, J. E., & Selinger, H. V. (1976). *Community psychology and the schools: A behaviorally oriented multilevel preventive approach.* New York: Wiley.

Asher, S.R. (1978). Children's peer relations. In M.E. Lamb (Ed.), *Social and Personality Development,* New York: Holt, Rinehart & Winston.

Asher, S.R., (1983). Social competence and peer status: Recent advances and future directions. *Child Development, 54,* 427-434.

Asher, S.R., & Renshaw, P.D. (1981). Children Without Friends: Social Knowledge and Social-Skill training. In S.R. Asher & J.M. Gottman (Eds.), *The Development of Children's Friendships,* (pp 273-296). New York: Cambridge University Press.

Bachman, J.G., Green, S., & Wirtanen, I.D. (1971). *Youth in transition: Dropping out-problem or symptom (Vol. 3).* Ann Arbor, MI: Institute for Social Research.

Bachman, J.G., Johnston, L.D., & O'Malley, P.M. (1981). *Monitoring the future: Questionnaire responses from the nation's high school seniors,* Ann Arbor: Institute for Social Research.

Bandura, A., (1977). *Social Learning Theory.* Englewood Cliffs, N.J.: Prentice Hall.

Bandura, A. & Wood, R.E. (1989). Effects of perceived controllability and performance standards on self-regulation of complex decision making. *Journal of Personality and Social Psychology, 56,* 805-814.

Barlow, D.H., Hayes, S.C., & Nelson, R.O. (1984). *The Scientist Practitioner: Research and accountability in clinical and educational settings.* Elmsford, New York: Pergamon.

Bellack, A.S., (1979) A critical appraisal of strategies for assessing social skills. *Behavioral Assessment, 1,* 157-176.

Bellack, A.S., & Hersen, M., (1977). *Behaviour Modification: An Introductory Text.* Baltimore: William & Wilkins.

Bernard, H.W. (1971). *Adolescent Development.* Scranton: Intext Educational Publishers.

Berndt, T.J. (1982). The features and effects of friendship in early adolescence. *Child Development, 53,* 1447-1460.

Blood, L., & D'Angelo, R. (1974). A progress report on value issues in conflict between runaways and their parents. *Journal of Marriage and the Family, 36,* 486-491.

Bois-Reymond, M., & Ravesloot, J. (1996). The roles of Parents and Peers in the sexual and relational socialization of adolescents. In K. Hurrelmann & S.F. Hamilton (Eds.), *Social problems and social contexts in adolescence*, (pp. 3-37), New York: de Gruyter

Bramston, P., & Spence, S.H. (1985). Behavioural Versus Cognitive social skills training with intellectually - handicapped adults. *Behaviour Research and Therapy, 23*, 239-246.

Butler, L., & Meichenbaum, D. (1981). The assessment of interpersonal problem-solving skills. In P.C. Kendall & S.D. Hollon (Eds.), *Assessment Strategies for Cognitive-behavioral Interventions*, (pp. 197-225), New York: Academic Press.

Camp, C.J., Doherty, K., Moody-Thomas, S., & Denney, N.W. (1989). Practical problem solving types and scoring methods. In J.D. Sinnott (Ed.), *Everyday Problem Solving: Theory and applications*, (pp. 211-228), New York: Praeger.

Cartledge, G., & Milburn, J.F. (1986). *Teaching social skills to children*. New York: Pergamon Press.

Cohen, M., Becker, M.G., & Campbell, R. (1989). Relationships among four methods of assessment of children with attention deficit-hyperactivity disorder. *The Journal of School Psychology, 28*, 189-202.

Conger, J.J. (1973). *Adolescence and Youth: Psychological development in a changing world.* New York: Harper & Row.

Conger, J.J. (1979). *Adolescence: Generation under pressure.* Harper & Row, Publishers.

Conger, J.C., & Conger, A.J. (1982). Components of heterosocial competence. In J.P. Curran & P.M. Monti (Eds.), *Social skill Training: A practical handbook for assessment and treatment*, (pp. 313-347), The Guildford Press.

Conner, C.K. (1990). *Conner's rating scales manual: Conners' teacher rating scales, Conners' patent rating scale. Instruments for use with children and adolescents*, Canada: Multi-Health Systems Inc.

Conner, C. K. (2000). *Conner's Rating Scales - Revised: Technical Manual*. Multi-Health Systems Inc.

Corah, N.C., & Boffa, J. (1970). Perceived control, self-observations, and response to aversive stimulation. *Journal of Personality and Social Psychology, 16*, 1-4.

Cormier, W.H., Otani, A., & Cormier, S. (1986). The effect of problem-solving training on two problem-solving tasks. *Cognitive Therapy and Research, 10*, 95-108.

Cowen, E.L., Pederson, A., Babigian, H., Izzo, L.D. & Trost, M.A. (1973). Long-term follow-up of early detected vulnerable children. *Journal of Consulting and Clinical Psychology, 41*, 438-446.

Craighead, W. E. (1991). Cognitive factors and classification issues in adolescent depression. *Journal of Youth & Adolescents, 20*, 311-326.

Crutchfield, R.S. (1969). Nurturing the cognitive skills of productive thinking. *In Life skills in school and society*, Washington, D.C.: Association for Supervision and Curriculum Development.

Davison, G.C., Robins, C., & Johnson, M.K. (1983). Articulated thoughts during simulated situations: A paradigm for studying cognition in emotion and behavior. *Cognitive Therapy and Research, 2.* 17-40.

Dereli-İman, E. (2013). The social problem-solving questionnaire: Evaluation of psychometric properties among Turkish primary school students. *Egitim Arastirmalari - Eurasian Journal of Educational Research*, 52, 97-116.

Desjardins, T. L., & Leadbeater, B. J. (2011). Relational victimisation and depressive symptoms in adolescence: Moderating effects of mother, father, and peer emotional support. *Journal of Youth and Adolescence, 40*, 531–544. doi:10.1007/s10964-010-9562-1.

Dishion, T.J. (1990). The family ecology of boy's peer relations in middle childhood. *Child Development, 61*, 874-892.

D'Hondt, W., & Vandeweile, M. (1984). Use of drugs among Senegalese school-going adolescents. *Journal of Youth and* Adolescence, 13, 326-341.

Dodge, K.A., Asher, S., & Parkhurst, J.T. (1989). Social life as a goal coordination task. In C. Ames & R. Ames (Eds.), *Research on motivations in education* (Vol. 3), New York: Academic Press.

Dodge, K.A., McClaskey, C.L. & Feldman, E. (1985). Situational approach to the assessment of social competence in children. *Journal of Consulting and Clinical Psychology, 53 (3)*, 344-353.

Dodge, K.A., & Murphy, R.R. (1984). The assessment of social competence in adolescents. In P. Karoly & J.J. Steffan (Eds.), *Adolescent behavior disorders: Current perspectives*, (pp. 61-96). Lexington, MA: D.C. Health.

Dodge, K.A., Murphy, R.R., & Buchsbaum, K. (1984). The assessment of intention-cue detection skills in children: Implications for developmental psychopathology. *Child Development, 55*, 163-173.

Doerfler, L.A., Mullins, L.L., Griffin, N.J., Siegel, L.J., & Richards, C.S. (1984). Problem-solving deficits in depressed children, adolescents, and adults. *Cognitive Therapy and Research, 8*, 489-499.

Dusek, J.B. (1991). *Adolescent development and behavior* (2nd Ed.). New Jersey: Prentice Hall.

D'Zurilla, T.J. (1986). *Problem-solving therapy: A social competence approach to clinical intervention.* New York: Springer.

D'Zurilla, T.J., & Goldfried, M. (1971). Problem-solving and behavior modification. *Journal of Abnormal Psychology, 78*, 104-126.

D'Zurilla, T.J, & Maydeu-Olivares, A. (1995). Conceptual and methodological issues in social problem-solving assessment. *Behavior Therapy, 26*, 409-432.

D'Zurilla, T.J, & Nezu, A. (1980). A study of the generation-of-alternatives process in social problem solving. *Cognitive Therapy and Research, 4*, 67-72.

D'Zurilla, T.J, & Nezu, A. (1982). Social problem solving in adults. In P.C Kendall (Ed.), *Advances in cognitive-behavioral research and therapy* (Vol. 1). New York: Academic Press.

D'Zurilla, T.J, & Nezu, A. (1990). Development and preliminary evaluation of the social problem-solving inventory. *Psychological Assessment: Journal of Consulting and Clinical Psychology, 2,* 156-163.

D'Zurilla, T. J., & Nezu, A. M. (2001). Problem-solving therapies. In K. S. Dobson (Ed.), *Handbook of Cognitive Behavioural Therapies* (pp. 211-245). New York, London: The Guildford Press.

D'Zurilla, T.J, Nezu, A. & Maydeu-Olivares, A. (1996). *Manual for the social problem solving inventory-revised* (SPSI-R). In press, North Tonawanda, N.Y: Multi-Health Systems, INC.

D'Zurilla, T. J., Nezu, A. M, & Maydeu-Olivares, A. (2002). *Social Problem-Solving Inventory–Revised (SPSI–R): Technical Manual.* North Tonawanda, NY: Multi-Health Systems, Inc.

D'Zurilla, T.J., & Sheedy, C.F. (1991). Relation between social problem solving ability and subsequent level of psychological stress in college students. *Journal of Personality and Social Psychology, 61*, 841- 846.

D'Zurilla, T.J., & Sheedy, C.F. (1992). The relation between social problem solving ability and subsequent level of academic competence in college students. *Cognitive Therapy and Research, 16*, 589-599.

Earls, F. (1986). Epidemiology of psychiatric disorders in children and adolescents. In G.L. Klerman, M.M. Weissman, P.S. Applebaum & L.H. Roth (Eds.), *Psychiatry: Social, Epidemiological, and Legal Psychiatry*, (pp. 123-152). New York: Basic Books.

Edelbrock, C., Greenbaum, R., & Conover, N.C. (1985). Reliability and concurrent relations between the teacher version of the child behavior profile and the Conners revised teacher rating scale. *Journal of Abnormal Child Psychology, 13,* 295-304.

Eichorn, D.H., Mussen, P.H., Clausen, N., Haan, M.P., & Honzik, M.P. (1981). Overview. In D.H. Eichorn, J.A. Clausen, N. Haan, M.P. Hanzik, & P.H. Mussen (Eds.), *Present and past in middle life*, (pp. 411-434), New York: Academic.

Epstein, S. (1982). Conflict and Stress. In L. Goldberger & S. Braznitz, (Eds.), *Handbook of Stress: Theoretical and Clinical aspects*. New York: Free Press.

Epstein, S. (1990). Cognitive-experiential self theory. In L.A. Pervin (Ed.), *Handbook of personality: Theory and Research*, (pp. 165-192). New York: Guilford Press.

Epstein, S. (1994). Integration of the cognitive and the psychodynamic unconscious. *American Psychologist, 49,* 709-724.

Epstein, S., Lipson, A., Holstein, C., & Huh, E. (1992). Irrational reactions to negative outcomes: Evidence for two conceptual systems. *Journal of Personality and Social Psychology, 63,* 328-339.

Epstein, S., & Meier, P. (1989). Constructive thinking: A broad coping variable with specific components. *Journal of Personality and Social Psychology, 57,* 332-350.

Fine, G.A. (1981). Friends, impressions: management and preadolescent behavior. In S.R. Asher, & J.M. Gottman (Eds.). *The development of children's friendships,* (pp. 29-52). Cambridge: Cambridge University Press.

Fischler, G.L., & Kendall, P.C. (1988). Social cognitive problem solving and childhood adjustment: Qualitative and topological analyses. *Cognitive Therapy and Research, 12,* 133-153.

Fitzpatrick, S., & Bussey, K. (2011). The development of the Social Bullying Involvement Scales. *Aggressive Behavior, 37,* 177–192.

Frauenknecht, M., Black, D.A. (1995). Social problem solving inventory for adolescents (SPSI-A): Development and preliminary psychometric evaluation. *Journal of Personality Assessment, 64,* 522-539.

Freedman, B. J., Rosenthal, L., Donahoe, Jr. C. P., Schlundt, D. G., & McFall, R. M. (1978). A social behavioral analysis of skill deficits in delinquent and nondelinquent adolescent boy. *Journal of Consulting and Clinical Psychology, 46,* 1448-1462.

French, D.C., & Tyne, T.F. (1982). The identification and treatment of children with peer-relationship difficulties. In J.P. Curran & P.M. Monti, *Social skills training: A practical handbook for assessment and treatment,* (pp. 280-308). New York: Guilford Press.

Friedenberg. L. (1995). *Psychological testing: Design, Analysis, and Use.* Allyn and Bacon.

Gaffney, L. R., & McFall, R. M. (1981). A comparison of social skills in delinquent and non-delinquent girls using a behavioral role-playing inventory. *Journal of Consulting and Clinical Psychology, 49,* 959-967.

Gesten, E.L., Weissberg, R.P., Amish, P.I., & Smith, J.K. (1987). Social problem-solving training: A skills-based approach to prevention and treatment. In C.A. Mather & J.E. Zins (Eds.), *Psychoeducational interventions in the schools,* (pp. 26-45). New York: Pergamon Press.

Getter, H., & Nowinski, J.K. (1981). A free response test of interpersonal effectiveness. *Journal of Personality Assessment, 45,* 301-308.

Goddard, P., & McFall, R.M. (1992). Decision-making skills and heterosexual competence in college women: An information-processing analysis. *Journal of Social and Clinical Psychology, 11,* 401-425.

Gotlib, I.H., & Asarnow, R.F. (1979). Interpersonal and impersonal problem solving skills in mildly and clinically depressed university students. *Journal of Counselling Psychology, 47*, 86-95.

Gottlieb, B.H. (1991). Social support in adolescence. In M.E. Colten & S. Gore (Eds.), *Adolescent stress causes and consequences*, (pp. 281-306). New York: de Gruyter.

Gresham, F. M., & Elliot, S. (1990). *Manual for the Social Skills Rating Scale*. Odessa, FL: Psychological Assessment Resources.

Guildford, J.P. (1977). *Way beyond the IQ: Guide to improving intelligence and creativity*. Great Neck, New York: Creative Synergetic Associates.

Hamberger, L.K., & Lohr, J.M. (1984). *Stress and stress management*. New York: Springer.

Hamilton, S.F., & Darling, N. (1989). Mentors in adolescents' lives. In K. Hurrelmann & U. Engel (Eds.). *The social world of adolescents*, (pp. 121-139). Berlin: de Gruyter.

Hartup, W.W., & Sancilio, M.F. (1986). Children's friendships. In E. Schopler & G.B. Mesibov (Eds.), *Social behavior in autism*, (pp. 61-80). New York: Plenum.

Hendry, L.B. (1989). The influence e of adults and peers on adolescents' lifestyles and leisure-styles", in K. Hurrelmann & U. Engel (Eds.), *The Social world of adolescents*, (pp. 245-263). Berlin: de Gruyter.

Hendry, L.B., Shucksmith, J.M., Love, J.G., & Glendining, A. (1993). *Young people's leisure and lifestyles*. London: Routlege.

Heppner, P.P., & Anderson, W.P. (1985). The relationship between problem solving self-appraisal and psychological adjustment. *Cognitive Therapy and Research, 9,* 415-427.

Heppner, P.P., Baumgardner, A., & Jackson, J. (1985). Problem solving self-appraisal, depression, and attribution styles: Are they related?. *Cognitive Therapy and Research, 9*, 105-113.

Heppner, P.P., Hibel, J.H., Neal, G.W., Weinstein, C.L., & Rabinowitz, F.E. (1982). Personal problem solving: A descriptive study of individual differences. *Journal of Counselling Psychology, 29*, 580-590.

Heppner, P.P., Neal, G.W., & Larson, L.M. (1984). Problem-solving training as prevention with college students. *Personnel and Guidance Journal, 62*, 514-519.

Heppner, P.P., & Petersen, C.H. (1982). The development and implications of a personal problem solving inventory. *Journal of Counselling Psychology, 29*, 66-75.

Hetherington, E.M. (1989). Coping with family transition: Winners, losers, and survivors. *Child Development, 60,* 1-14.

Hurrelmann, K. (1996). The social world of adolescents: A sociological perspective. In K. Hurrelmann & S.F. Hamilton (Eds.), *Social problems and social contexts in adolescence: Perspectives across boundaries*, (pp. 39-62). New York: de Gruyter.

Hurrelmann, K., Engel, U., Holler, B., & Nordlohne, E. (1988). Failure in school, family conflicts, and psychosomatic disorders. *Journal of Adolescence, 25,* 205-215.

Janis, I.L. (1982). Decision making under stress. In L. Goldberger & S. Breznitz (Eds.), *Handbook of Stress: Theoretical and clinical aspects*, New York: Free Press.

Joffe, R.D., Dobson, K.S., Fine, S., Marriage, K., & Haley, G. (1990). Social problem-solving in depressed, conduct-disordered, and normal adolescents. *Journal of Abnormal Child Psychology, 18 (5),* 565-575.

Kagan, C. (1984). Social problem solving and social skills training. *British Journal of Clinical Psychology, 23,* 161-173.

Kaplan, S.L., Hong, G.K., & Weinhold, C. (1984). Epidemiology of depressive symptomology in adolescents. *Journal of the American Academy of Child Psychiatry, 23,* 91-98.

Kasik, L. (2014). Development of Social Problem Solving – A Longitudinal Study (2009–2011) in a Hungarian Context. European Journal of Developmental Psychology, 12(2), 142–158.

Kathryn, S. W. (2011). Understanding How Social and Emotional Skill Deficits Contribute to School Failure. *Preventing School Failure, 55(1),* 10-16.

Kelly, J.A. (1982). *Social skills training: A practical guide for interventions.* New York: Springer Publishing Company.

Kendall, P.C., & Hollon, S.D. (Eds.). (1979). *Cognitive-behavioral interventions: Theory, research, and procedures.* New York: Academic Press.

Kendall, P.C., & Fischler, G.L. (1984). Behavioral and adjustment correlates of problem solving: Validational analyses of international cognitive problem solving measures. *Child Development, 55,* 879-892.

Kennedy, E., Spence, S.H., & Hensley, V.R. (1989). An examination of the relationship between childhood depression and social competence. *Journal of Child Psychology and Psychiatry, 30,* 305-315.

Klagholz, D.D. (1987). Adolescent social networks and social understanding. Paper presented at the Biennial Meeting of the Society for Research in Child Development, Baltimore.

Kleinmuntz, B. (Ed.), (1966). *Problem solving: Research, method and theory.* New York: Wiley.

Krasnor, L.R., & Rubin, K.H. (1981). The assessment of social problem-solving skills in young children. In T. Merluzzi, C. Glass, & M. Genest (Eds.), *Cognitive assessment.* New York: Guilford Press.

Larson, R., & Asmussen, L. (1991). Anger, worry, and hurt in early adolescence: An enlarging world of negative emotions. In M.E. Colten & S. Gore (Eds.), *Adolescent stress causes and consequences.* New York: de Gruyter.

Lazarus, R.S. (1966). *Psychological stress and the coping process.* New York: McGraw-Hill.

Lazarus, R.S. (1981). The stress and coping paradigm. In C. Eisdorfer, D. Cohen, A. Kleinman, & P. Maxim (Eds.), *Theoretical bases for psychopathology*. New York: Spectrum.

Lazarus, R.S. (1982). Thoughts on the relations between emotion and cognition. *American Psychologist, 37,* 1019-1024.

Lazarus, R.S., & Folkman, S. (1984). *Stress, appraisal, and coping*, New York: Springer.

Levine, J., & Zigler, E. (1973). The essential-reactive distinction in alcoholism: A developmental approach. *Journal of Abnormal Psychology, 81,* 242-249.

Lochman, J.E., & Lampron, L.B. (1986). Situational Social problem-solving skills and self-esteem of aggressiveand non aggressive boys. *Journal of Abnormal Child Psychology, 14,* 605-617.

Lochman, J.E., Wayland, K.K, & White, K.J. (1993). Social goals: Relationship to adolescent adjustment and to social problem solving. Journal of Abnormal Child Psychology, *21,* 135-151.

Logan, G.D. (1988). Toward and instance theory of automatization. *Psychological Review, 95,* 492-527.

Logan, G.D. (1989). Automaticity and cognitive control. In J.A. Bargh & J.S. Uleman (Eds.), *Unintended thought,* (pp. 52-74). New York: Guilford.

Mandler, G. (1982). Stress and thought processes. In L. Goldberger 7 S. Breznitz (Eds.), *Handbook of stress: Theoretical and clinical aspects*. New York: Free Press.

Marx, E.M., & Schulze, C.C. (1991). Interpersonal problem-solving in depressed students. *Journal of Clinical Psychology, 47,* 361-367.

Marx, E.M., Williams, J.M., & Claridge, G.C. (1992). Depression and social problem solving. *Journal of Abnormal Psychology, 101,* 78-86.

Mather, M.D. (1970). Obsession and compulsion. In C.G. Costello (ed.), *Symptoms of Psychopathology*. New York: Wiley.

Maydeu-Olivares, A., & D'Zurilla, T. (1996). A factor-analytic study of the Social Problem-Solving Inventory: an integration of theory and data. *Cognitive Therapy and Research, 20,* 115-133.

McFall, R.M. (1982). A review and reformulation of the concept of social skills. *Behavioral Assessment, 4,* 1-33.

McFall, R.M., & Dodge, K.A. (1982). Self-management and interpersonal skills learning. In P. Karoly & F.H. Kanfer (Eds.), *Self-management and behavior change: From theory to practice,* (pp. 353-392). New York: Pergamon Press.

McGrath, J.E. (ed.), (1970). *Social and psychological factors in stress*. New York: Holt, Rinehart, & Winston.

McGrath, J.E. (1976). Stress and behavior in organization. In M.D. Dunnette (ed.), *Handbook of industrial organizational psychology*. Chicago: Rand McNally.

McKenry, P.C., Walters, L.H., & Johnson, C. (1979). Adolescent pregnancy: A review of the literature. *Family Coordinator, 28*, 16-28.

McMurran, M., & McGuire, J. (2011). *Social problem solving and offending evidence, evaluation and evolution.* New York: John Willey Sons Ltd.

Meichenbaum, D., Henshaw, D., & Himel, N. (1982). Coping with stress as a problem-solving process. In H.W. Krohne & L. Laux (Eds.), *Achievement, stress and anxiety*, (pp. 127-142). New York: Hemisphere.

Messick, S. (1989). Meaning and values in test validation: The science and ethics of assessment. *Educational Researcher, 18*, 5-11.

Mitchell, J.J. (1974). *Human life: The early adolescent years.* Toronto: Holt, Rineharrt and Winston.

Montemayor, R. (1982). The relationship between parent-adolescent conflict and the amount of time adolescents spend alone and with parents and peers. *Child Development, 53*, 1512-1519.

Morales, B.A., & Atilano, V.J. (1977). *A survey of drug dependence in the student population of Barranquilla.* Ministry of Public health, Division of Mental Health, Bogota.

Morrison, R.L., & Bellack, A.S. (1981). The role of social perception in social skill. *Behavior Therapy, 12,* 69-79.

Mowrer, O.H. (1960a). *Learning theory and behavior.* New York: Wiley.

Mowrer, O.H. (1960b). *Learning theory and the symbolic processes.* New York: Wiley.

Murphy, G.E. 1985). A conceptual framework for the choice of interventions in cognitive therapy. *Cognitive Therapy and Research, 9.* 127-134.

Murphy, K.R., & Davidshofer, C.O. (1994). *Psychological testing: Principles and applications.* PRENTICE HALL, New Jersey.

Newell, A., & Simon, H.A. (1972). *Human problem solving.* Englewood Cliffs, NJ: Prentice-Hall.

Nezu, A M. (1985). Differences in psychological distress between effective and ineffective problem solvers. *Journal of counselling Psychology, 32*, 135-138.

Nezu, A., & D'Zurilla, T.J. (1979). An experimental evaluation of the decision-making process in social problem solving. *Cognitive Therapy and Research*, 3, 269-277.

Nezu, A., & D'Zurilla, T.J. (1981a). Effects of problem definition and formulation on decision making in the social problem-solving process. *Behavior Therapy, 12*, 100-106.

Nezu, A., & D'Zurilla, T.J. (1981b). Effects of problem definition and formulation on the generation of alternatives in the social problem-solving process. *Cognitive Therapy and Research, 5*, 265-271.

Nguyen, C. K. (1991). *The psychological characteristics of the puberty.* Unpublished document, the Centre of Child Bio-Psychology, National Institute of Educational Science (Vietnam).

Nguyen, C. K. (1993). *Values and oriented-values in Vietnamese high school students.* Unpublished document, National Institute of Educational Science (Vietnam).

Nguyen, C. K. (1994). *Parental role and adolescent education: Difficulties and potential educational resolutions.* Unpublished research report, the Youth Psychological Counselling Centre (YPCC), Vietnamese Youth Federal Association.

Nguyen, C. K. (2016). *Adolescents Psychological Counselling.* University of Pedagogy Publisher. ISBN 978-604-54-2358-5.

Nguyen, C. K. (2017). *Psychotherapy.* Ha Noi National University Publisher. ISBN 978-604-62-9668-3.

Nguyen, C. K. (2019). Development of the teacher rating scale of interpersonal problem solving in adolescents. *Current Psychology* (CUPS-D-18-00849R2). DOI: 10.1007/s12144-019-00427-2.

Nguyen, C. K., & Nguyen, T. M. L. (2017). Development of the social problem solving measure of adolescents' competences in dealing with interpersonal problems. *HNUE Journal of Science, Educational Sciences, Vol. 62, Iss. 12,* 12-24.

Nguyen, C. K., & Nguyen, T. M. L. (2019). Development and Psychometric Properties of a Social Problem Solving Test for Adolescents. *Journal of Rational-Emotive & Cognitive-Behavior Therapy,* pp. 1-20. https://doi.org/10.1007/s10942-019-00325-3.

Nguyen, C. K., Tran, T. H., & Nguyen, T. M. L. (2018). The problem-solving abilitiy of 4th and 5th grade elementary school students: the situation and factors affecting. In Proceedings the sixth international conference on school psychology: the role of school psychology in promoting well-being of students and families (pp. 182-194).

Nguyen, C. K., Tran, T. H., & Nguyen, T. M. L. (2019). The development of a social problem solving test for elementary school students. In press, Hanoi National University of Education.

O'Connor, R.D. (1969). Modification of social withdrawal through symbolic modelling. *Journal of Applied Behavior Analysis, 2,* 15-22.

O'Connor, R.D. (1972). Relative efficacy of modelling, shaping and the combined procedures for modification of social withdrawal. *Journal of Applied Behavior Analysis, 79,* 327-334.

Offer, D. (1969). *The psychological world of the teenager: A study of normal adolescent boys.* New York: Basic Books.

Offer, D. (1987). In defense of adolescents. JAMA, 257:3407.

Offer, D., & Offer, J.B. (1975). *From teenage to young manhood: A psychological study.* New York: Basic Books.

Offer, D., Ostrov, E., & Howard, K.I. (1981). *The adolescent: A psychological self-portrait.* New York: Basic Books.

Offer, D., Ostrov, E., Howard, K.I., & Atkinson, R. (1988). *The teenage world: The adolescents' self-image in ten countries.* New York: Plenum Press.

Offer, D., & Boxer, A.D. (1991). Normal adolescent development: Empirical Research findings. In M. Lewis (Ed.), *Child and adolescent psychiatry:* A comprehensive textbook. Williams & Wilkins Co, Baltimore, MD, US.

Offrey, L., & Rinaldi, C. (2017). Parent–child communication and adolescents' problem-solving strategies in hypothetical bullying situations. *International Journal of Adolescence and Youth, 22:3,* 251-267. https://doi.org/10.1080/02673843.2014.884006.

Orbach, I., BAR-Joseph, H., & Dror, N. (1990). Style of problem-solving in suicidal individuals. *Suicide and Life Threatening Behavior, 20,* 56-64.

Parker, G.J., & Asher, S.R. (1987). Peer relations and later personal adjustment: Are low accepted children at risk? *Psychology Bulletin, 102,* 357-389.

Parnes, S.J. (1967). *Creative behavior guidebook.* New York: Charles Scribner's Sons.

Parnes, S.J., Noller, R.B., & Biondi, A.M. (1977). *Guide to creative action: Revised edition of creative behavior guidebook.* New York: Charles Scribner's Sons.

Penn, D. L., Spaulding, W., & Hope, D. (1993). Problem solving from different perspectives: An investigation of instructional context on social problesolving ability. *Journal of Cognitive Psychotherapy: An International Quarterly, 7,* 49-61).

Petersen, A.C., & Ebata, A.T. (1987). Developmental transitions and adolescent problem behavior: Implications for prevention and intervention. In K. Hurrelmann (ed.), *Social prevention and intervention.* New York: de Gruyter.

Petersen, A.C., & Ebata, A.T., & Graber, J.A. (1987). *Coping with adolescence: The functions and dysfunctions of poor achievement.* Paper presented at the Biennital Meeting of the Society for Research in Child Development, Baltimore.

Petersen, A.C., & Hamburg, B.A. (1986). Adolescence: A developmental approach to problems and psychopathology. *Behavior Therapy, 17,* 480-499.

Petersen, A.C., Silbereisen, R.K., & S□rensen, S. (1996). Adolescent development: A global perspective. In K. Hurrelmann & S.F. Hamilton (Eds.), *Social problems and social contexts in adolescence,* (pp. 3-37). New York: de Gruyter.

Pham, H. G., Nguyen, M. D., & Nguyen, C. K. (1991). *An anticipateded model for Vietnamese youths in the year 2000 and later.* Unpublished document, Central Science and Education Commission (Vietnam).

Phillips, E.L. (1978). *The social skills basis of psychopathology: Alternatives to abnormal psychology and psychiatry.* New York: Grune & Stratton.

Phillips, L., & Zigler, E. (1961). Social competence: The action-thought parameter and vicariousness in normal and pathological behaviors. *Journal of Abnormal and Social Psychology, 63,* 137-146.

Platt, J.J., & Spivack, G. (1975). *Manual for the Means-Ends Problem-Solving Procedures (MEPS): A measure of international cognitive problem-solving skills.* Unpublished document, Philadelphia: Hahnemann Community Mental Health/Mental Retardation Center.

Platt, J.J., Spivack, G., Altman, N., Altman, D., & Peizer, S.B. (1974). Adolescent problem solving thinking. *Journal of Consulting and Clinical Psychology, 42,* 787-793.

Plienis, A.J., Hansen, D.J., Ford, F., Smith, S. Jnr., Stark, L.J., & Kelly, J.A. (1987). "Behavioral small group training to improve the social skills of emotionally-disordered adolescents. *Behavior Therapy, 18,* 17-32.

Rabichow, H.G., & Sklansky, M.A. (1980). *Effective counselling of Adolescents.* Chicago: Follett.

Ralph, A., Spano, A., Whitely, H., Strong, L., Parker, M., & Pailthorpe. (1991). Social traing for adolescents: Making positive steps. *Behaviour Change, 8,* 183-193. Rathjen, D.P. (1980). An overview of social competence. In D.P. Rathjen & J.P. Foreyt (Eds.), *Social competence: Interventions for children and adults.* New York: Pergamon Press.

Reynolds, W.M. (1986). *Assessment of depression in adolescents: Manual for the Reynolds Adolescent Depression Scale.* Odessa, FL: Psychological Assessment Resources.

Roff, J.D., & Wirt, R.D. (1984). Childhood social adjustment, adolescents status, and young adult mental health. *American Journal of Orthopsychiatry, 54,* 595-602.

Rotherham-Borus, M.J., Trautman, P.D., Dopkins, S.C., & Shrout, P.E. (1990). Cognitive style and pleasant activities among female adolescent suicide attempters. *Journal of Consulting and Clinical Psychology, 58,* 554-561.

Rotter, J.B. (1954). *Social learning and clinical psychology.* Englewood Cliffs, NJ: Prentice-Hall.

Rubin, K.H., & Krasnor, L.R. (1986). Social-cognitive and social behavioral perspective on problem-solving. In Perlmulter (Ed.), The Minnesota Symposium of Child Psychology: *Vol 18, Cognitive perspectives on children's social and behavioral development,* 1- 68. Hillsdale, NJ: Erbaum.

Rutter, M. (1986). The developmental psychopathology of depression: Issues and perspectives. In M. Rutter, C. Izard, & P. Read, (Eds.), *Depression in young people: Developmental and clinical perspectives,* (pp. 3-30). New York: Guilford.

Rutter, M., Graham, P., Chadwick, O., & Yule, W. (1976). Adolescent turmoil: Fact or fiction? *Journal of Child Psychology Psychiatry, 17,* 35-56.

Sacco, W. P., & Graves, D. J. (1984). Childhood depression, interpersonal problem-solving, and self-ratings of performance. *Journal of Clinical Child Psychology, 58,* 554-561.

Sadowski, C., & Kelly, M. L. (1993). Social problem solving in suicidal adolescents. *Journal of Consulting and Clinical Psychology, 61,* 121-127.

Sadowski, C., Moore, L. A., & Kelly, M. L. (1994). Psychometric properties of the social problem solving inventory (SPSI) with normal and emotionally disturbed adolescents. *Journal of Abnormal Chid Psychology, 22,* 565-575.

Sarason, B.R. (1981). The dimensions of social competence: Contributions from a variety of research areas. In J.D. Wine, & M.D. Smye (Eds.), *Social competence.* New York: Guilford.

Schinka. J. (1989). *Personal problems checklist for adolescents.* Odessa, FL: Psychological Assessment Resources.

Schmidt, C. R., Ollendick, T.H., & Stanowicz, L.B. (1988). Developmental changes in the influences of assigned goals on cooperation and competition. *Developmental Psychology, 23,* 574-579.

Sch"npflug, W. (1983). Coping efficiency and situational demands. In R. Hockey (ed.), *Stress and fatigue in human performance.* New York: Wiley.

Schotte, D.E., & Clum, G.A. (1987). Problem-solving skills in suicidal psychiatric patients. *Journal of Consulting and Clinical Psychology, 55,* 49-54.

Schroder, H.M., Driver, M.J., & Streufirt, S. (1967). *Human information processing.* New York: Holt, Rinehart & Winston.

Schulz, P., & Sch"npflug, W. (1982). Regulatory activity during states of stress. In H.W. Krohne & L. Laux (Eds.), *Achievement, stress and anxiety.* New York: Hemisphere.

Semrud-Clikeman, M. (2007): *Social competence in children.* New York: Springer.

Shantz, C.U. (1987). Conflicts between children. *Child Development, 58,* 283-305.

Sherry, P., Keitel, M., & Tracey, T.J. (1984). The relationship between person-environment fit, coping, and strain. Paper presented at the 92nd Annual Convention of the American Psychological Association, Toronto, Canada.

Shujja, S. & Malik, F. (2011). Cross cultural perspective on social Competence Children: Development and Validation of an Indigenous Scale for Children in Pakistan, *Journal of Behavioural Sciences, 21*(1), 13-32.

Shuller, D.Y., & MacNamara, J.R. (1976). Expectancy factors in behavioral observation. *Behavior Therapy, 7,* 519-527.

Shure, M.B. (1981). Social competence as a problem-solving skill. In J.D. Wine & M.D. Smye (Eds.), *Social Competence.* New York Guilford.

Shure, M.B., & Spivack, G. (1978). *Problem-solving techniques in childrearing.* San Francisco: Jossey-Bass.

Singh, A. (1984). The girls who ran away from home. *Child Psychiatry Quarterly, 17,* 1-8.

Smith, C.A., & Lazarus, R.S. (1990). Emotion and adaptation. In L. Pervin (Ed.), *Handbook of personality: Theory and research* (pp. 609-637). New York: Guilford Press.

Spence, S. H. (1980). *Social skills training with children and adolescents: A counsellor's manual.* Windsor: NFER Publishing Co.

Spence, S.H. (1988). The role of social-cognitive skills in the determination of children's social competence. *Behavior Change, 5,* 9-18.

Spence, S.H. (1991). Developments in the assessment of social skills and social competence in children. *Behavior Change, 8,* 148-166.

Spence, S.H., & Liddle, B. (1990). Self-report measures of social competence for children: An evaluation of the Mastson Evaluation of Social Skills for Youngers and the List of Social Situation Problems. *Behavioural Assessment, 12,* 310-321.

Spielberger, C.D., Gorsuch, R.L., & Lushene, R.E. (1970). *Manual for the State-Trait Anxiety Inventory (Self-Evaluation Questionair).* Palo Alto, CA: Consulting Psychologists Press.

Spivack, G., Platt, J.J., & Shure, M.B. (1976). *The problem-solving approach to adjustment.* San Francisco: Jossey-Bass.

Spivack, G., & Shure, M.B. (1974). *Social adjustment of young children: A cognitive approach to solving real-life problems.* San Francisco: Jossey-Bass.

Spivack, G., Shure, M.B., & Platt, J.J. (1985). *Means-Ends Problem Solving (MEPS): Stimuli and scoring procedures supplement.* Unpublished document, Hahnemann University.

Stein, M. A., & O'Donnell, J. P. (1985). Classification of childrens' behavior problems: Clinical and qualitative approaches. *Journal of Abnormal Child Psychiatry,* 13, 269-280.

Taylor, E., & Sandberg, S. (1984). Hyperactive behavior in English school children: A questionnaire survey. *Journal of Abnormal Child Psychiatry, 12,* 143-156.

Teichmann, M., Rahav, G., & Barnea, Z. (1987). Alcohol and psychoactive drug use among Israeli adolescents: An epidemiological and demographic investigation. *International Journal of Addictions, 22,* 81-92.

Tisdelle, D.A., & St. Lawrence, J.S. (1986). Interpersonal problem solving competence: Review and critique of the literature. *Clinical Psychology Review, 6,* 337-356.

Trower, P., Bryant, B., & Argyle, M. (1978). *Social skills and mental health.* London: Methuen.

Turk, D.C., & Salovey, P. (1985). Cognitive structures, cognitive processes, and cognitive-behavior modification: I Client issues. *Cognitive Therapy and Research, 9.* 1-17.

Tversky, A., & Kahneman, D. (1981). The framing of decisions and the psychology of choice. *Science,* 211, 453-458.

Tyne, T.F., & Flynn, J.T. (1979). The remediation of elementary school children's low social status through a teacher-centered consultation program. *Journal of School Psychology, 17,* 244-254.

Urbain, E.S., & Kendall, P.C. (1980). Review of social-cognitive problem-solving interventions with children. *Psychological Bulletin, 88,* 109-143.

Vitaro, F., & Pelletier, D. (1991). Assessment of children's social problem-solving skills in hypothetical and actual conflict situations. *Journal of Abnormal Child Psychology, 19,* 505-518.

Wakeling, H. (2007). The psychometric validation of the social problem-solving inventory - revised with UK incarcerated sexual offenders. *Sex Abuse: A Journal of Research and Treatment.* https://doi.org/10.1007/s11194-007-9038-3.

Webster-Stratton, C., Reid, M. J., & Hammond, M. (2001). Social skills and problem solving training for children with early-onset conduct problems: Who benefits? *Journal of Child Psychology and Psychiatry, 42* (7), 943–952.

Weiner, I.B. (1980). Psychopathology in adolescence. In J. Adelson (ed.), *Handbook of adolescent psychology,* (pp. 447-471). New York: Wiley.

Wentzel, R.R. (1991). Relation between social competence and academic achievement in early adolescence. *Child Development, 62,* 1066-1078.

Wrubel, J., Benner, P., & Lazarus, R.S. (1981). Social competence from the perspective of stress and coping. In J.D. Wine & M.D. Smye (Eds.), *Social competence.* New York: Guilford.

Yoman, J., & Edelstein, B. A. (1993). Relationship between solution effectiveness ratings and actual solution impact in social problem solving. *Behavior Therapy, 24,* 409-430.

Yong, A. G., & Pearce, S. (2013). A Beginner's Guide to Factor Analysis: Focusing on Exploratory Factor Analysis. *Tutorials in Quantitative Methods for Psychology,* Vol. 9(2), p. 79-94. DOI:10.20982/tqmp.09.2.p079.

Zsolnai, A., & Kasik, L. (2016). Coping Strategies and Social Problem Solving in Adolescence. In A. Surian (Ed.), *Open spaces for interactions and learning diversities.* Rotterdam: Sense Publishers.

Zsolnai, A., Kasik, L., & Braunitzer, G. (2014). Coping strategies at the ages 8, 10 and 12. *Educational Psychology.* https://doi.org/10.1080/01443410.2014.916397.

APPENDICES

APPENDIX A.

**The Social Problem Solving Test (SPST)
(full form)**

SOCIAL PROBLEM SOLVING TEST   (SPST)

Name: ....………….. Age: ...…... Gender (circle): M   F   Id. No: ....
Grade: ……… School: ………………………………. Date……./…./……

Instructions

Below are short stories about **social problem situations**. Please read each story carefully
and for each statement, choose (circle) **one** of the numbers (0 1 2) that best shows to what
extent the response is true of you, when responding to the following questions:

What would you think (or feel) and do?

> **0** = **Not at all**
> **1** = **Sometimes**
> **2** = **Usually**

For example: During break time some students come up to you in the playground, teasing
you and calling you stupid and dumb. **What would you think or feel and what would you
actually do?**

I would			I would		
1. Think they are bad people	0 1	2	1. Avoid playing with them	0 1	2
2. Feel frightened	⓪ 1	2	2. Tolerate their behaviour	0 1	2
3. Think about why they are behaving like they are	0 1 2		3. Ask them to stop behaving like they are	0 1	2
4. Feel insulted or upset	0 1	2	4. Hit them or throw a tantrum	⓪ 1	2
5. Other (describe)** _Eg. Feel unhappy_	0 1	2	5. Other reaction (describe)** _Eg. Stay in classroom during breaktime_	0 1	2

Story (b):

You are playing in the playground when two students who are chasing each other run into
you and fall down. When they stand up, they yell bad words at you.

What would you think or feel?	**What would you do?**
Eg. I would think these students have lost their temper due to being hurt	_Eg. I would leave without saying anything_
Eg. I would think their behaviour is not intentional	_Eg. I would ignore their bad language_
Eg. They are rude	Eg. I would pick a quarrel with them

** These free-response items are other feelings or solutions that are beyond the given solutions. The subject
can describe them

Here are the stories:

Story # 1

You are looking forward to watching your favourite television programme. When you go into the room to watch it you find another student has turned on a show you don't like.

I would think or feel		**I would**	
1. He/she is fond of this show 0 1 2		1. Find other place to watch TV 0 1 2	
2. It is unfair 0 1 2		2. Tell the person to turn on the show I like 0 1 2	
3. Unlucky, but I think the issue is solvable (Eg. I can ask for my turn or I can discuss other solutions with the student) 0 1 2		3. Ask the student how long he/she will be, then decide whether to wait/ leave or watch the show with him/her 0 1 2	
4. Upset or angry 0 1 2		4. Annoy the student in some way in order to drive him/her away 0 1 2	
5. Nothing can change the situation 0 1 2		5. Leave the room and do not watching TV 0 1 2	
6. Other (describe)**_____ 0 1 2		6. _____ 0 1 2	

Story # 1 (b)

You go to a library to borrow a book. It took you a long time to find a interesting book. You found it but you forgot your library card. Therefore, you have to leave the book and go to get your card. When you go back to get the book, you find an another student is reading it .

What would you think or feel?	**What would you do?**
_____	_____
_____	_____
_____	_____
_____	_____
_____	_____

Story # 2.

During a break time, a student group comes into the canteen for a drink and one of the students unintentionally spits on your foot (or your body). You ask the student to apologise, but the student refuses to do so.

I would think or feel					**I would**			
1. He/she is fond of this show	0	1	2	1.	Find other place to watch TV	0	1	2
2. It is unfair	0	1	2	2.	Tell the person to turn on the show I like	0	1	2
3. Unlucky, but I think the issue is solvable (Eg. I can ask for my turn or I can discuss other solutions with the student)	0	1	2	3.	Ask the student how long he/she will be, then decide whether to wait/ leave or watch the show with him/her	0	1	2
4. Upset or angry	0	1	2	4.	Annoy the student in some way in order to drive him/her away	0	1	2
5. Nothing can change the situation	0	1	2	5.	Leave the room and do not watching TV	0	1	2
6. Other (describe)**_____	0	1	2	6.	_____	0	1	2

Story # 2 (b)

When you go to a restaurant or a public place where a lot of people come and go, you find a younger group of people coming to your place to talk. You notice their behaviour is impolite and you don't want to talk to them. Therefore, you stand up and move to another place, but one of these youngsters stands up, tries to prevent you going and acts in a provoking way.

What would you think or feel?	**What would you do?**
_____	_____
_____	_____
_____	_____
_____	_____
_____	_____

Story # 3.

On the occasion of your birthday, your friend of the opposite sex gives you a bunch of roses and a valuable present, implying "I like you...I love you". However, you want to maintain a friendship only.

What would you think or feel?	**What would you do?**
I would think or feel	**I would**

	I would think or feel						**I would**			
1.	He/she is a good friend, but a love-affair can influence study in a bad way	0	1	2		1.	Take the flowers and gift, keep silent, then say "Sorry! I can't..." and return the gift after the birth day	0	1	2
2.	The friend is insensitive or is childish	0	1	2		2.	Refuse the roses and the gift and show a cold-greeting attitude	0	1	2
3.	About how to help my friend understand that this relationship is a friendship only, but I must speak politely, not rudely	0	1	2		3.	Take the roses but politely return the gift and act in a way that shows I regard the person as equal to other friends	0	1	2
4.	Feel insulted or upset	0	1	2		4.	Make fun of the person or tease him/her	0	1	2
5.	Frightened or troubled	0	1	2		5.	Avoid the person all the time if possible	0	1	2
6.	_____	0	1	2		6.	_____	0	1	2

Story # 3 (b)

Break time is over and you come into your class. You find a letter in your notebook and the contents of the letter reveal that the author likes you ...and loves you. However, you think you are too young to fall in love with the person, though you know the person is a good friend. However, you only want to spend time on your studies at this moment.

What would you think or feel?	**What would you do?**
_____	_____
_____	_____
_____	_____
_____	_____
_____	_____

Story # 4

Your friend suddenly stops an intimate relationship with you without any explanation. He/she has also made fun of you, or made unfriendly comments about you, and avoided you if possible.

What would you think or feel?	**What would you do?**

I would think or feel	**I would**

1. My friend may have personal reasons or has made mistakes that are "reasonable" 0 1 2

2. My friend is not good or is shallow 0 1 2

3. About why my friend acts like that or about the underlying causes of the misunderstanding 0 1 2

4. Insulted and/or upset 0 1 2

5. The friendship is over 0 1 2

6. _____ 0 1 2

1. Tolerate or ignore my friend's attitude 0 1 2

2. Demand the friend explains the reason 0 1 2

3. Find a chance to meet to identify the problem and discuss it with my friend 0 1 2

4. Violently criticize or blame my friend 0 1 2

5. Cut off any relationship with my friend without asking him/her what the problem was 0 1 2

6. _____ 0 1 2

Story # 4 (b)

You have a close friend (A) of the opposite sex. Since you want to expand your friendship, you help A make friends with B, a close, same-sexed friend. As time passes, you feel A and B become more intimate and leave you out. They usually avoid you, and are even unpleasant when you are present. You hear their unfriendly comments about you.

What would you think or feel?	**What would you do?**
_____	_____
_____	_____
_____	_____
_____	_____
_____	_____

Story # 5

You hardly ever watch TV, but while you are watching one of your favourite TV programme, one of your parents starts to nag you a lot to clean up your room. Finally, your parent comes in and turns the TV off.

What would you think or feel?			**What would you do?**		
I would think or feel			**I would**		
1. My parent is right or reasonable	0 1 2		1. Clean up my room	0 1 2	
2. My parent is strict	0 1 2		2. Clean in a reluctant manner	0 1 2	
3. About why my parents are behaving like they are and what can change them	0 1 2		3. Suggest to my parents that I could see the TV show and clean after the show or clean first, then continue watching	0 1 2	
4. Feel upset or angry	0 1 2		4. Throw a tantrum	0 1 2	
5. It is unfair because the cleaning can be done after the TV show	0 1 2		5. Go to my room and close the door without cleaning the room	0 1 2	
6. _____	0 1 2		6. _____	0 1 2	

Story # 5 (b)

You like dressing well and you like a fashionable way of dressing. However, your parents don't like the way you dress and always nag you about it.

What would you think or feel?	**What would you do?**
_____	_____
_____	_____
_____	_____
_____	_____
_____	_____
_____	_____

Story # 6.

You are studying for your examination (which happens next week), when your best friend comes to ask you to go out to a good film. Your friend met you at school the day before and offered you a ticket for a good new film, and you agreed as you feel well prepared for the exam and you need a bit of relaxation. When you ask your parents' permission to go, your parents refuse and nag you.

What would you think or feel?				**What would you do?**			
I would think or feel				**I would**			
1. Parents are right or reasonable	0 1 2			1. Say sorry and explain to my friend that my parents do not agree	0 1 2		
2. Parents are too strict or unsympathetic	0 1 2			2. Pretend to obey my parents, then find a false reason to go	0 1 2		
3. About why my parents don't agree and how to persuade my parents to my point of view	0 1 2			3. Discuss with my parents that I am well-prepared and need a bit of relaxation. If still not allowed, apologise to my friend and forget about it	0 1 2		
4. Upset or angry	0 1 2			4. Throw a tantrum	0 1 2		
5. Unhappy, but think that I can't change anything	0 1 2			5. Return the ticket, then go to my room without talking to parents	0 1 2		
6. _____	0 1 2			6. _____	0 1 2		

Story # 6 (b)

You have some friends of the opposite sex and you know they are good friends . However, your parents don't like you having friendships with people of a different sex. One day when your parents go out, one of these friends comes to see you. When your parents come home, they are irritable and ask your friend to leave the house.

What would you think or feel?	**What would you do?**
_____	_____
_____	_____
_____	_____
_____	_____
_____	_____

Story # 7

When you wash your Dad's clothes, you suddenly find a letter from a strange woman in his pocket. Out of curiosity, you read it. You find this letter is a declaration of her love for your Dad. You realise that it may threaten your peaceful family.

What would you think or feel?	**What would you do?**

I would think or feel				**I would**			
1. Dad must stop the unacceptable relationship	0	1	2	1. Talk to Dad, and ask him to cut off the relationship	0	1	2
2. Mum is betrayed	0	1	2	2. Tell Mum about the letter	0	1	2
3. About why Dad acts like he is and how to resolve the problem soon	0	1	2	3. Calm down, investigate/discuss the problem with Dad or find help from someone understanding and closely related to Dad if necessary	0	1	2
4. Upset that the woman is possibly the cause of breaking my family	0	1	2	4. Warn or threaten revenge on the woman	0	1	2
5. Depressed that my father is not acting like my Dad	0	1	2	5. Ignore the issue or avoid Dad	0	1	2
6. _____	0	1	2	6. _____	0	1	2

Story # 7 (b)

Your mum and dad have conflicts and one evening after a fight, your Dad left and moved out of home. After one week investigating, you find the flat your Dad is living in and you decide to go there. When you arrive you saw a young woman caring for your Dad.

What would you think or feel?	**What would you do?**
_____	_____
_____	_____
_____	_____
_____	_____
_____	_____
_____	_____

Story # 8

Your teacher accuses you of writing swear words on the toilet wall, and is threatening to put you down to a lower class. You know you didn't do it but that your close friend did.

What would you think or feel?			
I would think or feel			

What would you do?			
I would			

1. The teacher's anger is reasonable and understandable   0 1 2

2. The teacher is silly or unreasonable   0 1 2

3. About how to control the situation, or think of repairing the damage rather than tracking down the culprit   0 1 2

4. I am accused unfairly or feel upset   0 1 2

5. It is too difficult for me to solve the issue   0 1 2

6. _____   0 1 2

1. Show evidence that I am innocent   0 1 2

2. Say I didn't do this and that my friend did it   0 1 2

3. Say I didn't do it, but instead of finding the culprit, discuss how to clean the wall without a fuss   0 1 2

4. Talk angrily to the teacher   0 1 2

5. Avoid argument and suffer the punishment if it occurs   0 1 2

6. _____   0 1 2

Story # 8 (b)

One of your friends complains that he/she has a problem with his/her teacher. The teacher doesn't like him/her and the teacher is unfair to him/her. Hence, he/she feels depressed and intends suiciding.

What would you think or feel?	What would you do?
_____	_____
_____	_____
_____	_____
_____	_____
_____	_____
_____	_____

187

Story # 9

In the classroom, your teacher is writing on the blackboard. There is swearing and laughing behind him/her. The teacher suddenly turns around and sees you talking. The teacher becomes angry and says:

T: What are you doing? Why are you laughing?

You: Nothing! It was not me!

T   (more irritable): So! Who laughed?

You: I don't know.

T: If you don't know, you get out of my class.

You: No man! It was not my fault! Why do I have to get out?

T: If you don't, I will get you out!

The atmosphere becomes very tense.

(A) What would you think and do if you were the student?

I would think or feel		I would	
1. The teacher's reaction may be under-standable	0 1 2	1. Leave with an irritable attitude	0 1 2
2. The teacher is ridiculous	0 1 2	2. Refuse to go out	0 1 2
3. The matter may disrupt the lesson or disturb other students	0 1 2	3. Get out quietly and talk to the teacher after class or meet the principal to solve the problem	0 1 2
4. Upset or angry	0 1 2	4. Talk angrily to the teacher or throw a tantrum	0 1 2
5. It is a "good" reason to leave the class-room as well as school	0 1 2	5. Get out and leave school	0 1 2
6. _____	0 1 2	6. _____	0 1 2

(B) What would you think and do if you were not the student, but were the monitor of this class?

I would think or feel	I would do
_____	_____
_____	_____
_____	_____
_____	_____
_____	_____

Story # 10

You are lying down on your bed with a headache and the boy next door is playing his radio loudly, and it makes your head feel worse.

What would you think or feel?					**What would you do?**			
I would think or feel					**I would**			
1. He is very keen on the music	0	1	2		1. Ask the boy to stop or play the radio softly	0	1	2
2. He is a bad boy	0	1	2		2. Tell his parents	0	1	2
3. If the boy knew my problem he may stop or think about how to prevent the noise that upsets me	0	1	2		3. Say "Sorry, I am sick. Please turn the radio off or play it softly," or choose alternatives such as closing the door or moving to a quieter place	0	1	2
4. Upset at being irritated	0	1	2		4. Violently force him to turn the radio off	0	1	2
5. Nothing can change in any way	0	1	2		5. Try to put up with the noise	0	1	2
6. _____	0	1	2		6. _____	0	1	2

If you ask the boy to turn the radio down or off, but he ignores you,

What would you think or feel?	**What would you do?**
_____	_____
_____	_____
_____	_____
_____	_____

Story # 10 (b)

While you are studying, some children from next-door neighbouring families are playing and chasing each other outside. This makes a lot of noise and therefore disturbs you.

What would you think or feel?	**What would you do?**
_____	_____
_____	_____
_____	_____
_____	_____

Story # 11.

You are walking on a quiet road when suddenly you see a "thief" intending to snatch a handbag from a person walking in front of you. You look around but no one else is there.

What would you think or feel?				What would you do?			
I would think or feel				**I would**			
1. The person may not know the threat coming	0	1	2	1. Walk quickly to the person to warn him/her of the danger	0	1	2
2. I don't care what might happen to the person	0	1	2	2. Ignore what is going on	0	1	2
3. About how to help, but safeguard yourself (ie. how to warn the person of the risk without alarming the thief)	0	1	2	3. Do something to warn the person of the danger such as pretending accidentally to run into the thief or to become acquainted with the person	0	1	2
4. Of help from the police	0	1	2	4. Run quickly to warn the police	0	1	2
5. Frightened or worried	0	1	2	5. Run away or quickly leave the unsafe place	0	1	2
6. _____	0	1	2	6. _____	0	1	2

Story # 11 (b)

A group of adolescents make friends with you. You agree to be involved in their activities because you think they are good friends. However, as time passes, you gradually find that they will not be good friends and they intend to involve you in possible illegal action.

What would you think or feel?	What would you do?
_____	_____
_____	_____
_____	_____
_____	_____
_____	_____

Story # 12.

You are playing a game (eg., football or tennis) in a team, when a person in the opposite team collides with you and suddenly falls down. Although the person is in the wrong, you pick him/her up and say "Are you OK?". Responding to your polite help, the person uses bad language and insults you.

What would you think or feel?	**What would you do?**
I would think or feel	**I would**

1. Due to hurt the person has lost control and his/her temper   0 1 2

2. The person is wrong and/or impolite   0 1 2

3. About how to help if the person is hurt and/or how to reorganise the matter to continue the game if the person is not seriously hurt   0 1 2

4. Being insulted and/or upset   0 1 2

5. Frightened or worried   0 1 2

6. _____   0 1 2

1. Ignore the bad language   0 1 2

2. Blame or argue with the person and say that he/she is wrong   0 1 2

3. Call medical help if the person is badly hurt, or shake his/her hands as a gesture that there is "no problem" and continue playing   0 1 2

4. Hit the person or throw a tantrum   0 1 2

5. Avoid playing near the person or leave the game   0 1 2

6. _____   0 1 2

Story # 12 (b)

While you are riding on your bicycle, a youth riding in the opposite direction suddenly runs into you. Although you are both hurt and the youth was at fault, you say "Sorry!". Responding to your polite attitude, the youth becomes angry and insults you.

What would you think or feel?	**What would you do?**

APPENDIX B: Form A of the SPST

SOCIAL PROBLEM SOLVING TEST (SPST)

Name: ....…………….. Age: ….…... Gender (circle):   M   F   Id. No: ....

Grade: …….…   School: ……………………………….   Date......./…./.…...

Instructions

Below are short stories about **social problem situations**. Please read each story carefully
and for each statement, choose (circle) **one** of the numbers (0 1 2) that best shows to what
extent the response is true of you, when responding to the following questions:

What would you think (or feel) and do?

> **0 = Not at all**
>
> **1 = Sometimes**
>
> **2 = Usually**

For example: During break time some students come up to you in the playground, teasing
you and calling you stupid and dumb. **What would you think or feel and what would you
actually do?**

I would			I would		
1. Think they are bad people	0 1 2		1. Avoid playing with them	0 1 2	
2. Feel frightened	⓪ 1 2		2. Tolerate their behaviour	0 1 2	
3. Think about why they are behaving like they are	0 1 2		3. Ask them to stop behaving like they are	0 1 2	
4. Feel insulted or upset	0 1 2		4. Hit them or throw a tantrum	⓪ 1 2	
5. Other (describe)** _Eg. Feel unhappy_	0 1 2		5. Other reaction (describe)** _Eg. Stay in classroom during breaktime_	0 1 2	

Story (b):

You are playing in the playground when two students who are chasing each other run into you and fall down.
When they stand up, they yell bad words at you.

What would you think or feel?	What would you do?
Eg. I would think these students have lost their temper due to being hurt	_Eg. I would leave without saying anything_
Eg. I would think their behaviour is not intentional	_Eg. I would ignore their bad language_
Eg. They are rude	Eg. I would pick a quarrel with them

** These free-response items are other feelings or solutions that are beyond the given solutions. The
subject can describe them

Here are the stories:

Story # 1

You are looking forward to watching your favourite television programme. When you go into the room to watch it you find another student has turned on a show you don't like.

What would you think or feel?				**What would you do?**			
I would think or feel				**I would**			
1. He/she is fond of this show	0	1	2	1. Find other place to watch TV	0	1	2
2. It is unfair	0	1	2	2. Tell the person to turn on the show I like	0	1	2
3. Unlucky, but I think the issue is solvable (Eg. I can ask for my turn or I can discuss other solutions with the student)	0	1	2	3. Ask the student how long he/she will be, then decide whether to wait/ leave or watch the show with him/her	0	1	2
4. Upset or angry	0	1	2	4. Annoy the student in some way in order to drive him/her away	0	1	2
5. Nothing can change the situation	0	1	2	5. Leave the room and do not watching TV	0	1	2
6. Other (describe)_____	0	1	2	6. _____	0	1	2

Story # 1 (b)

You go to a library to borrow a book. It took you a long time to find a interesting book. You found it but you forgot your library card. Therefore, you have to leave the book and go to get your card. When you go back to get the book, you find an another student is reading it .

What would you think or feel?	**What would you do?**
_____	_____
_____	_____
_____	_____
_____	_____
_____	_____

Story # 2.

During a break time, a student group comes into the canteen for a drink and one of the students unintentionally spits on your foot (or your body). You ask the student to apologise, but the student refuses to do so.

What would you think or feel?   **What would you do?**

I would think or feel   **I would**

1. The student's behaviour may be a
   casual reaction; it is not intentional   0 1 2

2. The student is rude or disrespectful   0 1 2

3. About how to keep the problem under self-control "Eg. If I aggravate
   the situation, fighting may occur."
                                                       0 1 2

4. Insulted or upset/angry   0 1 2

5. Frightened and anxious   0 1 2

6. _____   0 1 2

1. Ignore the student's behaviour and
   attitude   0 1 2

2. Blame the student   0 1 2

3. Clean myself if necessary, then concentrate on other activities   0 1 2

4. Hit the student or throw a tantrum   0 1 2

5. Leave or avoid the person   0 1 2

6. _____   0 1 2

Story # 4

Your friend suddenly stops an intimate relationship with you without any explanation. He/she has also made fun of you, or made unfriendly comments about you, and avoided you if possible.

What would you think or feel?   **What would you do?**

I would think or feel   **I would**

1. My friend may have personal reasons or the mistakes are "reasona-
   ble"   0 1 2

2. My friend is not good or is shallow
                                                       0 1 2

3. About why my friend acts like that
   or about the underlying causes of
   the misunderstanding   0 1 2

4. Insulted and/or upset   0 1 2

5. The friendship is over   0 1 2

6. _____   0 1 2

1. Tolerate or ignore my friend's atti-
   tude   0 1 2

2. Demand the friend explains the rea-
   son   0 1 2

3. Find a chance to meet to identify the
   problem and discuss it with my
   friend   0 1 2

4. Violently criticize or blame my
   friend   0 1 2

5. Cut off any relationship with my
   friend without asking him/her what
   the problem was   0 1 2

6. _____   0 1 2

Story # 3.

On the occasion of your birthday, your friend of the opposite sex gives you a bunch of roses and a valuable present, implying "I like you...I love you". However, you want to maintain a friendship only.

What would you think or feel?				**What would you do?**			
I would think or feel				**I would**			
1. He/she is a good friend, but a love-affair can influence study in a bad way	0 1 2			1. Take the flowers and gift, keep silent, then say "Sorry! I can't..." and return the gift after the birth day	0 1 2		
2. The friend is insensitive or is childish	0 1 2			2. Refuse the roses and the gift and show a cold-greeting attitude	0 1 2		
3. About how to help my friend understand that this relationship is a friendship only, but I must speak politely, not rudely	0 1 2			3. Take the roses but politely return the gift and act in a way that shows I regard the person as equal to other friends	0 1 2		
4. Feel insulted or upset	0 1 2			4. Make fun of the person or tease him/her	0 1 2		
5. Frightened or troubled	0 1 2			5. Avoid the person all the time if possible	0 1 2		
6. _____	0 1 2			6. _____	0 1 2		

Story # 3 (b)

Break time is over and you come into your class. You find a letter in your notebook and the contents of the letter reveal that the author likes you... and loves you. However, you think you are too young to fall in love with the person, though you know the person is a good friend. However, you only want to spend time on your studies at this moment.

What would you think or feel?	**What would you do?**
_____	_____
_____	_____
_____	_____
_____	_____
_____	_____

Story # 5

You hardly ever watch TV, but while you are watching one of your favourite TV programme, one of your parents starts to nag you a lot to clean up your room. Finally, your parent comes in and turns the TV off.

What would you think or feel?	**What would you do?**

I would think or feel					**I would**			
1. My parent is right or reasonable	0	1	2	1. Clean up my room	0	1	2
2. My parent is strict	0	1	2	2. Clean in a reluctant manner	0	1	2
3. About why my parents are behaving like they are and what can change them	0	1	2	3. Suggest to my parents that I could see the TV show and clean after the show or clean first, then continue watching	0	1	2
4. Feel upset or angry	0	1	2	4. Throw a tantrum	0	1	2
5. It is unfair because the cleaning can be done after the TV show	0	1	2	5. Go to my room and close the door without cleaning the room	0	1	2
6. _____	0	1	2	6. _____	0	1	2

Story # 5 (b)

You like dressing well and you like a fashionable way of dressing. However, your parents don't like the way you dress and always nag you about it.

What would you think or feel?	**What would you do?**
_____	_____
_____	_____
_____	_____
_____	_____
_____	_____
_____	_____

Story # 6.

You are studying for your examination (which happens next week), when your best friend comes to ask you to go out to a good film. Your friend met you at school the day before and offered you a ticket for a good new film, and you agreed as you feel well prepared for the exam and you need a bit of relaxation. When you ask your parents' permission to go, your parents refuse and nag you.

What would you think or feel? I would think or feel				What would you do? I would			
1. Parents are right or reasonable	0	1	2	1. Say sorry and explain to my friend that my parents do not agree	0	1	2
2. Parents are too strict or unsympathetic	0	1	2	2. Pretend to obey my parents, then find a false reason to go	0	1	2
3. About why my parents don't agree and how to persuade my parents to my point of view	0	1	2	3. Discuss with my parents that I am well-prepared and need a bit of relaxation. If still not allowed, apologize to my friend and forget about it	0	1	2
4. Upset or angry	0	1	2	4. Throw a tantrum	0	1	2
5. Unhappy, but think that I can't change anything	0	1	2	5. Return the ticket, then go to my room without talking to parents	0	1	2
6. _____	0	1	2	6. _____	0	1	2

Story # 8

Your teacher accuses you of writing swear words on the toilet wall, and is threatening to put you down to a lower class. You know you didn't do it but that your close friend did.

What would you think or feel? I would think or feel				What would you do? I would			
1. The teacher's anger is reasonable and understandable	0	1	2	1. Show evidence that I am innocent	0	1	2
2. The teacher is silly or unreasonable	0	1	2	2. Say I didn't do this and that my friend did it	0	1	2
3. About how to control the situation, or think of repairing the damage rather than tracking down the culprit	0	1	2	3. Say I didn't do it, but instead of finding the culprit, discuss how to clean the wall without a fuss	0	1	2
4. I am accused unfairly or feel upset	0	1	2	4. Talk angrily to the teacher	0	1	2
5. It is too difficult for me to solve the issue	0	1	2	5. Avoid argument and suffer the punishment if it occurs	0	1	2
6. _____	0	1	2	6. _____	0	1	2

Story # 7

When you wash your Dad's clothes, you suddenly find a letter from a strange woman in his pocket. Out of curiosity, you read it. You find this letter is a declaration of her love for your Dad. You realise that it may threaten your peaceful family.

What would you think or feel?	**What would you do?**
I would think or feel	**I would**

	I would think or feel						I would			
1.	Dad must stop the unacceptable relationship	0	1	2		1.	Talk to Dad, and ask him to cut off the relationship	0	1	2
2.	Mum is betrayed	0	1	2		2.	Tell Mum about the letter	0	1	2
3.	About why Dad acts like he is and how to resolve the problem soon	0	1	2		3.	Calm down, investigate/discuss the problem with Dad or find help from someone understanding and closely related to Dad if necessary	0	1	2
4.	Upset that the woman is possibly the cause of breaking my family	0	1	2		4.	Warn or threaten revenge on the woman	0	1	2
5.	Depressed that my father is not acting like my Dad	0	1	2		5.	Ignore the issue or avoid Dad	0	1	2
6.	_____	0	1	2		6.	_____	0	1	2

Story # 7 (b)

Your mum and dad have conflicts and one evening after a fight, your Dad left and moved out of home. After one week investigating, you find the flat your Dad is living in and you decide to go there. When you arrive you saw a young woman caring for your Dad.

What would you think or feel?	**What would you do?**
_____	_____
_____	_____
_____	_____
_____	_____
_____	_____
_____	_____

Story # 9

In the classroom, your teacher is writing on the blackboard. There is swearing and laughing behind him/her. The teacher suddenly turns around and sees you talking. The teacher becomes angry and says:

T: What are you doing? Why are you laughing?

You: Nothing! It was not me!

T   (more irritable): So! Who laughed?

You: I don't know.

T: If you don't know, you get out of my class.

You: No man! It was not my fault! Why do I have to get out?

T: If you don't, I will get you out!

The atmosphere becomes very tense.

(A) What would you think and do if you were the student?

I would think or feel				I would		
1. The teacher's reaction may be understandable	0 1 2		1. Leave with an irritable attitude	0 1 2
2. The teacher is ridiculous	0 1 2		2. Refuse to go out	0 1 2
3. The matter may disrupt the lesson or disturb other students	0 1 2		3. Get out quietly and talk to the teacher after class or meet the principal to solve the problem	0 1 2
4. Upset or angry	0 1 2		4. Talk angrily to the teacher or throw a tantrum	0 1 2
5. It is a good reason to leave the classroom as well as school	0 1 2		5. Get out and leave school	0 1 2
6. _____	0 1 2		6. _____	0 1 2

(B) What would you think and do if you were the monitor of this class?

      I would think   **I would do**

_____   _____

_____   _____

_____   _____

_____   _____

_____   _____

Story # 10

You are lying down on your bed with a headache and the boy next door is playing his radio loudly, and it makes your head feel worse.

What would you think or feel?		**What would you do?**	
I would think or feel		**I would**	
1. He is very keen on the music	0 1 2	1. Ask the boy to stop or play the radio softly	0 1 2
2. He is a bad boy	0 1 2	2. Tell his parents	0 1 2
3. If the boy knew my problem he may stop or think about how to prevent the noise that upsets me	0 1 2	3. Say "Sorry, I am sick. Please turn the radio off or play it softly," or choose alternatives such as closing the door or moving to a quieter place	0 1 2
4. Upset at being irritated	0 1 2	4. Violently force him to turn the radio off	0 1 2
5. Nothing can change in any way	0 1 2	5. Try to put up with the noise	0 1 2
6. _____	0 1 2	6. _____	0 1 2

If you ask the boy to turn the radio down or off, but he ignores you,

What would you think or feel?	**What would you do?**
_____	_____
_____	_____
_____	_____
_____	_____
_____	_____
_____	_____

Story # 11.

You are walking on a quiet road when suddenly you see a "thief" intending to snatch a handbag from a person walking in front of you. You look around but no one else is there.

What would you think or feel?				**What would you do?**			
I would think or feel				**I would**			
1. The person may not know the threat coming	0	1	2	1. Walk quickly to the person to warn him/her of the danger	0	1	2
2. I don't care what might happen to the person	0	1	2	2. Ignore what is going on	0	1	2
3. About how to help, but safeguard yourself (ie. how to warn the person of the risk without alarming the thief)	0	1	2	3. Do something to warn the person of the danger such as pretending accidentally to run into the thief or to become acquainted with the person	0	1	2
4. Of getting help from the police	0	1	2	4. Run quickly to warn the police	0	1	2
5. Frightened or worried	0	1	2	5. Run away or quickly leave the unsafe place	0	1	2
6. _____	0	1	2	6. _____	0	1	2

Story # 11 (b)

A group of adolescents make friends with you. You agree to be involved in their activities because you think they are good friends. However, as time passes, you gradually find that they will not be good friends and they intend to involve you in possible illegal action.

What would you think or feel?	**What would you do?**
_____	_____
_____	_____
_____	_____
_____	_____
_____	_____

Story # 12.

You are playing a game (e.g., football or tennis) in a team, when a person in the opposite team collides with you and suddenly falls down. Although the person is in the wrong, you pick him/her up and say "Are you OK?". Responding to your polite help, the person uses bad language and insults you.

What would you think or feel?	**What would you do?**
I would think or feel	**I would**

1. Due to being hurt the person has lost control and his/her temper	0 1 2	
2. The person is wrong and/or impolite	0 1 2	
3. About how to help if the person is hurt and/or how to reorganise the matter to continue the game if the person is not seriously hurt	0 1 2	
4. Insulted and/or upset	0 1 2	
5. Frightened or worried	0 1 2	
6. _____	0 1 2	

1. Ignore the bad language	0 1 2	
2. Blame or argue with the person and say that he/she is wrong	0 1 2	
3. Call medical help if the person is badly hurt, or shake his/her hands as a gesture that there is "no problem" and continue playing	0 1 2	
4. Hit the person or throw a tantrum	0 1 2	
5. Avoid playing near the person or leave the game	0 1 2	
6. _____	0 1 2	

APPENDIX C. Form B of the SPST

SOCIAL PROBLEM SOLVING TEST   (SPST)

Name: ....…........ Age: ...….... Gender (circle): M   F   Id. No: ....
Grade: ....   School: ………………………………….   Date......./..../......

Instructions

Below are short stories about **social problem situations**. Please read each story carefully
and for each statement, choose (circle) **one** of the numbers (0 1 2) that best shows to what
extent the response is true of you, when responding to the following questions:

What would you think (or feel) and do?

$$0 \;=\; \textbf{Not at all}$$
$$1 \;=\; \textbf{Sometimes}$$
$$2 \;=\; \textbf{Usually}$$

For example: During break time some students come up to you in the playground, teasing
you and calling you stupid and dumb. **What would you think or feel and what would you
actually do?**

I would				**I would**		
1. Think they are bad people	0	1	2	1. Avoid playing with them	0	1 2
2. Feel frightened	⓪	1	2	2. Tolerate their behaviour	0	1 2
3. Think about why they are behaving like they are	0	1	2	3. Ask them to stop behaving like they are	0	1 2
4. Feel insulted or upset	0	1	2	4. Hit them or throw a tantrum	⓪	1 2
5. Other (describe)** _Eg. Feel unhappy_	0	1	2	5. Other reaction (describe)** _Eg. Stay in classroom during breaktime_	0	1 2

Story (b):

You are playing in the playground when two students who are chasing each other run into
you and fall down. When they stand up, they yell bad words at you.

What would you think or feel?	**What would you do?**
Eg. I would think these students have lost their temper due to being hurt	_Eg. I would leave without saying anything_
Eg. I would think their behaviour is not intentional	_Eg. I would ignore their bad language_
Eg. They are rude	Eg. I would pick a quarrel with them

** These free-response items are other feelings or solutions that are beyond the given solutions. The subject can
describe them

Here are the stories:

Story # 1.

You are looking forward to watching your favourite television programme. When you go into the room to watch it you find another student has turned on a show you don't like.

What would you think or feel?				**What would you do?**			
I would think or feel				**I would**			

1. He/she is fond of this show	0 1 2			1. Find other place to watch TV	0 1 2		
2. It is unfair	0 1 2			2. Tell the person to turn on the show I like	0 1 2		
3. Unlucky, but I think the issue is solvable (Eg. I can ask for my turn or I can discuss other solutions with the student)	0 1 2			3. Ask the student how long he/she will be, then decide whether to wait/ leave or watch the show with him/her	0 1 2		
4. Upset or angry	0 1 2			4. Annoy the student in some way in order to drive him/her away	0 1 2		
5. Nothing can change the situation	0 1 2			5. Leave the room and do not watchingTV	0 1 2		
6. Other (describe)_____	0 1 2			6. _____	0 1 2		

Story # 3.

On the occasion of your birthday, your friend of the opposite sex gives you a bunch of roses and a valuable present, implying "I like you...I love you". However, you want to maintain a friendship only.

What would you think or feel?				**What would you do?**			
I would think or feel				**I would**			

1. He/she is a good friend, but a love-affair can influence study in a bad way	0 1 2			1. Take the flowers and gift, keep silent, then say "Sorry! I can't..." and return the gift after the birth day	0 1 2		
2. The friend is insensitive or is child-ish	0 1 2			2. Refuse the roses and the gift and show a cold-greeting attitude	0 1 2		
3. About how to help my friend understand that this relationship is a friendship only, but I must speak politely, not rudely	0 1 2			3. Take the roses but politely return the gift and act in a way that shows I regard the person as equal to other friends	0 1 2		
4. Feel insulted or upset	0 1 2			4. Make fun of the person or tease him/her	0 1 2		
5. Frightened or troubled	0 1 2			5. Avoid the person all the time ifpossible	0 1 2		
6. _____	0 1 2			6. _____	0 1 2		

Story # 2.

During a break time, a student group comes into the canteen for a drink and one of the students unintentionally spits on your foot (or your body). You ask the student to apologise, but the student refuses to do so.

What would you think or feel?	**What would you do?**

I would think or feel		**I would**	
1. The student's behaviour may be a casual reaction; it is not intentional	0 1 2	1. Ignore the student's behaviour and attitude	0 1 2
2. The student is rude or disrespectful	0 1 2	2. Blame the student	0 1 2
3. About how to keep the problem under self-control "Eg. if I aggravate the situation, fighting may occur."	0 1 2	3. Clean myself if necessary, then concentrate on other activities	0 1 2
4. Insulted or upset/angry	0 1 2	4. Hit the student or throw a tantrum	0 1 2
5. Frightened and anxious	0 1 2	5. Leave or avoid the person	0 1 2
6. _____	0 1 2	6. _____	0 1 2

Story # 2 (b)

When you go to a restaurant or a public place where a lot of people come and go, you find a younger group of people coming to your place to talk. You notice their behaviour is impolite and you don't want to talk to them. Therefore, you stand up and move to another place, but one of these youngsters stands up, tries to prevent you going and acts in a provoking way.

What would you think or feel?	**What would you do?**
_____	_____
_____	_____
_____	_____
_____	_____
_____	_____
_____	_____

Story # 4

Your friend suddenly stops an intimate relationship with you without any explanation. He/she has also made fun of you, or made unfriendly comments about you, and avoided you if possible.

What would you think or feel?	**What would you do?**
I would think or feel	**I would**

#	I would think or feel				#	I would			
1.	My friend may have personal reasons or the mistakes are "reasonable"	0	1	2	1.	Tolerate or ignore my friend's attitude	0	1	2
2.	My friend is not good or is shallow	0	1	2	2.	Demand the friend explains the reason	0	1	2
3.	About why my friend acts like that or about the underlying causes of the mis-understanding	0	1	2	3.	Find a chance to meet to identify the problem and discuss it with my friend	0	1	2
4.	Insulted and/or upset	0	1	2	4.	Violently criticize or blame my friend	0	1	2
5.	The friendship is over	0	1	2	5.	Cut off any relationship with my friend without asking him/her what the problem was	0	1	2
6.	_____	0	1	2	6.	_____	0	1	2

Story # 4 (b)

You have a close friend (A) of the opposite sex. Since you want to expand your friendship, you help A make friends with B, a close, same-sexed friend. As time passes, you feel A and B become more intimate and leave you out. They usually avoid you, and are even unpleasant when you are present. You hear their unfriendly comments about you.

What would you think or feel?	**What would you do?**
_____	_____
_____	_____
_____	_____
_____	_____
_____	_____
_____	_____

Story # 5

You hardly ever watch TV, but while you are watching one of your favourite TV programme, one of your parents starts to nag you a lot to clean up your room. Finally, your parent comes in and turns the TV off.

What would you think or feel?				**What would you do?**			
I would think or feel				**I would**			
1. My parent is right or reasonable	0 1 2			1. Clean up my room	0 1 2		
2. My parent is strict	0 1 2			2. Clean in a reluctant manner	0 1 2		
3. About why my parents are behaving like they are and what can change them	0 1 2			3. Suggest to parents that I could see the TV show and clean after the show or clean first, then continue watching	0 1 2		
4. Feel upset or angry	0 1 2			4. Throw a tantrum	0 1 2		
5. It is unfair because the cleaning can be done after the TV show	0 1 2			5. Go to my room and close the door without cleaning the room	0 1 2		
6. _____	0 1 2			6. _____	0 1 2		

Story # 7

When you wash your Dad's clothes, you suddenly find a letter from a strange woman in his pocket. Out of curiosity, you read it. You find this letter is a declaration of her love for your Dad. You realise that it may threaten your peaceful family.

What would you think or feel?				**What would you do?**			
I would think or feel				**I would**			
1. Dad must stop the unacceptable relationship	0 1 2			1. Talk to Dad, and ask him to cut off the relationship	0 1 2		
2. Mum is betrayed	0 1 2			2. Tell Mum about the letter	0 1 2		
3. About why Dad acts like he is and how to resolve the problem soon	0 1 2			3. Calm down, investigate/discuss the problem with Dad or find help from someone understanding and closely related to Dad if necessary	0 1 2		
4. Upset that the woman is possibly the cause of breaking my family	0 1 2			4. Warn or threaten revenge on the woman	0 1 2		
5. Depressed that my father is not acting like my Dad	0 1 2			5. Ignore the issue or avoid Dad	0 1 2		
6. _____	0 1 2			6. _____	0 1 2		

Story # 6.

You are studying for your examination (which happens next week), when your best friend comes to ask you to go out to a good film. Your friend met you at school the day before and offered you a ticket for a good new film, and you agreed as you feel well prepared for the exam and you need a bit of relaxation. When you ask your parents' permission to go, your parents refuse and nag you.

What would you think or feel?					**What would you do?**			
I would think or feel					**I would**			
1. Parents are right or reasonable	0	1	2	1.	Say sorry and explain to my friend that my parents do not agree	0	1	2
2. Parents are too strict or unsympathetic	0	1	2	2.	Pretend to obey my parents, then find a false reason to go	0	1	2
3. About why my parents don't agree and how to persuade my parents to my point of view	0	1	2	3.	Discuss with my parents that I am well-prepared and need a bit of relaxation. If still not allowed, apologize to my friend and forget about it	0	1	2
4. Upset or angry	0	1	2	4.	Throw a tantrum	0	1	2
5. Unhappy, but think that I can't change anything	0	1	2	5.	Return the ticket, then go to my room without talking to parents	0	1	2
6. _____	0	1	2	6.	_____	0	1	2

Story # 6 (b)

You have some friends of the opposite sex and you know they are good friends . However, your parents don't like you having friendships with people of a different sex. One day when your parents go out, one of these friends comes to see you. When your parents come home, they are irritable and ask your friend to leave the house.

What would you think or feel?	**What would you do?**
_____	_____
_____	_____
_____	_____
_____	_____
_____	_____

Story # 8

Your teacher accuses you of writing swear words on the toilet wall, and is threatening to put you down to a lower class. You know you didn't do it but that your close friend did.

What would you think or feel?		**What would you do?**	
I would think or feel		**I would**	

1. The teacher's anger is reasonable and understandable	0 1 2	
2. The teacher is silly or unreasonable	0 1 2	
3. About how to control the situation, or think of repairing the damage rather than tracking down the culprit	0 1 2	
4. I am accused unfairly or feel upset	0 1 2	
5. It is too difficult for me to solve the issue	0 1 2	
6. _____	0 1 2	

1. Show evidence that I am innocent	0 1 2
2. Say I didn't do this and that my friend did it	0 1 2
3. Say I didn't do it, but instead of finding the culprit, discuss how to clean the wall without a fuss	0 1 2
4. Talk angrily to the teacher	0 1 2
5. Avoid argument and suffer the punishment if it occurs	0 1 2
6. _____	0 1 2

Story # 8 (b)

One of your friends complains that he/she has a problem with his/her teacher. The teacher doesn't like him/her and the teacher is unfair to him/her. Hence, he/she feels depressed and intends suiciding.

What would you think or feel?	**What would you do?**
_____	_____
_____	_____
_____	_____
_____	_____
_____	_____
_____	_____

Story # 9

In the classroom, your teacher is writing on the blackboard. There is swearing and laughing behind him/her. The teacher suddenly turns around and sees you talking. The teacher becomes angry and says:

T: What are you doing? Why are you laughing?

You: Nothing! It was not me!

T   (more irritable): So! Who laughed?

You: I don't know.

T: If you don't know, you get out of my class.

You: No man! It was not my fault! Why do I have to get out?

T: If you don't, I will get you out!

The atmosphere becomes very tense.

(A) What would you think and do if you were the student?

I would think or feel		I would	
1. The teacher's reaction may be understandable	0 1 2	1. Leave with an irritable attitude	0 1 2
2. The teacher is ridiculous	0 1 2	2. Refuse to go out	0 1 2
3. The matter may disrupt the lesson or disturb other students	0 1 2	3. Get out quietly and talk to the teacher after class or meet the principal to solve the problem	0 1 2
4. Upset or angry	0 1 2	4. Talk angrily to the teacher or throw a tantrum	0 1 2
5. It is a good reason to leave the classroom as well as school	0 1 2	5. Get out and leave school	0 1 2
6. _____	0 1 2	6. _____	0 1 2

Story # 10

You are lying down on your bed with a headache and the boy next door is playing his radio loudly, and it makes your head feel worse.

What would you think or feel?				What would you do?			
I would think or feel				**I would**			
1. He is very keen on the music	0	1	2	1. Ask the boy to stop or play the radio softly	0	1	2
2. He is a bad boy	0	1	2	2. Tell his parents	0	1	2
3. If the boy knew my problem he may stop or think about how to prevent the noise that upsets me	0	1	2	3. Say "Sorry, I am sick. Please turn the radio off or play it softly," or choose alternatives such as closing the door or moving to a quieter place	0	1	2
4. Upset at being irritated	0	1	2	4. Violently force him to turn the radio off	0	1	2
5. Nothing can change in any way	0	1	2	5. Try to put up with the noise	0	1	2
6. _____	0	1	2	6. _____	0	1	2

If you ask the boy to turn the radio down or off, but he ignores you,

What would you think or feel?	What would you do?
_____	_____
_____	_____
_____	_____
_____	_____

Story # 10 (b)

While you are studying, some children from next-door neighbouring families are playing and chasing each other outside. This makes a lot of noise and therefore disturbs you.

What would you think or feel?	What would you do?
_____	_____
_____	_____
_____	_____
_____	_____

Story # 11.

You are walking on a quiet road when suddenly you see a "thief" intending to snatch a handbag from a person walking in front of you. You look around but no one else is there.

What would you think or feel?				**What would you do?**			
I would think or feel				**I would**			

#	I would think or feel				#	I would			
1.	The person may not know the threat coming	0	1	2	1.	Walk quickly to the person to warn him/her of the danger	0	1	2
2.	I don't care what might happen to the person	0	1	2	2.	Ignore what is going on	0	1	2
3.	About how to help, but safeguard yourself (ie. how to warn the person of the risk without alarming the thief)	0	1	2	3.	Do something to warn the person of the danger such as pretending accidentally to run into the thief or to become acquainted with the person	0	1	2
4.	Of getting help from the police	0	1	2	4.	Run quickly to warn the police	0	1	2
5.	Frightened or worried	0	1	2	5.	Run away or quickly leave the unsafe place	0	1	2
6.	_____	0	1	2	6.	_____	0	1	2

Story # 12.

You are playing a game (eg., football or tennis) in a team, when a person in the opposite team collides with you and suddenly falls down. Although the person is in the wrong, you pick him/her up and say "Are you OK?". Responding to your polite help, the person uses bad language and insults you.

What would you think or feel?	**What would you do?**

I would think or feel	**I would**

1. Due to being hurt the person has lost control and his/her temper	0 1 2	1. Ignore the bad language	0 1 2
2. The person is wrong and/or impolite	0 1 2	2. Blame or argue with the person and say that he/she is wrong	0 1 2
3. About how to help if the person is hurt and/or how to reorganise the matter to continue the game if the person is not seriously hurt	0 1 2	3. Call medical help if the person is badly hurt, or shake his/her hands as a gesture that there is "no problem" and continue playing	0 1 2
4. Insulted and/or upset	0 1 2	4. Hit the person or throw a tantrum	0 1 2
5. Frightened or worried	0 1 2	5. Avoid playing near the person or leave the game	0 1 2
6. _____	0 1 2	6. _____	0 1 2

Story # 12 (b)

While you are riding on your bicycle, a youth riding in the opposite direction suddenly runs into you. Although you are both hurt and the youth was at fault, you say "Sorry!". Responding to your polite attitude, the youth becomes angry and insults you.

What would you think or feel?	**What would you do?**
_____	_____
_____	_____
_____	_____
_____	_____
_____	_____
_____	_____

APPENDIX D.

Rater's manual for the response coding of the SPST-B

A MANUAL FOR THE CODING OF THE SPST-b

(Stories-b)

This is a description of the *coding* of responses that is used for scoring the Stories-b (SPST-b). Each item (problematic situation) of the SPST-b is scored at two levels: *problem affect-cognitions* ("I would think and/or feel") and *problem-soving actions* ("I would do").

Problem affect-cognitions	**Problem-solving actions**
0 POINT - This level involves emotional arousal, insulted feelings, impulsive, or distorted cognitions.	0 POINT- This level involves the application of avoidance, impulsive, or irrational negative strategies to resolve problems.
1 POINT - This level refers to positive beliefs/ expectations/ thinkings such as: admitting a problem exists, viewing it as a challenge and perceiving a problem from an "empathic" or "forgivable/ tolerable" perspectives.	1 POINT - This level refers to "acceptable" positive solutions which involve emotion-focused coping strategies or tolerating a problem rather than resolving it thoroughly through evaluation of consequences and alternatives.
2 POINT - This reflects rational positive beliefs/ expectations/cognitions such as: understanding why a problem occurs like it is, recognizing self-responsibility to resolve it as soon as possible, and how to keep it under self-control.	2 POINT - This level refers to effective, deliberate, adaptive and rational positive strategies to resolve a problem soon and as well as possible.

Here are examples of specific response codings for each story in Stories-b (SPST-b):

Story # 1 (b)

You go to a library to borrow a book. It took you a long time to find an interesting book. You found it but you forgot your library card. Hence, you have to leave the book and go to get your card. When you go back to get the book, you find an another student is reading it.

What would you think or feel?	What would you do?
I would think and feel?	I would do?

0 --- Subject feels upset, thinks it is unfair. For example: "This book is mine…"; "I found the book first…"

1 --- Subject feels depressed, but thinks it is his/her fault. Examples: "If I didn't forget the card, I could borrow the book." or "If I told the library personell to keep the book for me…it was my fault."

2 --- Subject feels unlucky, thinks "The student likes/needs the book as much as me and he/she is lucky…but I think I can ask if the library has other copies…"

0 --- Subject gives up, goes home, or argues with the student about his/her *right* to borrow. Examples: "I'd go home." or "I need the book, I found it before you came…"

1 --- Subject leaves it for another time, or finds other books as alternatives. Examples: "I'd wait for my turn or leave for a next time to come to get it." or "I'd look for other books as alternatives."

2 --- Subject asks the student for the time/need involved in having the book or attempt to persuade nicely that "The book is important for my exam study…" or "I would go to the personell to ask for another copy before chosing other solutions."

Story # 2 (b)

When you go to a restaurant or a public place where a lot of people come and go, you find a younger group of people coming to your place to talk. You notice their behaviour is impolite and you don't want to talk to them. Hence, you stand up and move to another place, but one of these youngsters stands up, tries to prevent you going and acts in a provoking way.

What would you think or feel?	What would you do?
I would think and feel?	I would do?

0 --- Subject feels upset/nervous, thinks: "They are bad people and are trying to tease me…" or "They are impolite and rude…they need to have a lesson in politeness …"

1 --- Subject thinks that the people are young teens, and not conscious of their behaviour. Example: "They are too

0 --- Subject irritatively warns/threatens them or uses physical force or avoids them. Examples: "I'd curse/insult or attack them if I can" or "I'd quickly avoid the rude/ impolite people."

1 --- Subject ignores the uncultured attitude and leaves the place without speaking to them. Example: "I'd ignore their behaviour and walk away and not say anything to them."

young to have pro-social comunication skills."

2 --- Subject thinks of the reason underlying their behaviour or how to resolve the problem peacefully. Examples: "why do the people act like they are ? ...it is true if they have poor social skills." or "If they want to make a friend of me they should be polite."

2 --- Subject calmy/politely asks the people what they want and whether they can behave politely as friends. Examples: "What do you want?." or "Would you please behave politely if you want to talk to me or make a friend of me ?."

Story # 3 (b)

Break time is over and you come into your class. You find a letter in your note book and the contents of the letter reveal that the author likes you ...and loves you. However, you think you are too young to fall in love with the person, though you know the person is a good friend. However, you only want to spend time on your studies at this moment.

What would you think or feel?	**What would you do?**
I would think and feel?	**I would do?**

0 --- Subject feels upset or insulted. Examples: "The person is insensitive or childish." or "The person makes me embarrassed/ troubled."

2 --- Subject thinks the person has fallen in love with him/her and is too young to have a love-affair while in schooling. Examples: "I feel pleasant that someone loves me, but it is too young/dangerous at school age." or "A love-affair can influence my study."

3 --- Subject thinks that "The friendship is important and useful if it is preserved as a kind/pure friendship in school." and that "If I explain about the pros and cons of schooling and a love-fair my friend may agree to keeping it as a pure friendship while in schooling."

0 --- Subject pretends he/she doesn't know or keeps/remains silent or attempts to avoid the person if possible. Examples: "I'd better maintain a silent attitude." or "I'd avoid or stop having comunication with the person."

1 --- Subject overtly shows an unacceptable attitude that the love-affair disrupts the study and does not care about the possible consequences of his/her attitude. Example: "I'd express my opinion that a love-fair is unacceptable while in schooling."

2 --- Subject looks for a good chance to meet and explain/persuade and behave kindly/ politely, but keep a pure friendship. Example: "We'd stay at the level of a pure friendship while at school, but say to the friend that it may be a good basis for faithful love in the future."

Story # 4 (b)

You have a close friend (A) of the opposite sex. Since you want to expand your friendship you help A make friends with B, a close, same-sexed friend. As time passes, you feel A and B become more intimate and leave you out. They usually avoid you, and are even indirectly unpleasant when you are present. You hear their unfriendly comments about you.

What would you think or feel?	**What would you do?**
I would think and feel?	**I would do?**

0 --- Subject feels depressed or upset at being dropped, thinks that A is not a good friend. Examples: "A is not good friend as A betrays my kindness." or "I am betrayed and dropped or left out."

1 --- Subject feels sad, but thinks that it is a personal feeling or it is not reasonable to

0 --- Subject acts in a hostile way against A or makes an unfriendly comment about A or cuts any relationship with A without checking if the rumour is true. Example: "I'd consider A as not my friend."

1 --- Subject ignores unfriendly comment and behaves towards A as with other friends or as before, or patiently waits for a time

blame A and B, but their unfriendly comments are not good. Examples: "They are matched and my presence appears to be inconvenient for them." or "Friendship is something private/ personal, yet A should not stab me in the back."

2 --- Subject thinks of why A acts like he/she is, if there is a misunderstanding or certain reasons behind the problem. Examples: "A may have certain reasons to act like that…" or "If there is a misunderstanding between A and me."

when things will change. Examples: "I'd still behave kindly toward A and wait for a time to make A think again." or "I don't care about the negative attitude of A."

2 --- Subject detects the true reason causing the problem or looks for a good chance to meet and ask A for a clear explaination. Examples: "I'd meet A to ask for a clear explaination of this matter." or "I'd tell A that I respect the friendship between A and B…and ask them if the unfriendly comments are true?"

Story # 5 (b)

You like dressing well and you like a fashionable way of dressing. However, your parents don't like the way you dress and always nag you about it.

What would you think or feel?

I would think and feel?

0 --- Subject feels upset, thinks parents are too old to understand a youth's needs. Examples: "My friends dress the same way, but their parents don't object." or "Parents are too old to see its beauty."

1--- Subject feels sad since parents don't understand a youth's needs, but doesn't want to upset them. Examples: "These clothes are suitable for me, but not for my parents." or "The dress is colourful and fashionable, thus my parents don't like it."

2--- Subject thinks that parents have personal reasons to object and that is why they don't like it, or thinks about how he/she can explain feelings to parents. Examples: "Is it true that the dress is not good or not suitable for me?" or "If the dress is good/beautiful/suitable, how can I explain my feelings or persuade parents to change their minds."

What would you do?

I would do?

0 ---Subject ignores or objects to the parent's attitudes and acts as he/she likes. Examples: "I still wear what I like." or "I'd nag or get angry with my parents."

1 ---Subject gives up what his/her parents don't like or only wears it when parents are absent. Examples: "I obey my parents and don't wear those dresses." or "I only wear it in suitable places such as at parties or dances."

2 ---Subject asks parents the reason for the aversion and finds a good chance to explain. If parents still keep their ideas and object, the subject accepts, and looks for another chance to convince. Examples: "I ask my parents why they don't like those clothes and why they are not suitable." or "I assess if the clothes are well matched for me. If so, I attempt to convince my parents, or ask another adult to persuade my parents."

Story # 6 (b)

You have some friends of the opposite sex to you and you know they are good friends. However, your parents don't like you to have friendships with people of the opposite sex. One day when your parents go out, one of these friends comes to see you. When your parents come home, they are irritable and ask your friend leave the house.

What would you think or feel?	**What would you do?**
I would think and feel?	**I would do?**

0 --- Subject feels upset/depressed/ashamed or insulted, thinks parents are rude or too strict. Examples: "My parents don't have respect for my friends." or "Parents are too strict or unsympathetic or rude."

1 --- Subject thinks that parents want me to concentrate on study, but they don't understand my psychological needs. Examples: "Parents did so because they were worried about my study." or "As parents only want me focusing on study…"

2 --- Subject thinks parents do not understand him/her and the friend or they have personal reasons not to trust the friendship. Examples: "Why did parents behave as uncultured people." or "What have I done, so that my parent don't trust me."

0 --- Subject shows negative attitude or objection. Examples: "I'd keep a cold/ unfeeling or negative attitude towards parents." or "I'd threaten to leave home, if parents do it again."

1 --- Subject apologises to parents and tells the friend not to come to his/her house as parents don't like it. Examples: "I'd meet my friend to say sorry and ask the friend not to come." or "As my parents don't like you to come, we should meet at school or other places."

2 --- Subject attempts to explain to parents, so that they understand and respect the friendship and apologise to the friends. Examples: "I'd meet my friend to apologise to him/her for my parents' behaviour and explain to my parents"

Story # 7 (b)

When you wash your Dad's clothes, you suddenly find a letter from a strange woman in his pocket. Out of curiosity, you read it. You find this letter is a declaration of her love for your Dad. You realise that it appears to threaten your peaceful family.

What would you think or feel?	**What would you do?**
I would think and feel?	**I would do?**

0 --- Subject feels depressed, thinks Mum is betrayed by Dad. Examples: "Dad is a bad man, he is hard-hearted to leave the family for another woman." or "I hate Dad and love Mum much more as she is betrayed by Dad."

1 --- Subject thinks Dad is depressed/

0 --- Subject has negative attitude or threatening behaviour or avoids Dad/the woman or goes home to tell Mun the truth and asks Mum to divoce Dad. Examples: "I'd do something to warn/threaten the woman" or "I'd ask Mum to part with Dad"

disappointed about the family or Dad is attracted/seduced by the woman. Examples: "Constant family conflicts made Dad tired/depressed." or "The young woman seduced Dad."

2 --- Subject thinks that a peaceful/happy family is threatened or what caused the problem and whether I can help Dad understand and return to Mum. Examples: "Why would Dad leave Mum/family for a woman." or "Whether Mum and Dad no longer love each other or how to persuade Dad to leave the woman for the family."

1 --- Subject meets Dad and asks him to immediately leave the woman for the family. Example: "I'd meet Dad to ask him to leave the woman for Mum/family immediately."

2 --- Subject calmly enters and discusses with Dad the consequences involving the matter or quietly goes home, then investigates the relationship and talks with the woman or finds help from someone understanding/ closely related to Dad. Examples: "I'd ask Dad whether he still loves me/Mum…then persuade/advise him to think about the consequences of the situation and discuss consequent resolutions." or "I'd talk with the woman and then persuade Dad. If difficult, I'd find help from someone who can influence Dad."

Story # 8 (b)

One of your friends complains that he/she has a problem with his/her teacher, that the teacher doesn't like him/her and that the teacher is unfair to him/her. Hence, he/she feels depressed and intends suiciding.

What would you think or feel?
I would think and feel?

What would you do?
I would do?

0 --- Subject thinks the friend's suicidal intent is stupid/silly or the teacher is faulty. Examples: "Suicidal intent is stupid." or "The teacher causes the depressed mood of my friend."

1 --- Subject thinks the friend's problem seems to be serious/dangerous or the problem needs the help from adults. Examples: "It is a serious problem which needs help from adults." or "Parents or teachers may help the friend."

2 ---Subject thinks that the friend is depressed/shocked/dispointed, and thus needs help, and that suicide is not a good resolution for the problem. Examples: "My friend is shocked/ depressed, thus she/he thinks of suicide and I should help him/her." or "I need to explain to my friend that suicide is silly and help him/her discard it."

0 --- Subject blames the friend for the idea or blames the teacher or advises the friend to leave school/move to another school or threatens the teacher. Examples: "Are you crazy/mad or suicide is stupid." or "I'd advise my friend to leave school or move to another school."

1 --- Subject warns parents or school of the problem and asks for help. Example: "I'd warn the friend's parents or the school of the problem and ask them for help."

2 --- Subject expresses sympathy and does something to exclude the suicidal idea from the friend's mind or discusses positive alternative solutions with the friend. Examples: "I'd show sympathy and advise my friend that suicide is not a good solution, then help him/her meet the teacher to resolve the problem" or "I'd persuade the friend to discard the suicidal intent, then meet a good teacher or a significant adult to ask for help".

Story # 9

In the classroom, your teacher is writing on the blackboard. There is swearing and laughing behind him/her. The teacher suddenly turns around and sees a student laughing. The teacher becomes angry and says:

T: What are you doing? Why are you laughing?

You: Nothing! It was not me!

T   (more irritable): So! Who laughed?

You: I don't know.

T: If you don't know, you get out of my class.

You: No man! It was not my fault! Why do I have to get out?

T: If you don't, I will get you out!

The atmosphere becomes very tense.

(B) What would you think and do if you were not the student, but were the monitor of this class?

I would think and feel?

0 --- Subject thinks teacher is too hot-tempered or teacher has poor classroom management skills or teacher makes it more serious/complicated. Examples: "The problem is real simple, but the teacher makes it more serious." or "The student's behaviour is not worth being thrown out of class."

1 --- Subject thinks the teacher's irritation is reasonable or the student insults the teacher or the classroom discipline is violated. Examples: "The teacher is irritated by the student." or "The student is at fault for the disrupted lesson."

2 --- Subject thinks the tense atmosphere may disrupt the class lesson or thinks of the responsibility of a class monitor for the problem. Examples: "I am a class monitor, thus I am responsible for the situation." or "The class atmosphere is tense or disrupted, I need to deflate the tension."

I would do?

0 --- Subject doesn't care or keeps silent or objects to the teacher or shows support for the student's behaviour. Examples: "I'd keep silent." or "I'd apologise to the teacher and explain that the student is not at fault."

1 --- Subject goes out to seek the management staff or principal to resolve the issue. Example: "I'd go out and seek the management teacher or principal to report."

2 --- Subject stands up to apologise to the teacher for the class indiscipline and asks the student to leave and resolve the matter after class. Then subject stabilizes classroom law and order to help continuing the lesson. Example: "I'd apologise to the teacher for the student's shortcoming and tell the student to go out so that the class could continue and ask the student to go with me to meet the teacher to resolve the problem after class".

Story # 10.1 (b)

You are lying down on your bed with a headache and the boy next door is playing his radio loudly, and it makes your head feel worse.

What would you think/feel and what would you do, if you ask the boy to turn the radio down or off, but he ignores you.

I would think and feel?

0 --- Subject feels upset or irritated/insulted, thinks the boy is stubborn. Examples: "The boy attempts to irritate me." or "The boy is stubborn, thus he needs to be taught a lesson."

1 --- Subject thinks the boy is interested in music or he is very intent on his job. Examples: "The boy is too keen on the music, thus doesn't want to turn it down." or "He is too intent on the music and he didn't hear me."

2 --- Subject thinks the boy may not know his/her sickness or he is too intent on his music, or is not aware that his behaviour is disturbing other people. Examples: "The boy may not understand my sickness." or "He is not conscious of his radio disturbing me as he is too intent on his interesting music."

I would do?

0 --- Subject shouts or slaps the boy or uses other physical force. Examples: "I'd shout and force him to turn radio off." or "I'd slap the boy."

1 --- Subject suffers the loud noise or moves to another room or closes the door. Examples: "I'd close the door and attempt to suffer the noise." or "I'd move to another room, if I can."

2 --- Subject patiently explains about his/her sickness and asks the boy again. If he still ignores or refuses, subject talks to his parents/adults or find alternative solutions. Examples: "I'd explain about my sickness to the boy and ask him again to turn the radio off or down." or "If the boy ignores me again, I'd meet his parents to talk."

Story # 10.2 (b)

While you are studying, some children from next-door neighbouring families are playing and chasing each other outside. This makes a lot of noise and therefore disturbs you.

What would you think or feel?

I would think and feel?

0 --- Subject feels upset at being disturbed, thinks the children are mischievous or prankish. Examples: "The children are mischievous." or "I can no longer stand the mischievous children." or "Who are they?... why don't their parents advise them?."

What would you do?

I would do?

0 --- Subject shouts/threatens or uses physical force to drive the children out. Examples: "I'd drive the children out of the place." or "I'd ask the children to go away and if they are stubborn, I'd threaten or slap them."

1 --- Subject suffers the noise or closes the door or moves to another room or stops

1 --- Subject thinks the children have the natural need of playing or they are playing an interesting game or when playing children often make a lot of noise. Examples: "The children may be playing an interesting game." or "Children playing often make loud noise."

2 --- Subject thinks children do not know that they make a lot of noise disturbing other people or they do not know he/she needs quiet for exam study. Examples: "Children make a lot of noise as they play because they are too young to be conscious of their behaviour." or "They may not know that their playing is disturbing my exam study."

studying. Example: "I don't drive children out, but I close the door or move to another room."

2 --- Subject explains/persuades the children to play quietly or asks them to move to other place because the subject needs quietness for exam study. Examples: "Hey! I am studying for an examination. Can you play quietly or move to another place?." or "I need quiet for exam study. Please move to another place, I promise to tell you an interesting story after my exam."

Story # 11 (b)

A group of adolescents made friends with you. You agree to be involved in their activities because you think they were good friends. However, as time passes, you gradually find that they will not be good friends and they intend to involve you in a possible illegal action.

What would you think or feel?
I would think and feel?

0 --- Subject feels depressed/worried or feels stupid when he/she agreed to be involved in the gang or thinks of punishment or revenge occuring if he/she does not obey the practices of the group. Example: "I can be punished If I do not obey the practices of the group." or "I regret becoming involved in the group."

1 --- Subject thinks that it is more dangerous for him/her if he/she continues to be involved in the group or it is unsafe to continue to be involved in the group. Examples: "It is too dangerous to obey the practices of the gang" or "It is unsafe if I get involved in the activities of the group."

2 --- Subject thinks the practices of the group are anti-social and wonders how to turn/reverse the anti-social behaviour into pro-social behaviour. Examples: "The practices of the group are not as I think and I think that it is important to change the anti-social behaviour into pro-social behaviour." or "How can I influence the group to prevent their illegal activities."

What would you do?
I would do?

0 --- Subject avoids the members of the group if possible or refuses to participate in illegal behhaviour if possible. Examples: "I'd pretend to be sick to avoid them."; "I look for a way not to meet them." or "If they ask me to do an illegal thing with the group, I'll invent an excuse to refuse to do the task."

1 --- Subject pretends to obey, but sabotages the illegal practices of the group or gradually withdraws. If found out the subject immediately warns parents or police of the illegal practice of the group. Example: "I pretend to obey, but gradually withdraw or sabotage the anti-social practices."

2 --- Subject looks for a good way to advise/persuate the members of the group not to get involved in the anti-social practices. If they do not change, the subject asks for help from parents or police. Example: "I'd look for a good way to advise the friends only to do pro-social practices. If they refuse I ask for help from parents or police."

Story # 12 (b)

While you are riding on your bicycle, a youth riding in the opposite direction suddenly runs into you. Although you are both hurt and the youth was at fault, you say "Sorry!". Responding to your polite attitude, the youth becomes angry and insults you.

<table>
<tr><th>What would you think or feel?</th><th>What would you do?</th></tr>
<tr><th>I would think and feel?</th><th>I would do?</th></tr>
</table>

0 --- Subject feels upset, thinks the teenager is wrong and impolite/uncultured/ aggressive. Examples: "The person is at fault, but rude/ impolite." or "The person is aggressive, he/she has to pay for the insult."

1 --- Subject thinks the youth may be hurt or he/she has lost control due to being hurt. Examples: "The knock hurt and makes him/her upset or furious with me." or "Due to being hurt, the youth is not conscious of his/her behaviour."

2 --- Subject thinks about how to help if youth is seriously hurt or how to resolve the knock peacefully. Examples: "Having a stormy quarrel with the youth is not good, even leads to fighting." or "Arguing who/what is wrong is not a good solution." or "Could the youth need medical help?."

0 --- Subject argues/shouts or uses physical force to teach the person a lesson. Examples: "What are you saying?... you are wrong, and impolite." or "I'd give him/her a lesson for the insult."

1 --- Subject goes away without saying anything. Example: "I would go away and not say anything to the person."

2 --- Subject ignores the person's insult and/or calmly explains or calls medical help if the person is badly hurt or calls police/asks near-by adults for help if the subject has been hurt by the youth's aggressive behaviour. Examples: "I'd ignore the insult and ask him/her whether he/she is badly hurt. If not badly hurt, I go away." or "I'd explain that I am not at fault and ask the person if he/she needs medical help. If not seriously hurt, I'd go away without saying anymore."

APPENDIX E.

Teacher Rating Scale of Interpersonal Problem Solving (TRSIPS)

TEACHER RATING SCALE OF INTERPERSONAL PROBLEM SOLVING

Student's Name:...................................……… Teacher's Name: ....

Student's age:........   Grade:..........   School:...

Male/Female...........   Today's Date:...../...../..........

Below is a list of statements that describe students. Read **each item carefully** and decide **how much** you think the student has been bothered by this problem between now and the last three months. Please circle **one** of the numbers (0 1 2) below :

> **0 = Not true at all**
> **1 = Sometimes true**
> **2 = Often true**

For example, if you find this student often is poorly coordinated or clumsy you would **circle 2** like this: 0 1 2

This student:

1. Has problems making or keeping friends	0 1 2
2. Doesn't get along well with other students	0 1 2
3. Gets into more trouble than other students the same age	0 1 2
4. Gets in many fights	0 1 2
5. Makes fun of or teases other students	0 1 2
6. Is impulsive	0 1 2
7. Has disruptive behaviors	0 1 2
8. Displays avoidance or reserved behaviors in social settings	0 1 2
9. Shows inappropriate behaviors when dealing with conflict with others	0 1 2
10. Threatens people with physical violence or acts like a bully	0 1 2
11. Abuses people verbally	0 1 2
12. Is unresponsive	0 1 2
13. Isolates him/herself from other students	0 1 2
14. Is unsympathetic	0 1 2
15. Thinks about likely consequences before making decisions	0 1 2
16. Acts without stopping to think	0 1 2
17. Has temper tantrums or is hot tempered	0 1 2
18. Has a poor or negative attitude toward him or herself	0 1 2
19. Has poor understanding of the attitudes, feelings, and perspectives of others when he/she goes about problem solving	0 1 2
20. Has poor consciousness of the playing regulation: "need to be honest" or "fair play"	0 1 2

21. Is teased or annoyed by other students   0 1 2

22. Has bossy words that make classmates unhappy   0 1 2

23. Is isolated by classmates   0 1 2

24. Doesn't get along well with friends (different sex)   0 1 2

25. Doesn't get along well with friends (same sex)   0 1 2

26. Avoids or is afraid of facing problematic situations which he/she is responsible for   0 1 2

27. Is explosive or anti-social   0 1 2

28. Doesn't get along well with teacher   0 1 2

29. Is uncooperative with other students   0 1 2

30. Thinks of alternative solutions and consequences when he/she goes about problem solving   0 1 2

31. Denies having done wrong or blames other students for mistakes he/she has made   0 1 2

32. Uses different strategies to solve conflictive situations   0 1 2

33. Approaches problems from different angles in order to find an effective solution   0 1 2

34. Easily gets angry in playing with other students   0 1 2

35. Has good self-control when in conflict with other students   0 1 2

36. Has a positive attitude in a failing case   0 1 2

37. Maintains positive attitudes even if he/she feels unfairly treated   0 1 2

38. Has a negative attitude and inappropriate behaviors in conflictive situations   0 1 2

39. Tries to identify and resolve problems from the perspectives of others   0 1 2

40. Shows withdrawal or avoidance behaviors when frustrated   0 1 2

Printed by Books on Demand GmbH, Norderstedt / Germany